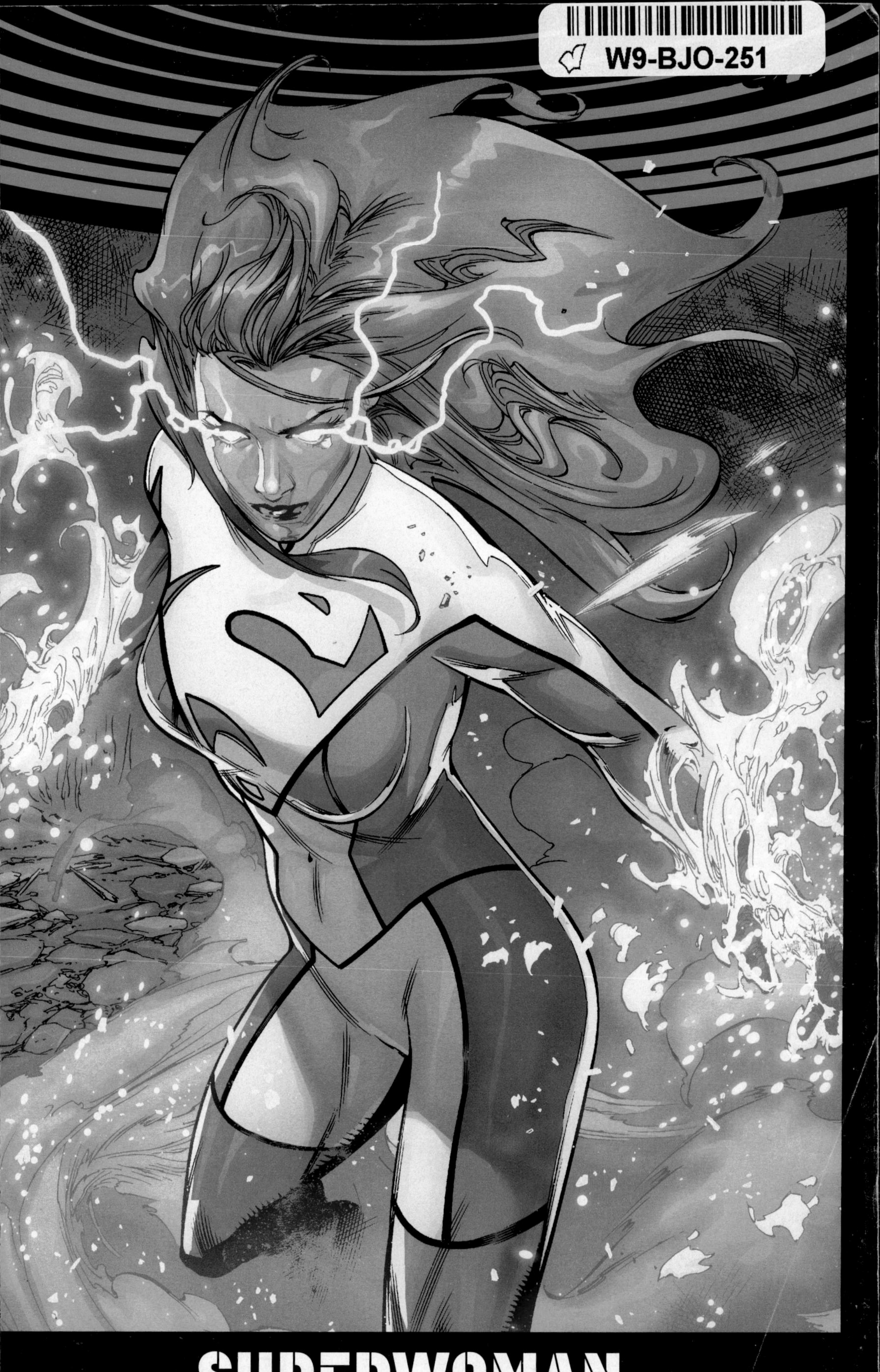

SUPERWOMAN

VOL.3 THE MIDNIGHT HOUR

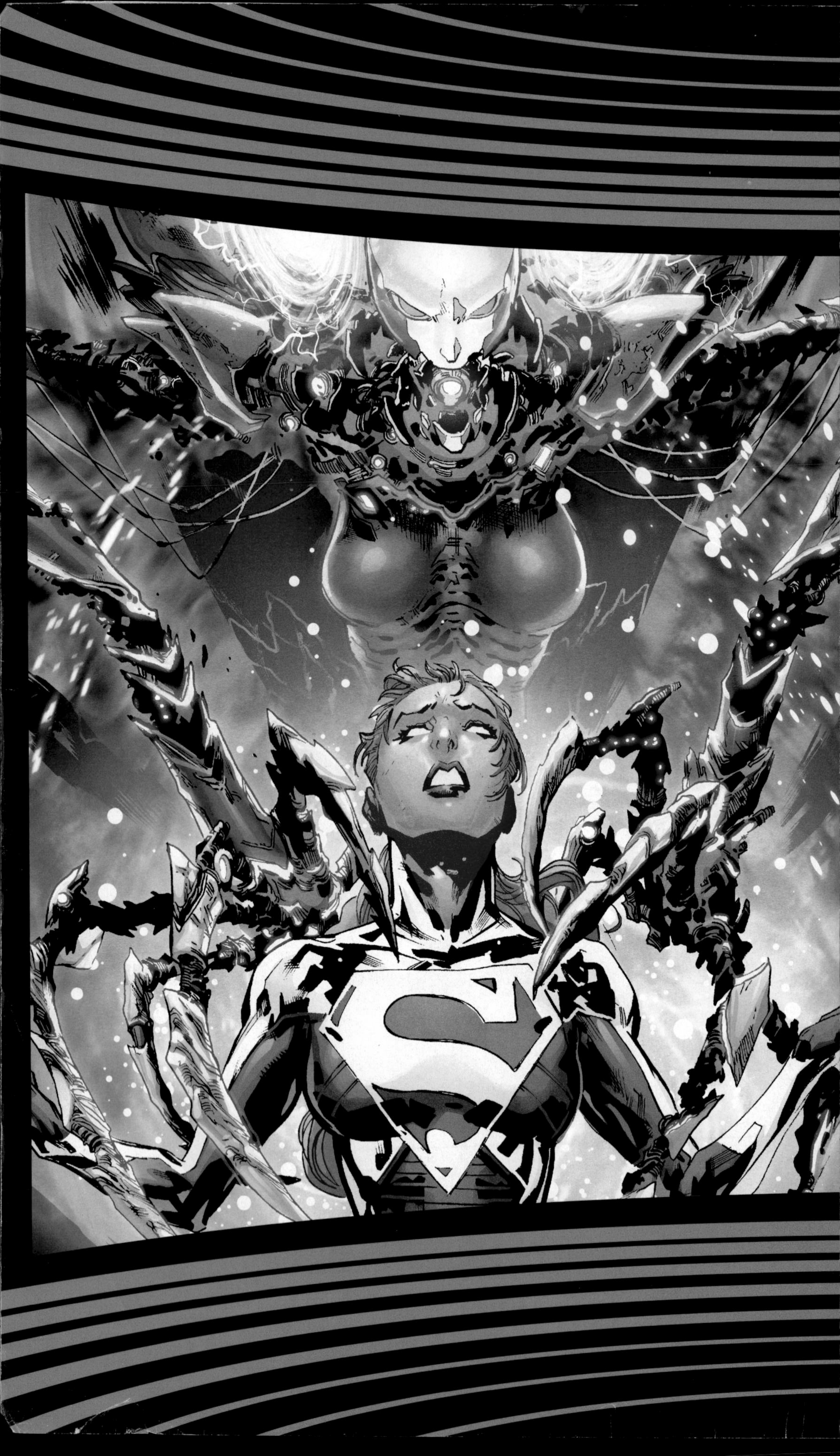

SUPERWOMAN

VOL.3 THE MIDNIGHT HOUR

K. PERKINS
writer

STEPHEN SEGOVIA * SAMI BASRI
FEDERICO DALLOCCHIO * MAX RAYNOR
pencillers

ART THIBERT * SAMI BASRI * FEDERICO DALLOCCHIO
JAIME MENDOZA * SCOTT HANNA
inkers

HI-FI
colorist

JOSH REED
CARLOS M. MANGUAL
letterers

EMANUELA LUPACCHINO and TOMEU MOREY
collection cover artists

STEEL created by LOUISE SIMONSON and JON BOGDANOVE
SUPERMAN created by JERRY SIEGEL and JOE SHUSTER
SUPERGIRL based on characters created by JERRY SIEGEL and JOE SHUSTER
By special arrangement with the Jerry Siegel family

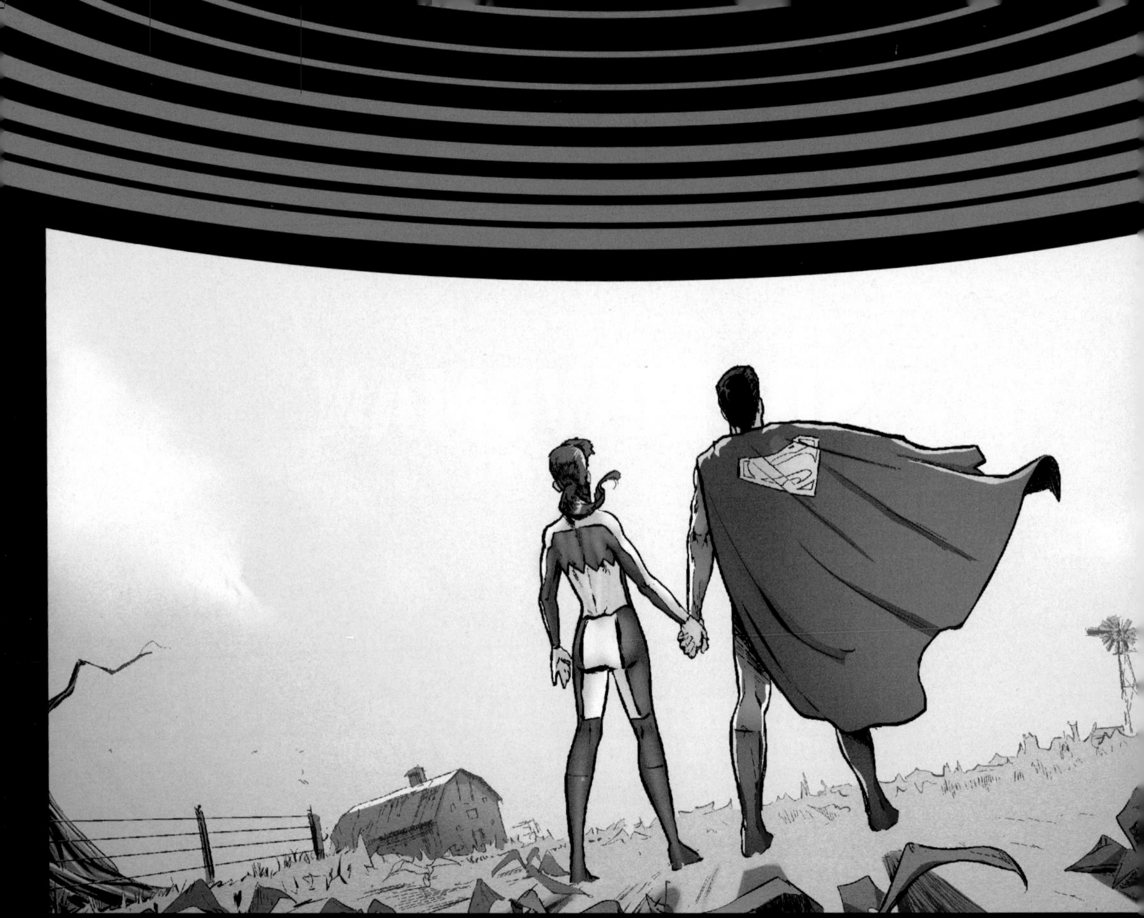

PAUL KAMINSKI EDDIE BERGANZA JESSICA CHEN Editors - Original Series * **ANDREA SHEA** Assistant Editor - Original Series
JEB WOODARD Group Editor - Collected Editions * **ERIKA ROTHBERG** Editor - Collected Edition
STEVE COOK Design Director - Books * **MONIQUE NARBONETA** Publication Design

BOB HARRAS Senior VP - Editor-in-Chief, DC Comics
PAT McCALLUM Executive Editor, DC Comics

DIANE NELSON President * **DAN DiDIO** Publisher * **JIM LEE** Publisher * **GEOFF JOHNS** President & Chief Creative Officer
AMIT DESAI Executive VP - Business & Marketing Strategy, Direct to Consumer & Global Franchise Management
SAM ADES Senior VP & General Manager, Digital Services * **BOBBIE CHASE** VP & Executive Editor, Young Reader & Talent Development
MARK CHIARELLO Senior VP - Art, Design & Collected Editions * **JOHN CUNNINGHAM** Senior VP - Sales & Trade Marketing
ANNE DePIES Senior VP - Business Strategy, Finance & Administration * **DON FALLETTI** VP - Manufacturing Operations
LAWRENCE GANEM VP - Editorial Administration & Talent Relations * **ALISON GILL** Senior VP - Manufacturing & Operations
HANK KANALZ Senior VP - Editorial Strategy & Administration * **JAY KOGAN** VP - Legal Affairs * **JACK MAHAN** VP - Business Affairs
NICK J. NAPOLITANO VP - Manufacturing Administration * **EDDIE SCANNELL** VP - Consumer Marketing
COURTNEY SIMMONS Senior VP - Publicity & Communications * **JIM (SKI) SOKOLOWSKI** VP - Comic Book Specialty Sales & Trade Marketing
NANCY SPEARS VP - Mass, Book, Digital Sales & Trade Marketing * **MICHELE R. WELLS** VP - Content Strategy

SUPERWOMAN VOL. 3: THE MIDNIGHT HOUR

DC Comics, 2900 West Alameda Ave., Burbank, CA 91505
Printed by LSC Communications, Kendallville, IN, USA. 4/20/18. First Printing.
ISBN: 978-1-4012-7852-6

Library of Congress Cataloging-in-Publication Data is available.

PEFC Certified
Printed on paper from sustainably managed forests, controlled sources
www.pefc.org
PEFC/29-31-337

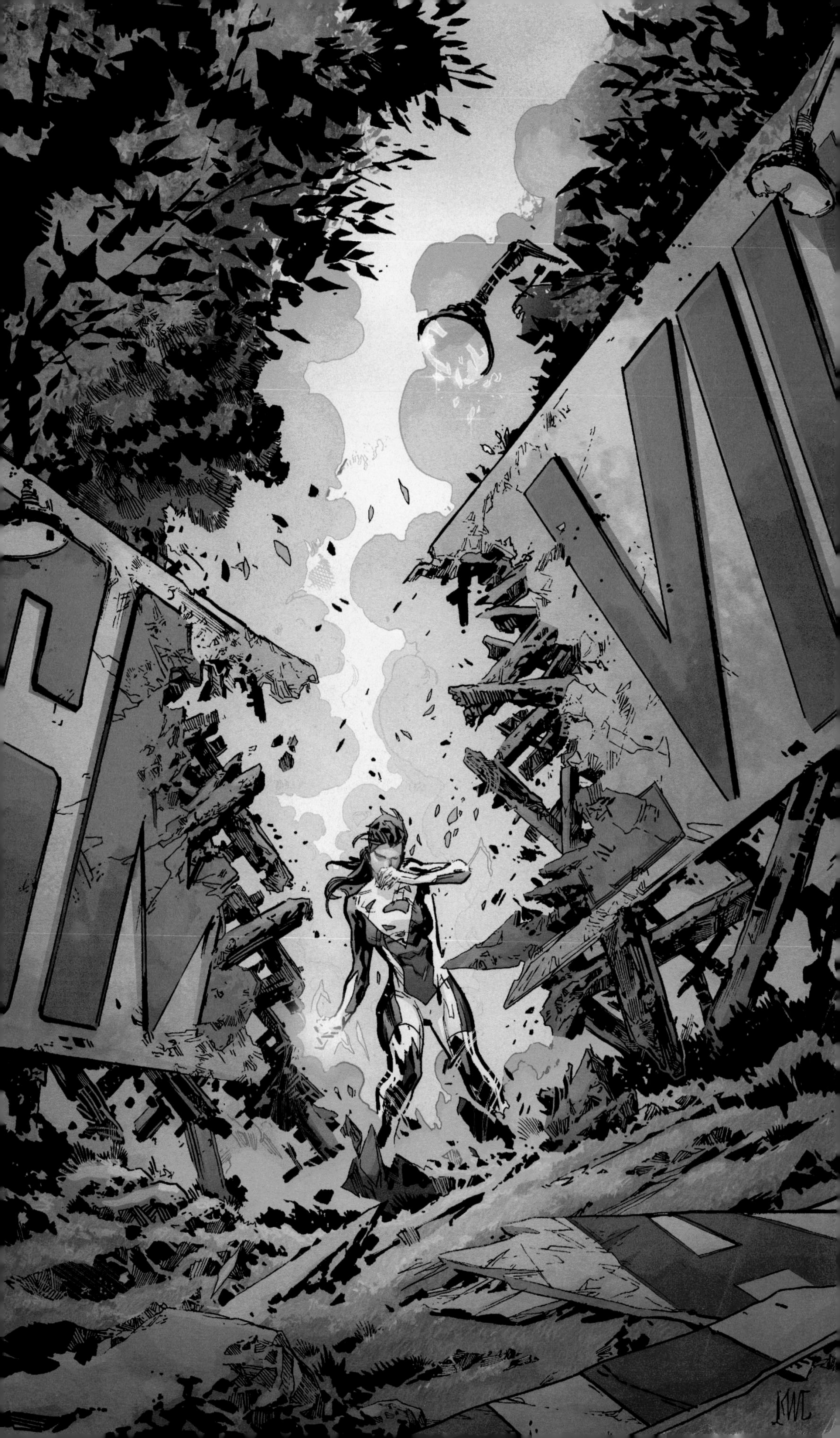

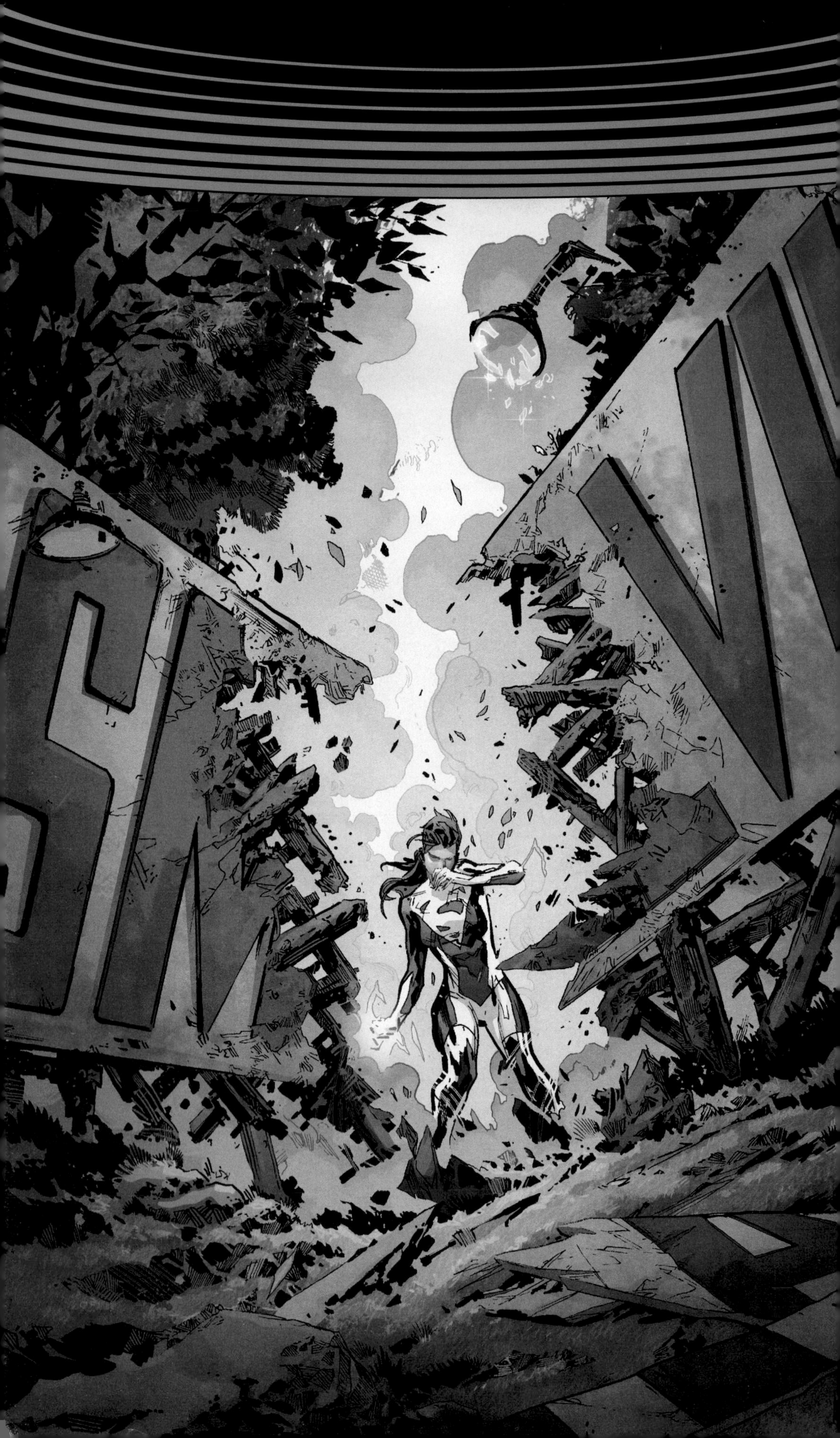

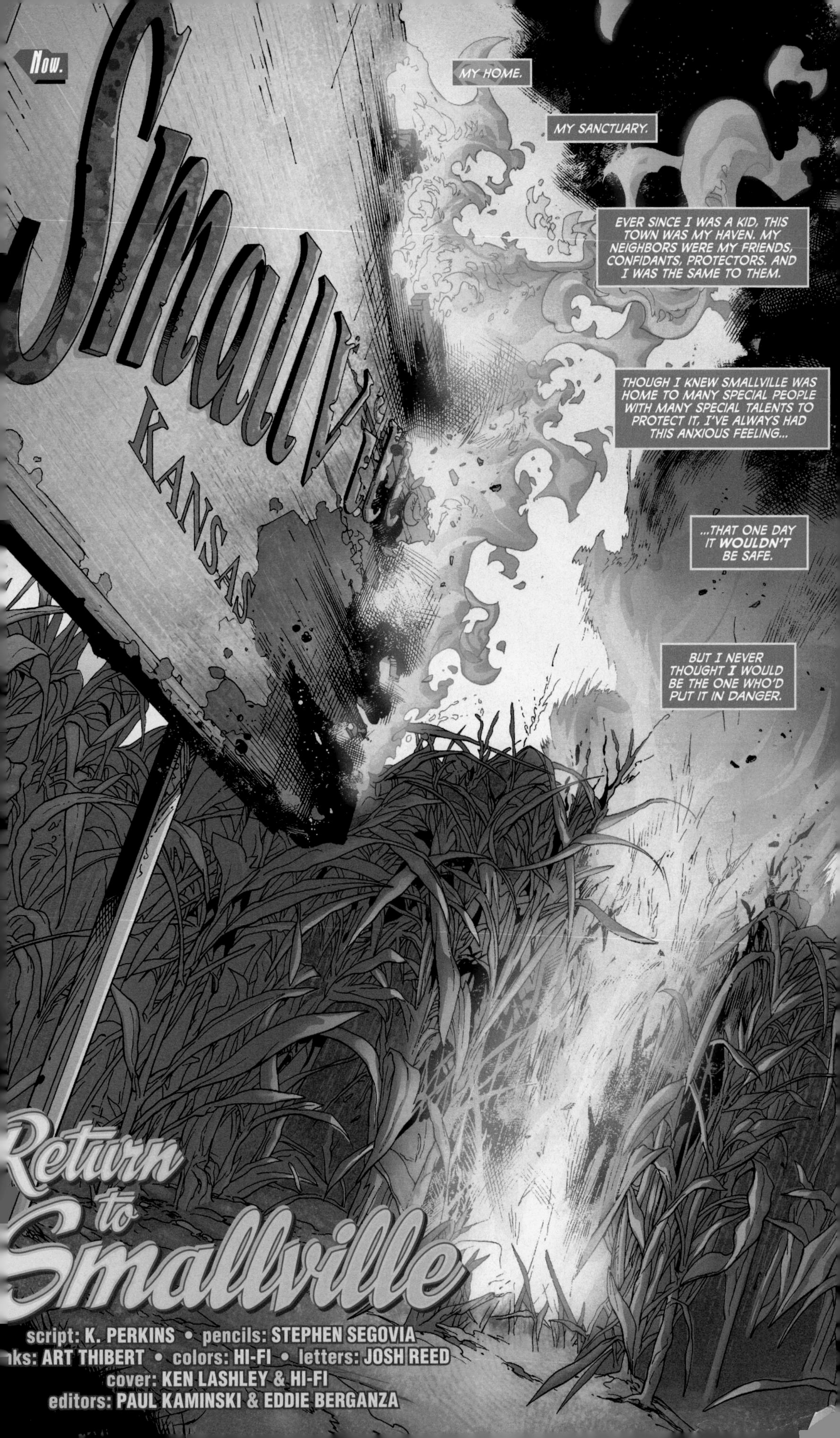
Now.
Smallville
KANSAS
MY HOME.
MY SANCTUARY.
EVER SINCE I WAS A KID, THIS TOWN WAS MY HAVEN. MY NEIGHBORS WERE MY FRIENDS, CONFIDANTS, PROTECTORS. AND I WAS THE SAME TO THEM.
THOUGH I KNEW SMALLVILLE WAS HOME TO MANY SPECIAL PEOPLE WITH MANY SPECIAL TALENTS TO PROTECT IT, I'VE ALWAYS HAD THIS ANXIOUS FEELING...
...THAT ONE DAY IT WOULDN'T BE SAFE.
BUT I NEVER THOUGHT I WOULD BE THE ONE WHO'D PUT IT IN DANGER.
Return to Smallville
script: K. PERKINS • pencils: STEPHEN SEGOVIA
nks: ART THIBERT • colors: HI-FI • letters: JOSH REED
cover: KEN LASHLEY & HI-FI
editors: PAUL KAMINSKI & EDDIE BERGANZA

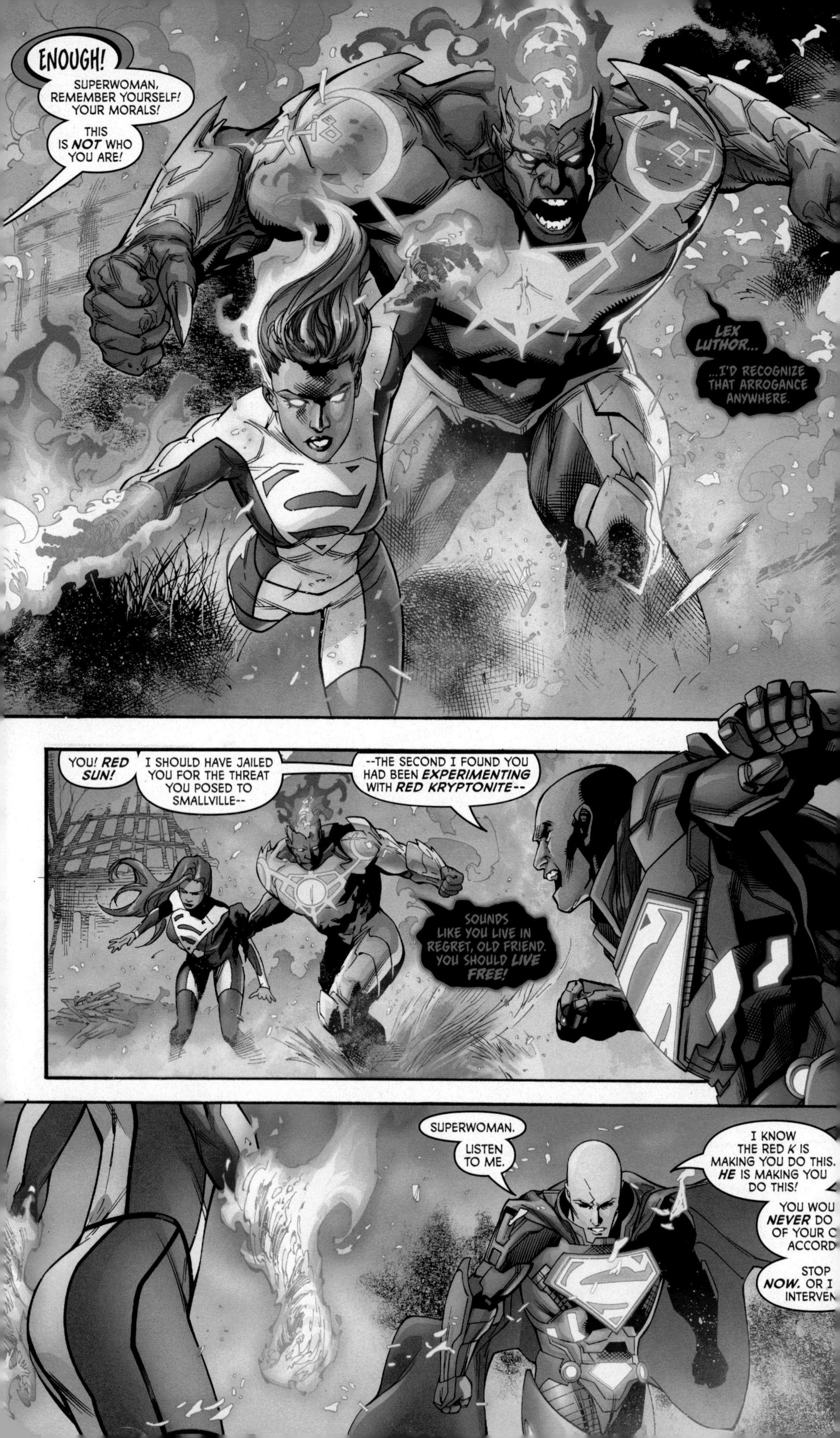

ENOUGH!
SUPERWOMAN, REMEMBER YOURSELF! YOUR MORALS!
THIS IS NOT WHO YOU ARE!
LEX LUTHOR...
...I'D RECOGNIZE THAT ARROGANCE ANYWHERE.
YOU! RED SUN!
I SHOULD HAVE JAILED YOU FOR THE THREAT YOU POSED TO SMALLVILLE--
--THE SECOND I FOUND YOU HAD BEEN EXPERIMENTING WITH RED KRYPTONITE--
SOUNDS LIKE YOU LIVE IN REGRET, OLD FRIEND. YOU SHOULD LIVE FREE!
SUPERWOMAN.
LISTEN TO ME.
I KNOW THE RED K IS MAKING YOU DO THIS. HE IS MAKING YOU DO THIS!
YOU WOU NEVER DO OF YOUR C ACCORD
STOP NOW. OR I INTERVEN

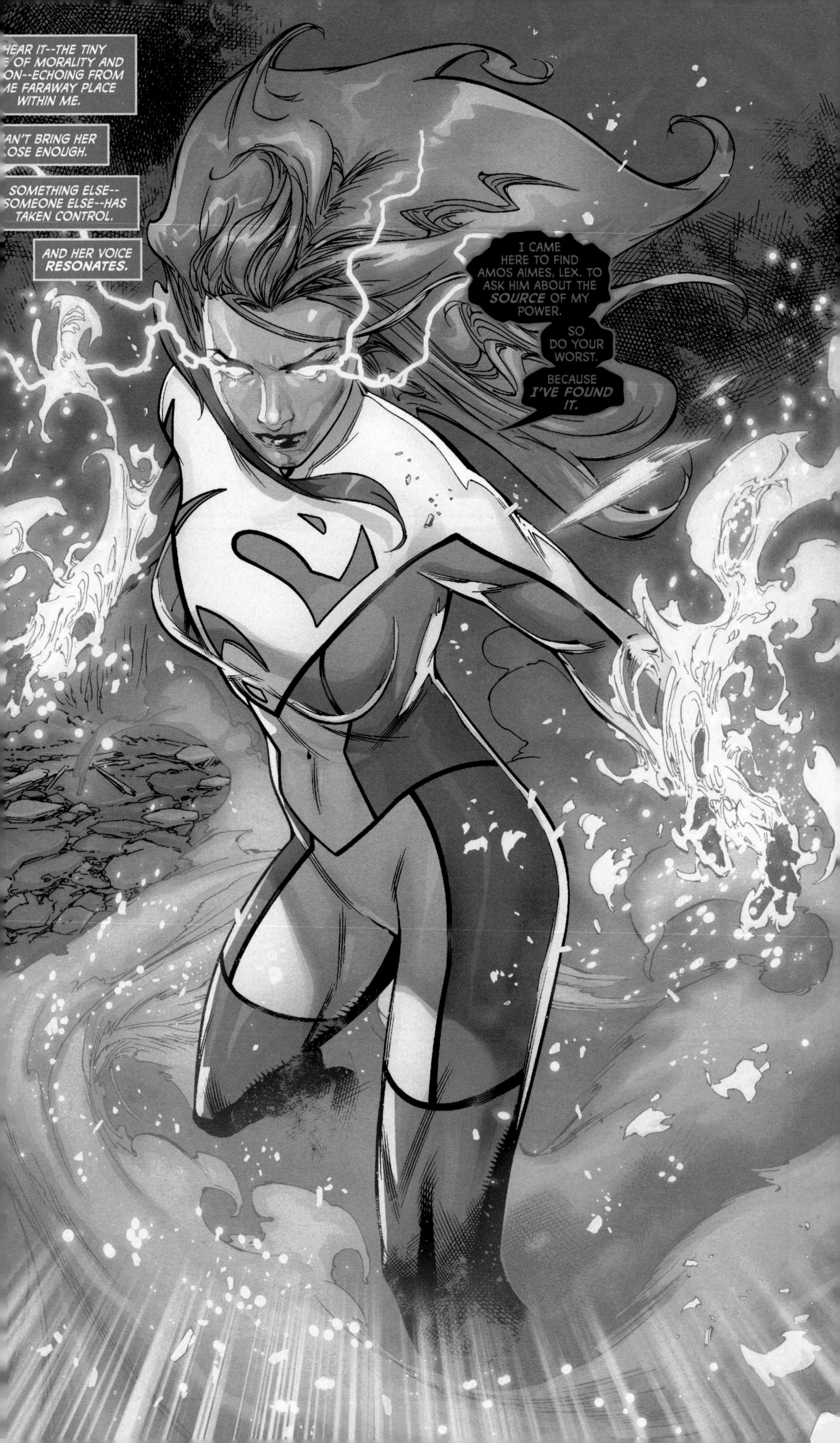

HEAR IT--THE TINY
E OF MORALITY AND
ON--ECHOING FROM
ME FARAWAY PLACE
WITHIN ME.
AN'T BRING HER
OSE ENOUGH.
SOMETHING ELSE--
SOMEONE ELSE--HAS
TAKEN CONTROL.
AND HER VOICE **RESONATES.**
I CAME HERE TO FIND AMOS AIMES, LEX. TO ASK HIM ABOUT THE ***SOURCE*** OF MY POWER.
SO DO YOUR WORST.
BECAUSE ***I'VE FOUND IT.***

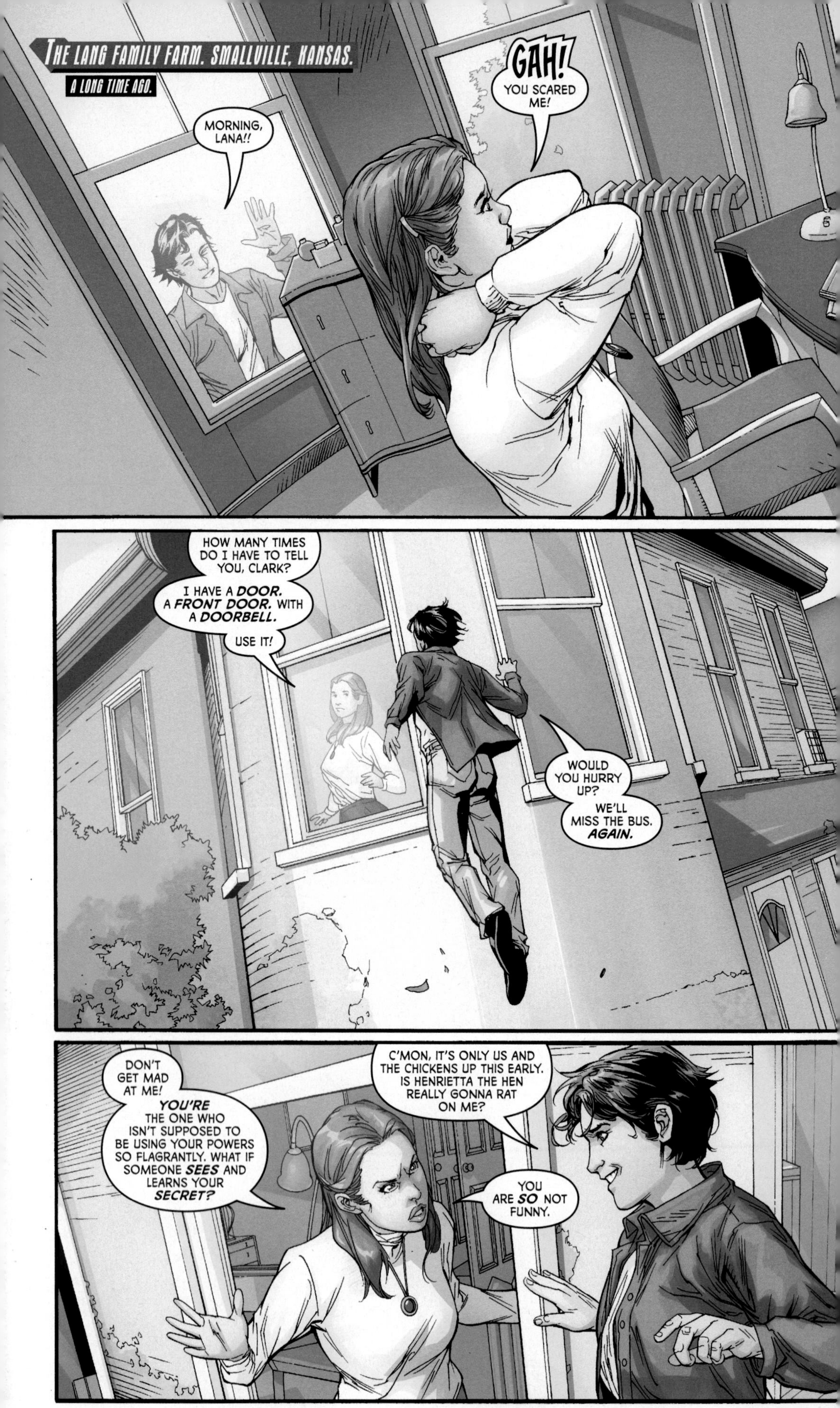
THE LANG FAMILY FARM. SMALLVILLE, KANSAS.
A LONG TIME AGO.
MORNING, LANA!!
GAH! YOU SCARED ME!
HOW MANY TIMES DO I HAVE TO TELL YOU, CLARK?
I HAVE A **DOOR.** A **FRONT DOOR.** WITH A **DOORBELL.**
USE IT!
WOULD YOU HURRY UP?
WE'LL MISS THE BUS. ***AGAIN.***
DON'T GET MAD AT ME! ***YOU'RE*** THE ONE WHO ISN'T SUPPOSED TO BE USING YOUR POWERS SO FLAGRANTLY. WHAT IF SOMEONE ***SEES*** AND LEARNS YOUR ***SECRET?***
C'MON, IT'S ONLY US AND THE CHICKENS UP THIS EARLY. IS HENRIETTA THE HEN REALLY GONNA RAT ON ME?
YOU ARE ***SO*** NOT FUNNY.

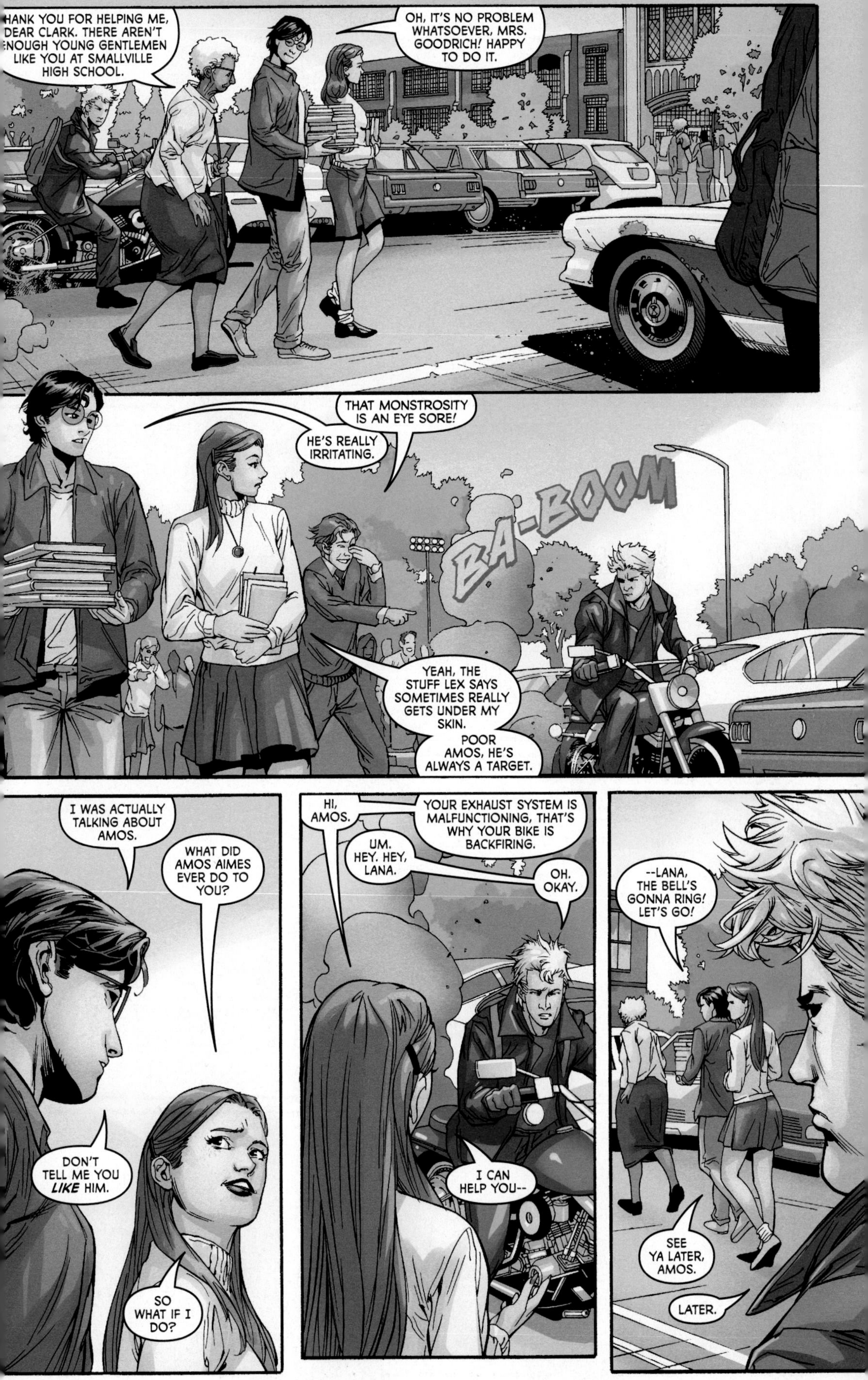
HANK YOU FOR HELPING ME, DEAR CLARK. THERE AREN'T ENOUGH YOUNG GENTLEMEN LIKE YOU AT SMALLVILLE HIGH SCHOOL.
OH, IT'S NO PROBLEM WHATSOEVER, MRS. GOODRICH! HAPPY TO DO IT.
THAT MONSTROSITY IS AN EYE SORE!
HE'S REALLY IRRITATING.
BA-BOOM
YEAH, THE STUFF LEX SAYS SOMETIMES REALLY GETS UNDER MY SKIN.
POOR AMOS, HE'S ALWAYS A TARGET.
I WAS ACTUALLY TALKING ABOUT AMOS.
WHAT DID AMOS AIMES EVER DO TO YOU?
DON'T TELL ME YOU *LIKE* HIM.
SO WHAT IF I DO?
HI, AMOS.
UM. HEY. HEY, LANA.
YOUR EXHAUST SYSTEM IS MALFUNCTIONING, THAT'S WHY YOUR BIKE IS BACKFIRING.
OH. OKAY.
I CAN HELP YOU--
--LANA, THE BELL'S GONNA RING! LET'S GO!
SEE YA LATER, AMOS.
LATER.

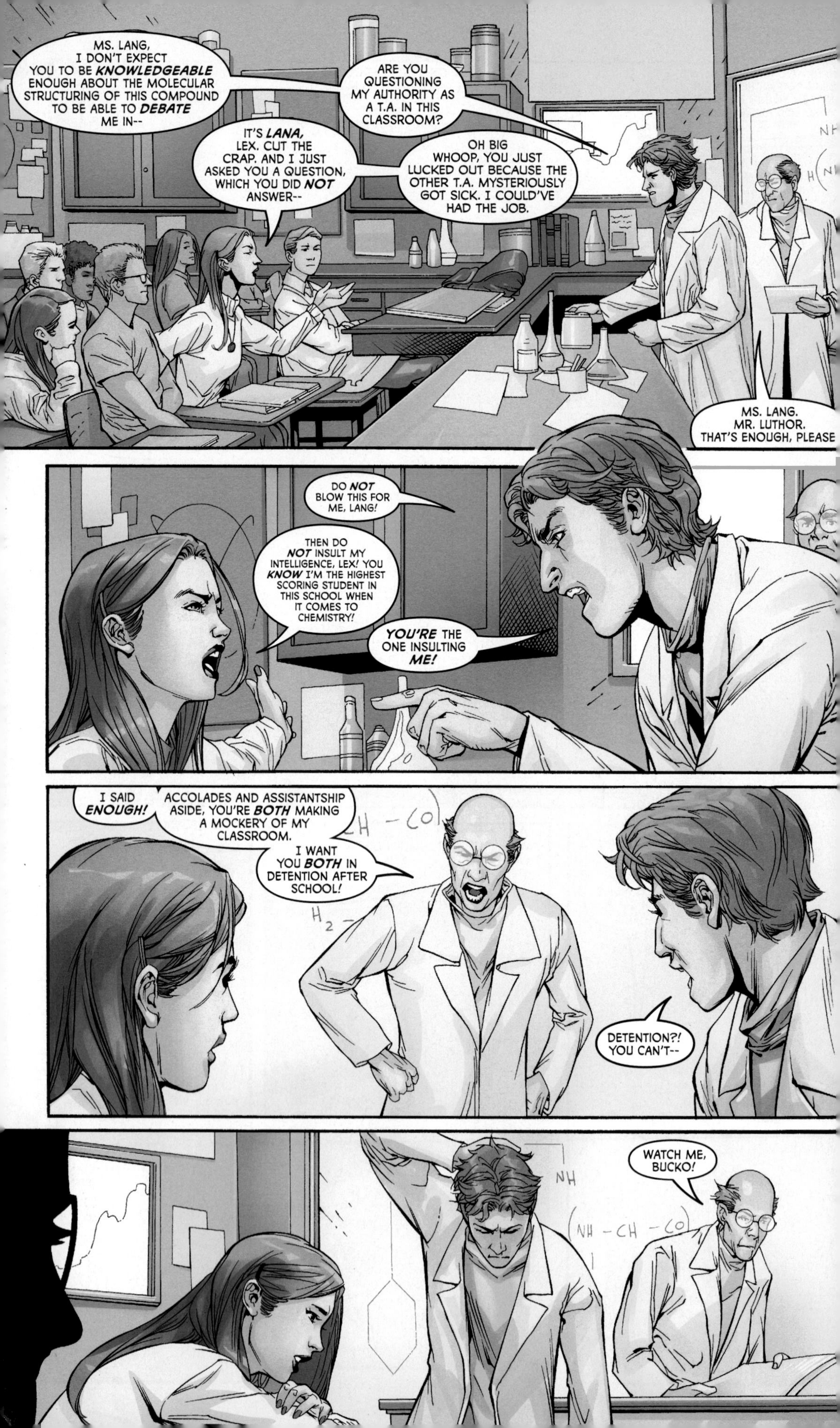
MS. LANG, I DON'T EXPECT YOU TO BE KNOWLEDGEABLE ENOUGH ABOUT THE MOLECULAR STRUCTURING OF THIS COMPOUND TO BE ABLE TO DEBATE ME IN--
ARE YOU QUESTIONING MY AUTHORITY AS A T.A. IN THIS CLASSROOM?
IT'S LANA, LEX. CUT THE CRAP. AND I JUST ASKED YOU A QUESTION, WHICH YOU DID NOT ANSWER--
OH BIG WHOOP, YOU JUST LUCKED OUT BECAUSE THE OTHER T.A. MYSTERIOUSLY GOT SICK. I COULD'VE HAD THE JOB.
MS. LANG. MR. LUTHOR. THAT'S ENOUGH, PLEASE
DO NOT BLOW THIS FOR ME, LANG!
THEN DO NOT INSULT MY INTELLIGENCE, LEX! YOU KNOW I'M THE HIGHEST SCORING STUDENT IN THIS SCHOOL WHEN IT COMES TO CHEMISTRY!
YOU'RE THE ONE INSULTING ME!
I SAID ENOUGH!
ACCOLADES AND ASSISTANTSHIP ASIDE, YOU'RE BOTH MAKING A MOCKERY OF MY CLASSROOM.
I WANT YOU BOTH IN DETENTION AFTER SCHOOL!
DETENTION?! YOU CAN'T--
WATCH ME, BUCKO!

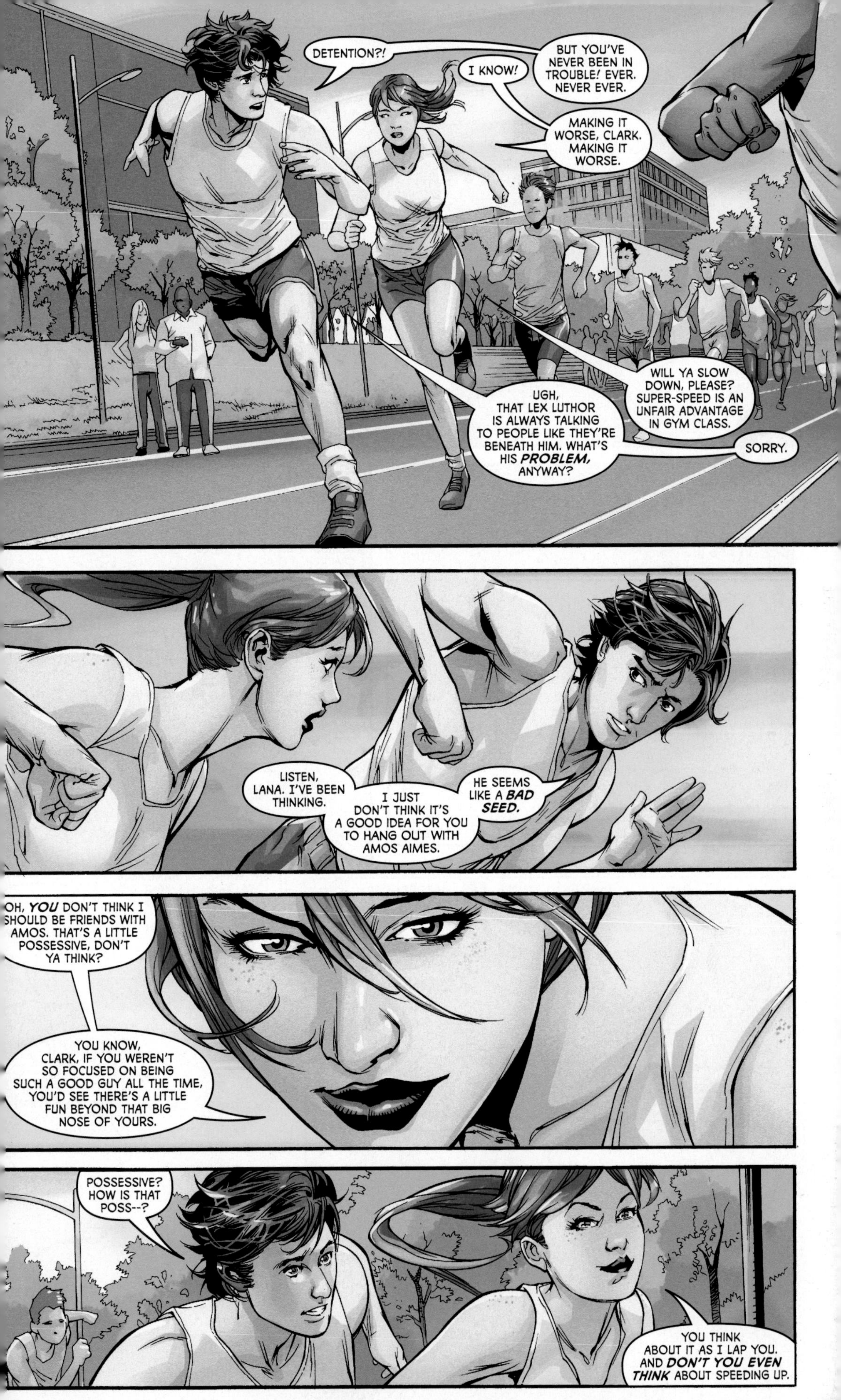

DETENTION?!
BUT YOU'VE NEVER BEEN IN TROUBLE! EVER. NEVER EVER.
I KNOW!
MAKING IT WORSE, CLARK. MAKING IT WORSE.
UGH, THAT LEX LUTHOR IS ALWAYS TALKING TO PEOPLE LIKE THEY'RE BENEATH HIM. WHAT'S HIS *PROBLEM,* ANYWAY?
WILL YA SLOW DOWN, PLEASE? SUPER-SPEED IS AN UNFAIR ADVANTAGE IN GYM CLASS.
SORRY.
LISTEN, LANA. I'VE BEEN THINKING.
I JUST DON'T THINK IT'S A GOOD IDEA FOR YOU TO HANG OUT WITH AMOS AIMES.
HE SEEMS LIKE A ***BAD SEED.***
OH, ***YOU*** DON'T THINK I SHOULD BE FRIENDS WITH AMOS. THAT'S A LITTLE POSSESSIVE, DON'T YA THINK?
YOU KNOW, CLARK, IF YOU WEREN'T SO FOCUSED ON BEING SUCH A GOOD GUY ALL THE TIME, YOU'D SEE THERE'S A LITTLE FUN BEYOND THAT BIG NOSE OF YOURS.
POSSESSIVE? HOW IS THAT POSS--?
YOU THINK ABOUT IT AS I LAP YOU. AND ***DON'T YOU EVEN THINK*** ABOUT SPEEDING UP.

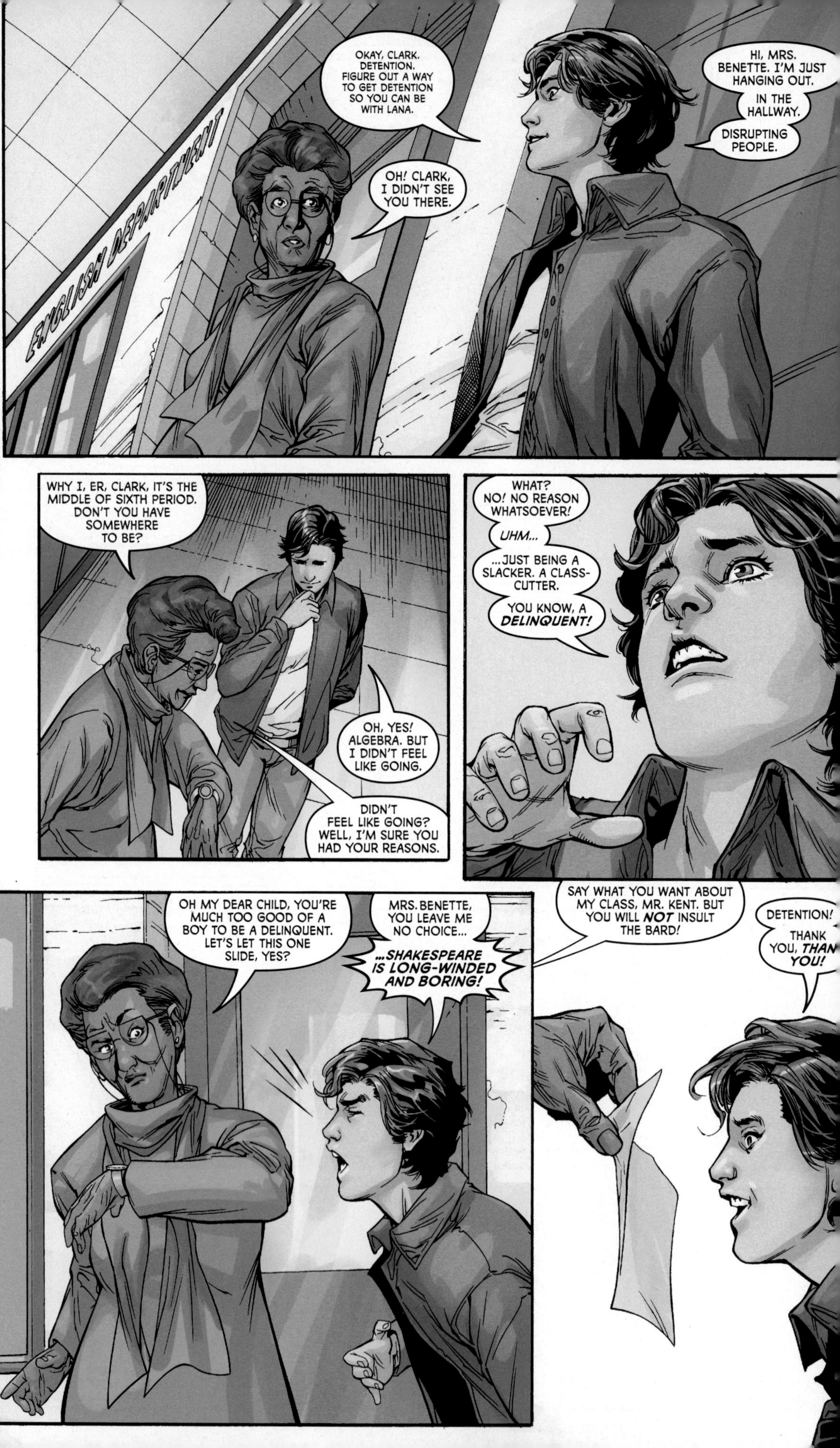
OKAY, CLARK. DETENTION. FIGURE OUT A WAY TO GET DETENTION SO YOU CAN BE WITH LANA.
HI, MRS. BENETTE. I'M JUST HANGING OUT.
IN THE HALLWAY.
DISRUPTING PEOPLE.
OH! CLARK, I DIDN'T SEE YOU THERE.
ENGLISH DEPARTMENT
WHY I, ER, CLARK, IT'S THE MIDDLE OF SIXTH PERIOD. DON'T YOU HAVE SOMEWHERE TO BE?
OH, YES! ALGEBRA. BUT I DIDN'T FEEL LIKE GOING.
DIDN'T FEEL LIKE GOING? WELL, I'M SURE YOU HAD YOUR REASONS.
WHAT? NO! NO REASON WHATSOEVER!
UHM...
...JUST BEING A SLACKER. A CLASS-CUTTER.
YOU KNOW, A ***DELINQUENT!***
OH MY DEAR CHILD, YOU'RE MUCH TOO GOOD OF A BOY TO BE A DELINQUENT. LET'S LET THIS ONE SLIDE, YES?
MRS. BENETTE, YOU LEAVE ME NO CHOICE...
...SHAKESPEARE IS LONG-WINDED AND BORING!
SAY WHAT YOU WANT ABOUT MY CLASS, MR. KENT. BUT YOU WILL ***NOT*** INSULT THE BARD!
DETENTION!
THANK YOU, ***THAN*** ***YOU!***

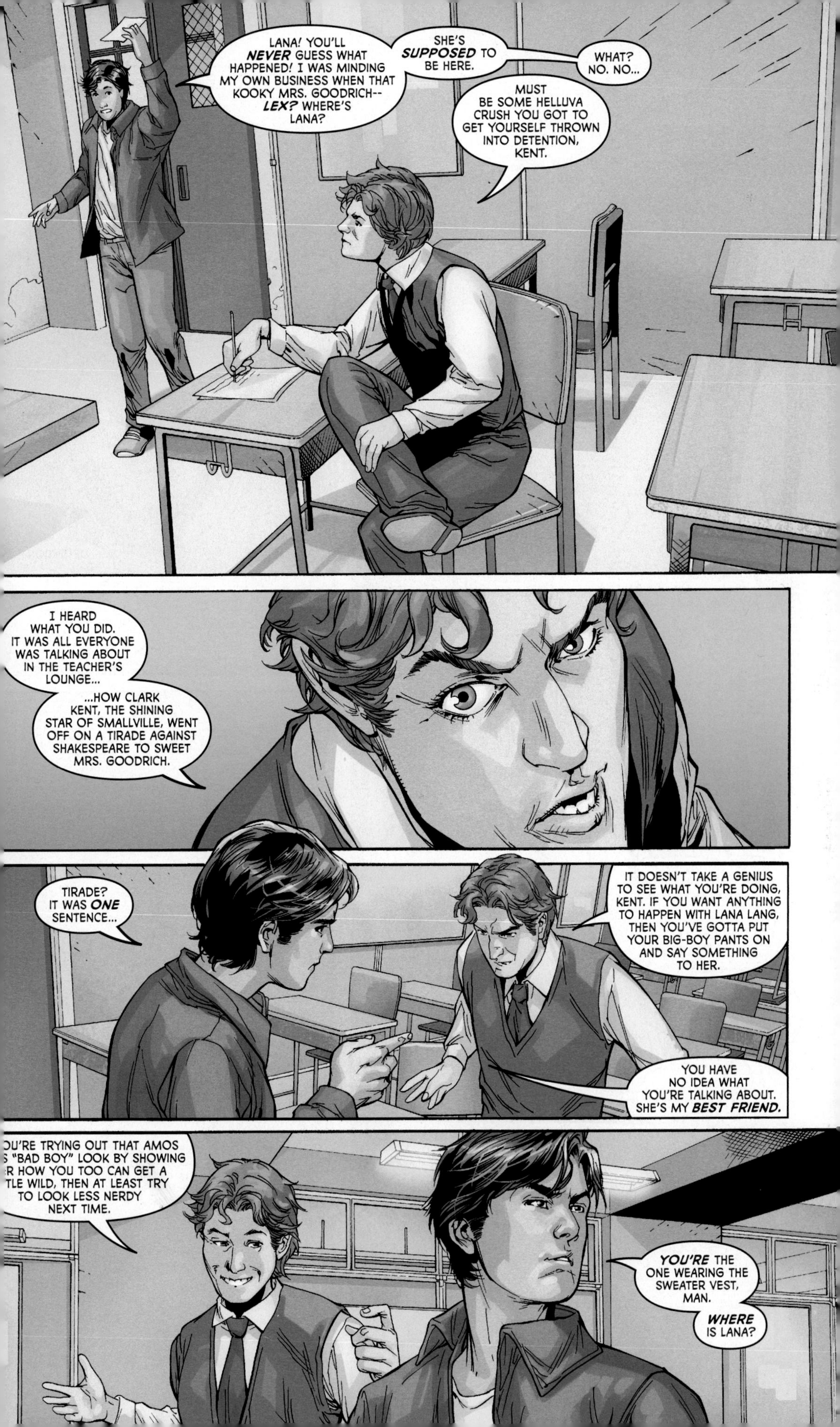
LANA! YOU'LL NEVER GUESS WHAT HAPPENED! I WAS MINDING MY OWN BUSINESS WHEN THAT KOOKY MRS. GOODRICH-- LEX? WHERE'S LANA?
SHE'S SUPPOSED TO BE HERE.
WHAT? NO. NO...
MUST BE SOME HELLUVA CRUSH YOU GOT TO GET YOURSELF THROWN INTO DETENTION, KENT.
I HEARD WHAT YOU DID. IT WAS ALL EVERYONE WAS TALKING ABOUT IN THE TEACHER'S LOUNGE...
...HOW CLARK KENT, THE SHINING STAR OF SMALLVILLE, WENT OFF ON A TIRADE AGAINST SHAKESPEARE TO SWEET MRS. GOODRICH.
TIRADE? IT WAS ONE SENTENCE...
IT DOESN'T TAKE A GENIUS TO SEE WHAT YOU'RE DOING, KENT. IF YOU WANT ANYTHING TO HAPPEN WITH LANA LANG, THEN YOU'VE GOTTA PUT YOUR BIG-BOY PANTS ON AND SAY SOMETHING TO HER.
YOU HAVE NO IDEA WHAT YOU'RE TALKING ABOUT. SHE'S MY BEST FRIEND.
OU'RE TRYING OUT THAT AMOS S "BAD BOY" LOOK BY SHOWING R HOW YOU TOO CAN GET A TLE WILD, THEN AT LEAST TRY TO LOOK LESS NERDY NEXT TIME.
YOU'RE THE ONE WEARING THE SWEATER VEST, MAN.
WHERE IS LANA?

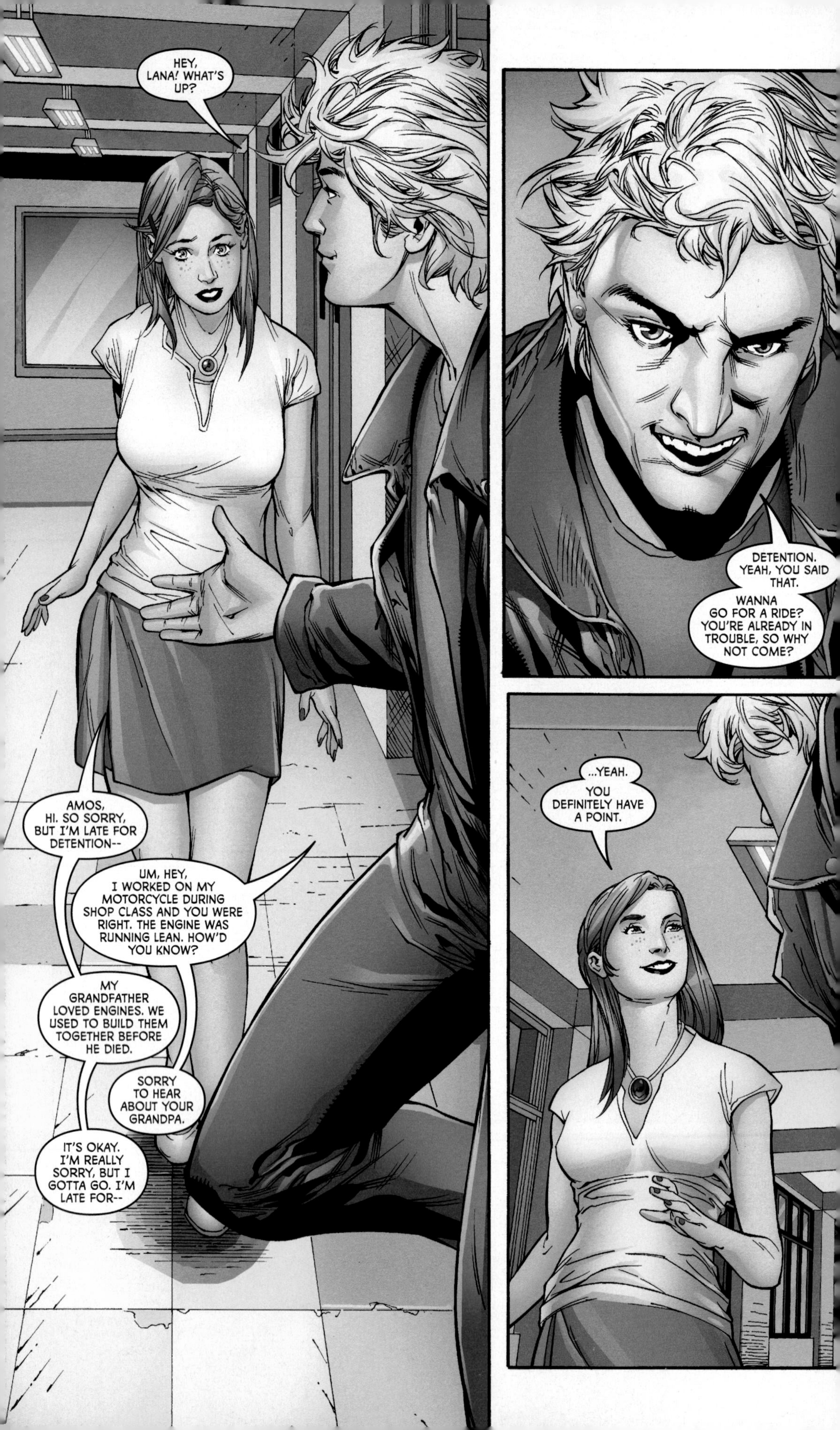
HEY, LANA! WHAT'S UP?
AMOS, HI. SO SORRY, BUT I'M LATE FOR DETENTION--
UM, HEY, I WORKED ON MY MOTORCYCLE DURING SHOP CLASS AND YOU WERE RIGHT. THE ENGINE WAS RUNNING LEAN. HOW'D YOU KNOW?
MY GRANDFATHER LOVED ENGINES. WE USED TO BUILD THEM TOGETHER BEFORE HE DIED.
SORRY TO HEAR ABOUT YOUR GRANDPA.
IT'S OKAY. I'M REALLY SORRY, BUT I GOTTA GO. I'M LATE FOR--
DETENTION. YEAH, YOU SAID THAT.
WANNA GO FOR A RIDE? YOU'RE ALREADY IN TROUBLE, SO WHY NOT COME?
...YEAH.
YOU DEFINITELY HAVE A POINT.

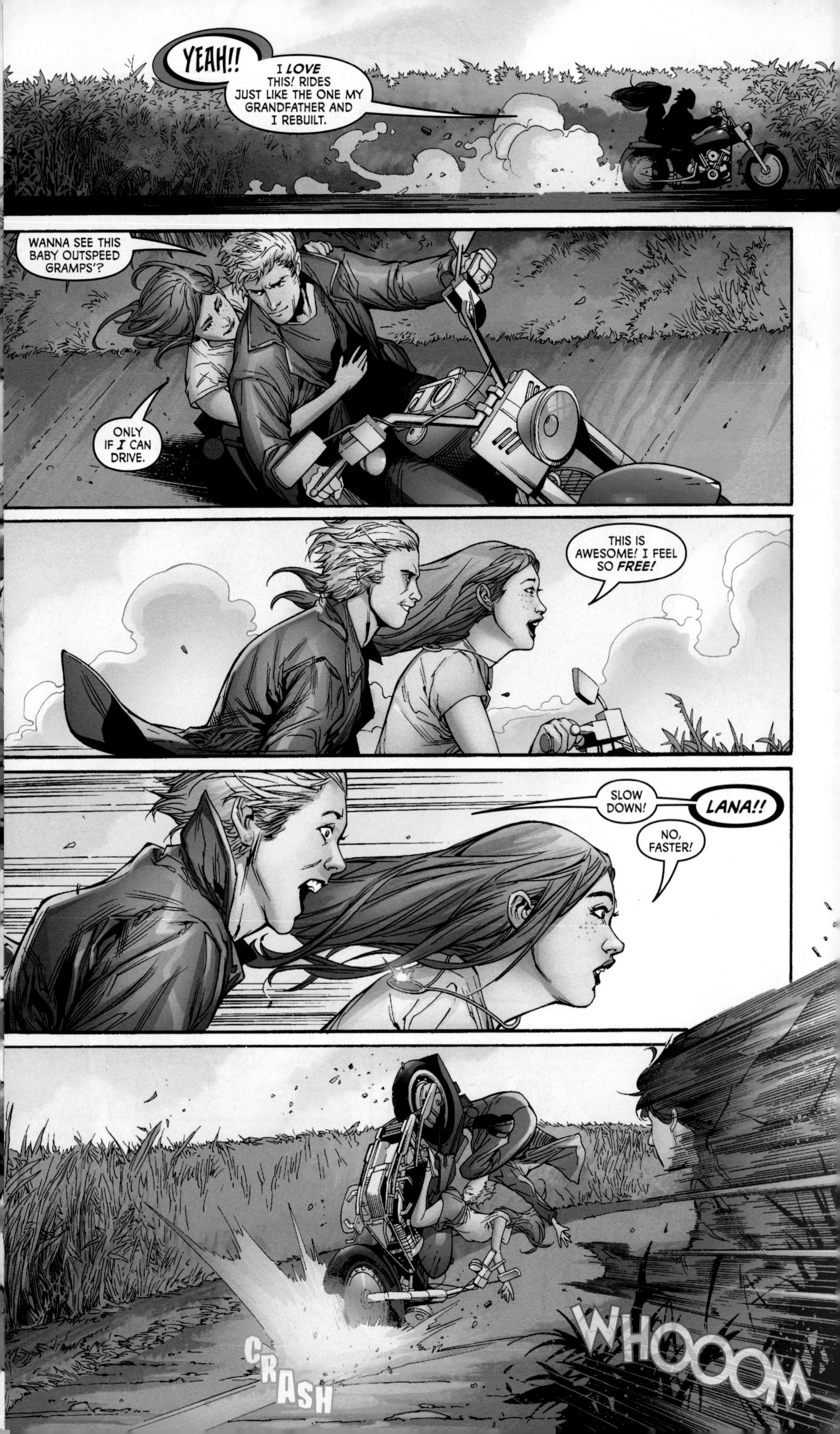
YEAH!!
I LOVE THIS! RIDES JUST LIKE THE ONE MY GRANDFATHER AND I REBUILT.
WANNA SEE THIS BABY OUTSPEED GRAMPS'?
ONLY IF I CAN DRIVE.
THIS IS AWESOME! I FEEL SO FREE!
SLOW DOWN!
LANA!!
NO, FASTER!
CRASH
WHOOOM

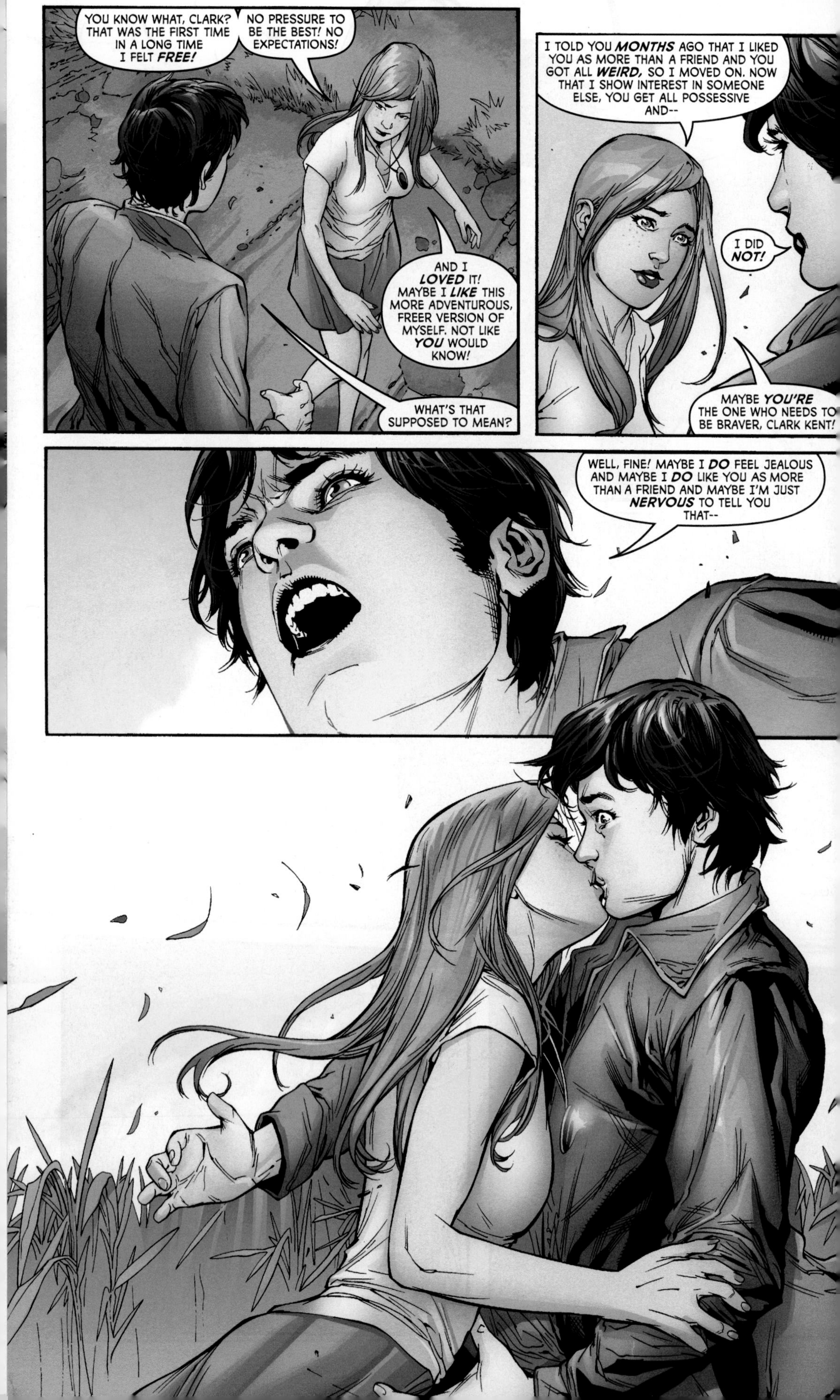
YOU KNOW WHAT, CLARK? THAT WAS THE FIRST TIME IN A LONG TIME I FELT FREE!
NO PRESSURE TO BE THE BEST! NO EXPECTATIONS!
AND I LOVED IT! MAYBE I LIKE THIS MORE ADVENTUROUS, FREER VERSION OF MYSELF. NOT LIKE YOU WOULD KNOW!
WHAT'S THAT SUPPOSED TO MEAN?
I TOLD YOU MONTHS AGO THAT I LIKED YOU AS MORE THAN A FRIEND AND YOU GOT ALL WEIRD, SO I MOVED ON. NOW THAT I SHOW INTEREST IN SOMEONE ELSE, YOU GET ALL POSSESSIVE AND--
I DID NOT!
MAYBE YOU'RE THE ONE WHO NEEDS TO BE BRAVER, CLARK KENT!
WELL, FINE! MAYBE I DO FEEL JEALOUS AND MAYBE I DO LIKE YOU AS MORE THAN A FRIEND AND MAYBE I'M JUST NERVOUS TO TELL YOU THAT--

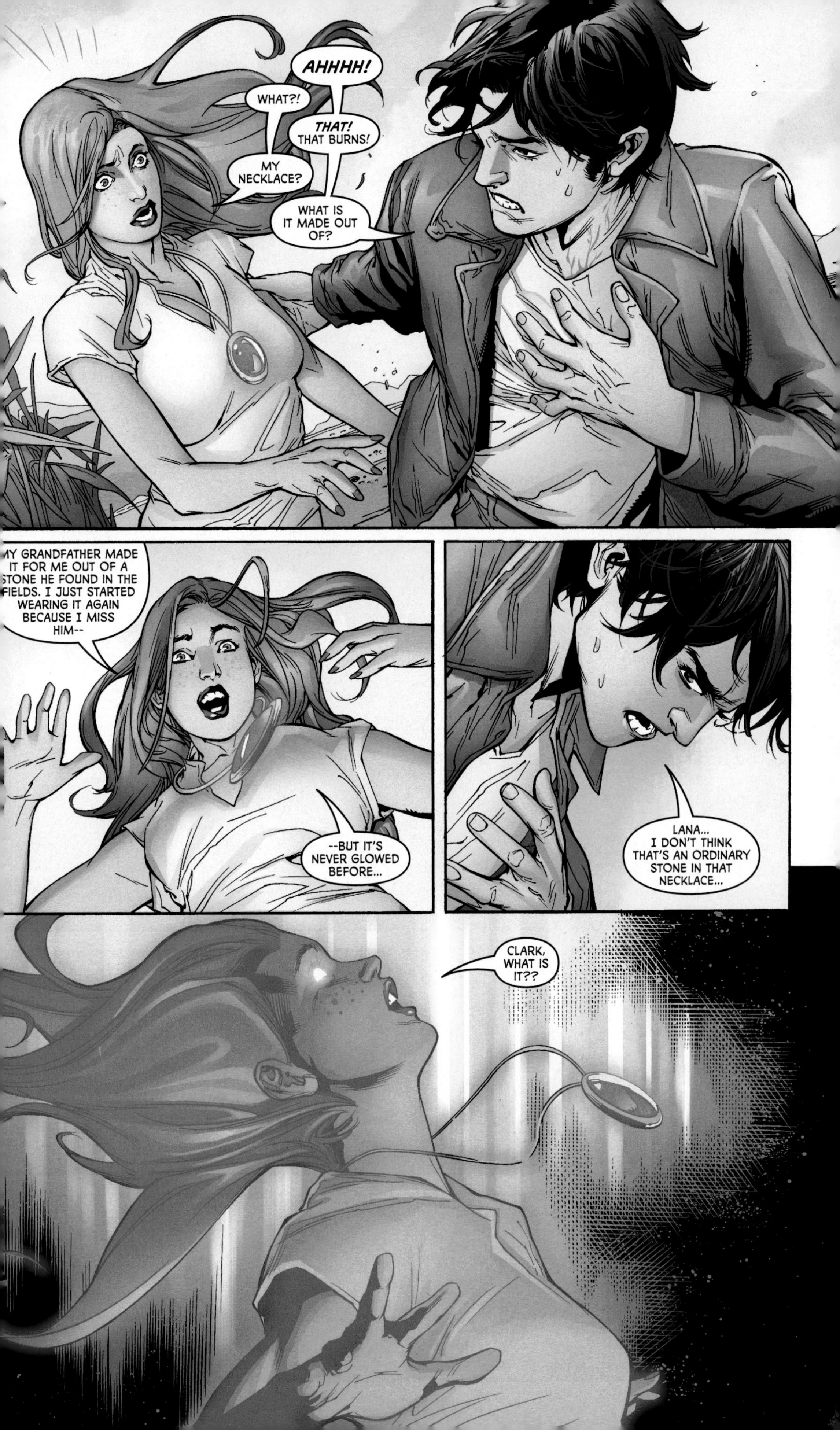
AHHHH!
WHAT?!
THAT! THAT BURNS!
MY NECKLACE?
WHAT IS IT MADE OUT OF?
MY GRANDFATHER MADE IT FOR ME OUT OF A STONE HE FOUND IN THE FIELDS. I JUST STARTED WEARING IT AGAIN BECAUSE I MISS HIM--
--BUT IT'S NEVER GLOWED BEFORE...
LANA... I DON'T THINK THAT'S AN ORDINARY STONE IN THAT NECKLACE...
CLARK, WHAT IS IT??

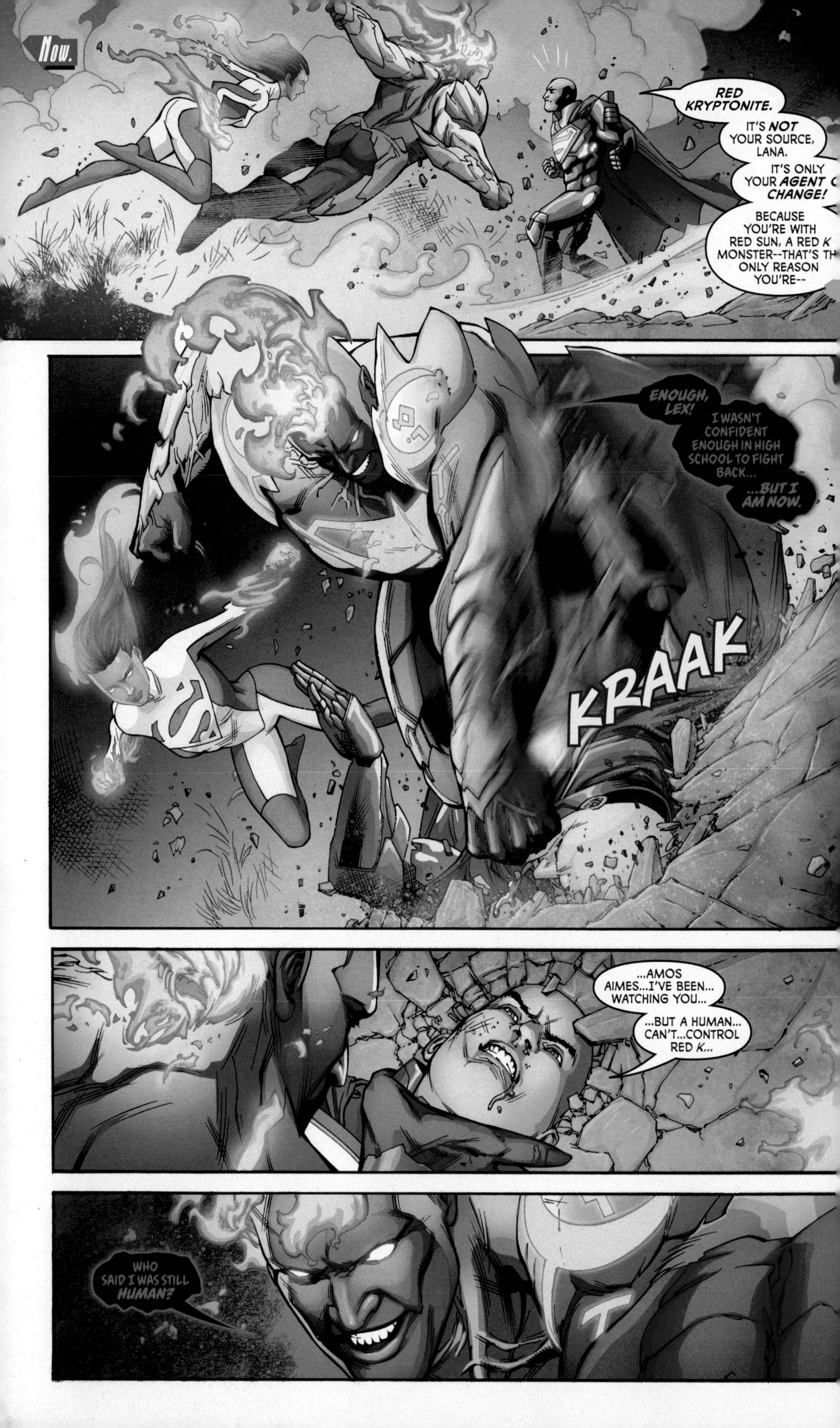
Now.
RED KRYPTONITE.
IT'S NOT YOUR SOURCE, LANA.
IT'S ONLY YOUR AGENT OF CHANGE!
BECAUSE YOU'RE WITH RED SUN, A RED K MONSTER--THAT'S THE ONLY REASON YOU'RE--
ENOUGH, LEX!
I WASN'T CONFIDENT ENOUGH IN HIGH SCHOOL TO FIGHT BACK...
...BUT I AM NOW.
KRAAK
...AMOS AIMES...I'VE BEEN... WATCHING YOU...
...BUT A HUMAN... CAN'T...CONTROL RED K...
WHO SAID I WAS STILL HUMAN?

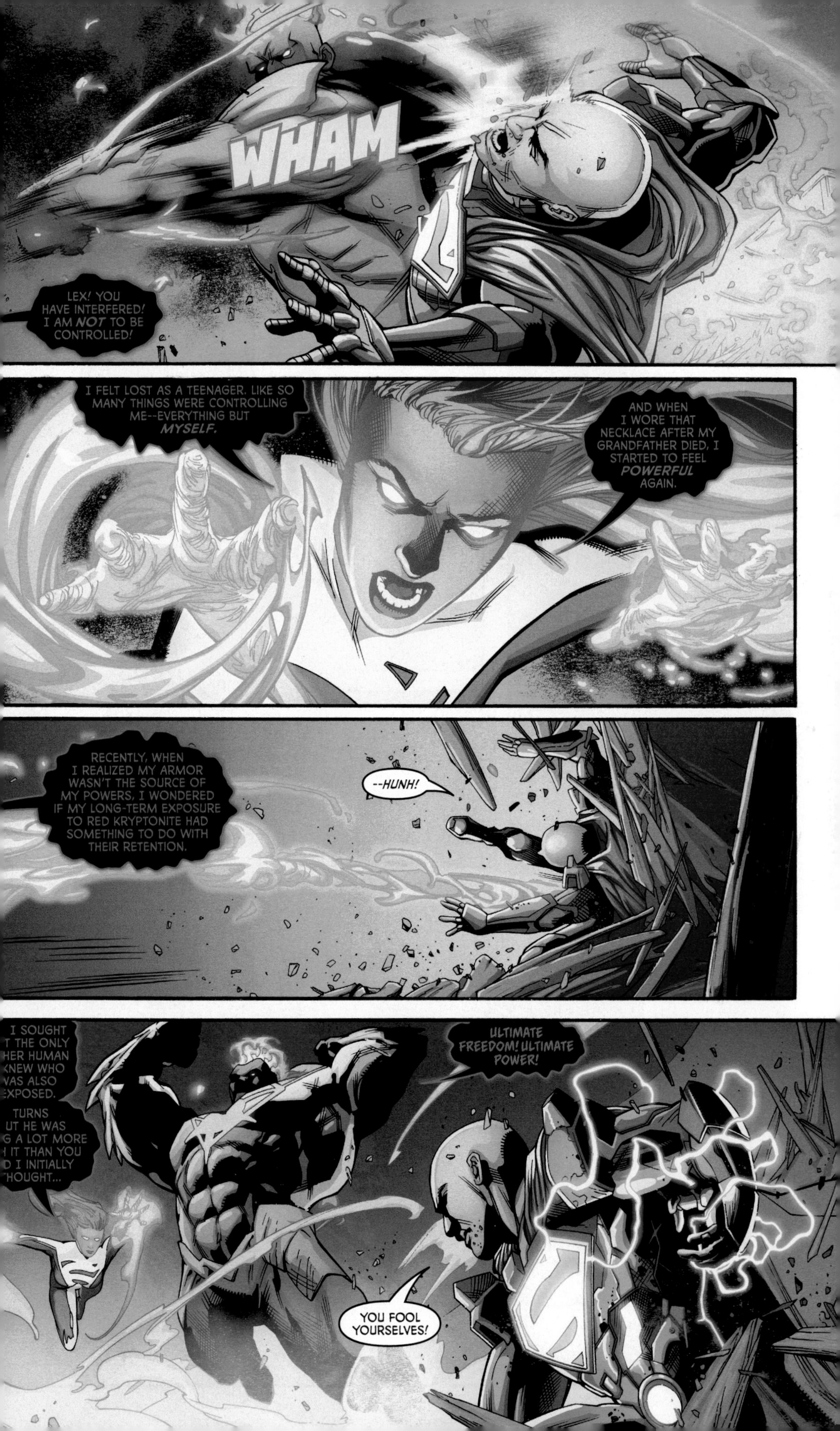
WHAM
LEX! YOU HAVE INTERFERED! I AM *NOT* TO BE CONTROLLED!
I FELT LOST AS A TEENAGER. LIKE SO MANY THINGS WERE CONTROLLING ME--EVERYTHING BUT *MYSELF.*
AND WHEN I WORE THAT NECKLACE AFTER MY GRANDFATHER DIED, I STARTED TO FEEL *POWERFUL* AGAIN.
RECENTLY, WHEN I REALIZED MY ARMOR WASN'T THE SOURCE OF MY POWERS, I WONDERED IF MY LONG-TERM EXPOSURE TO RED KRYPTONITE HAD SOMETHING TO DO WITH THEIR RETENTION.
--HUNH!
I SOUGHT T THE ONLY HER HUMAN KNEW WHO VAS ALSO EXPOSED.
TURNS UT HE WAS G A LOT MORE H IT THAN YOU D I INITIALLY THOUGHT...
ULTIMATE FREEDOM! ULTIMATE POWER!
YOU FOOL YOURSELVES!

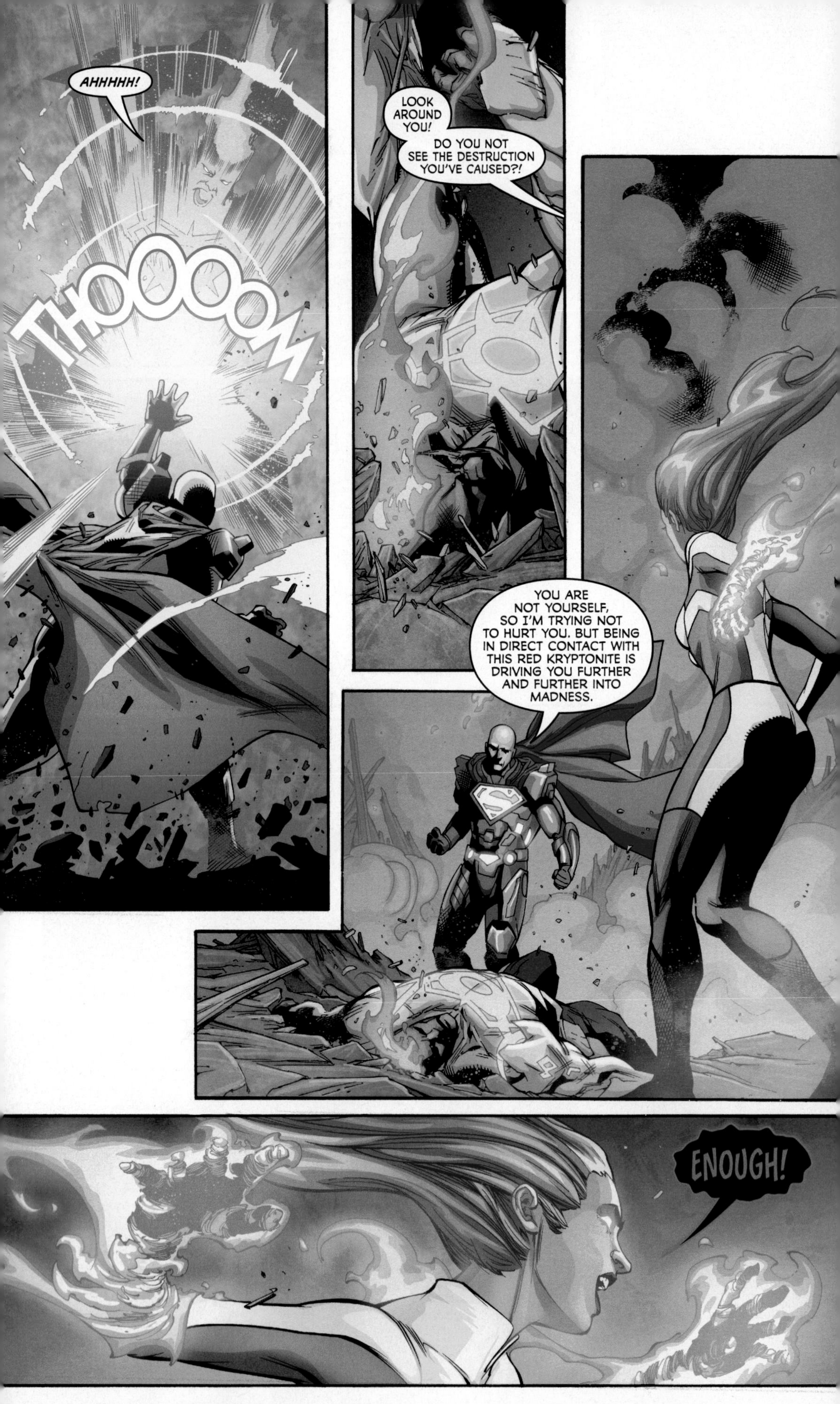
AHHHHH!
THOOOOM
LOOK AROUND YOU!
DO YOU NOT SEE THE DESTRUCTION YOU'VE CAUSED?!
YOU ARE NOT YOURSELF, SO I'M TRYING NOT TO HURT YOU. BUT BEING IN DIRECT CONTACT WITH THIS RED KRYPTONITE IS DRIVING YOU FURTHER AND FURTHER INTO MADNESS.
ENOUGH!

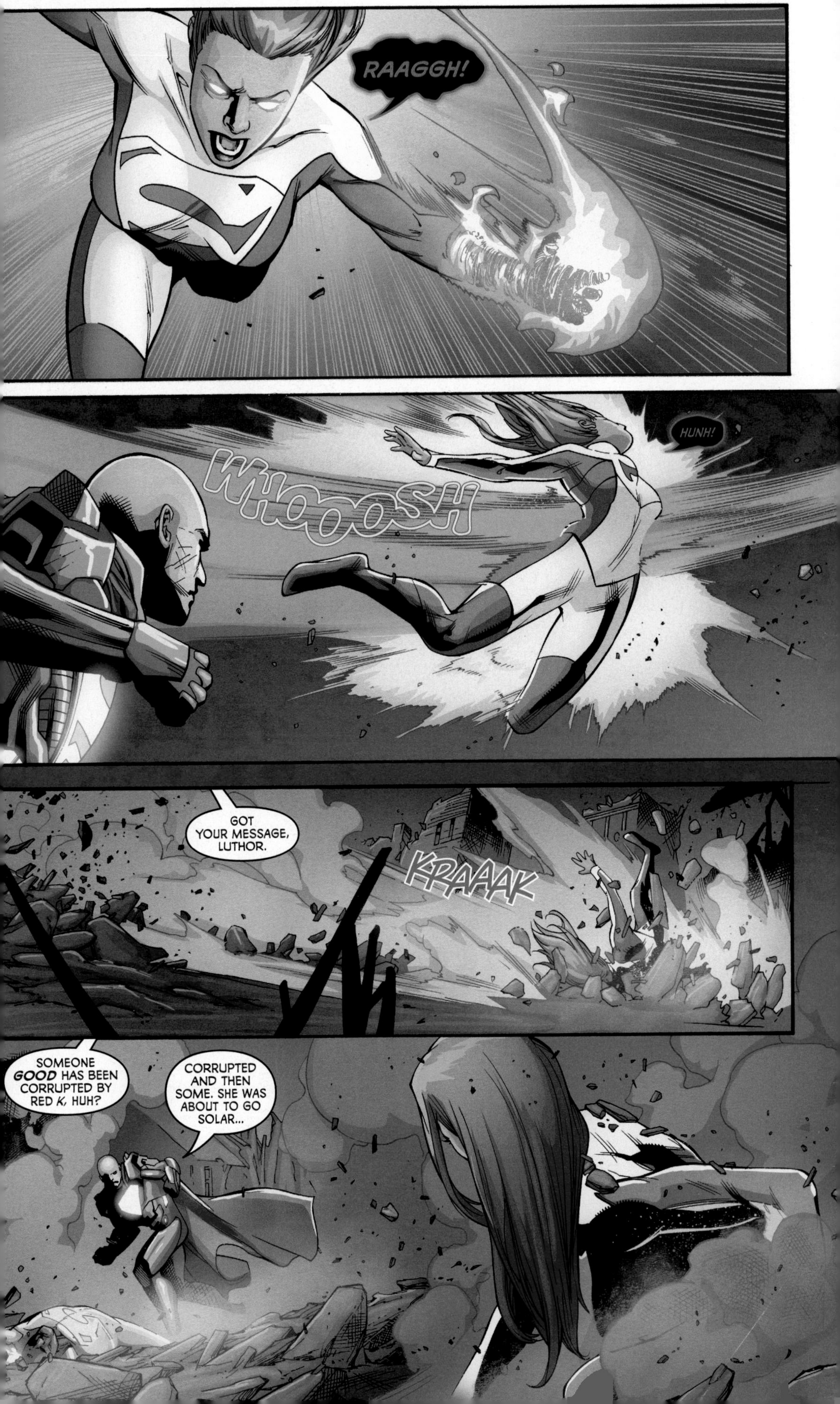
RAAGGH!
HUNH!
WHOOOSH
GOT YOUR MESSAGE, LUTHOR.
KRAAAK
SOMEONE **GOOD** HAS BEEN CORRUPTED BY RED *K*, HUH?
CORRUPTED AND THEN SOME. SHE WAS ABOUT TO GO SOLAR...

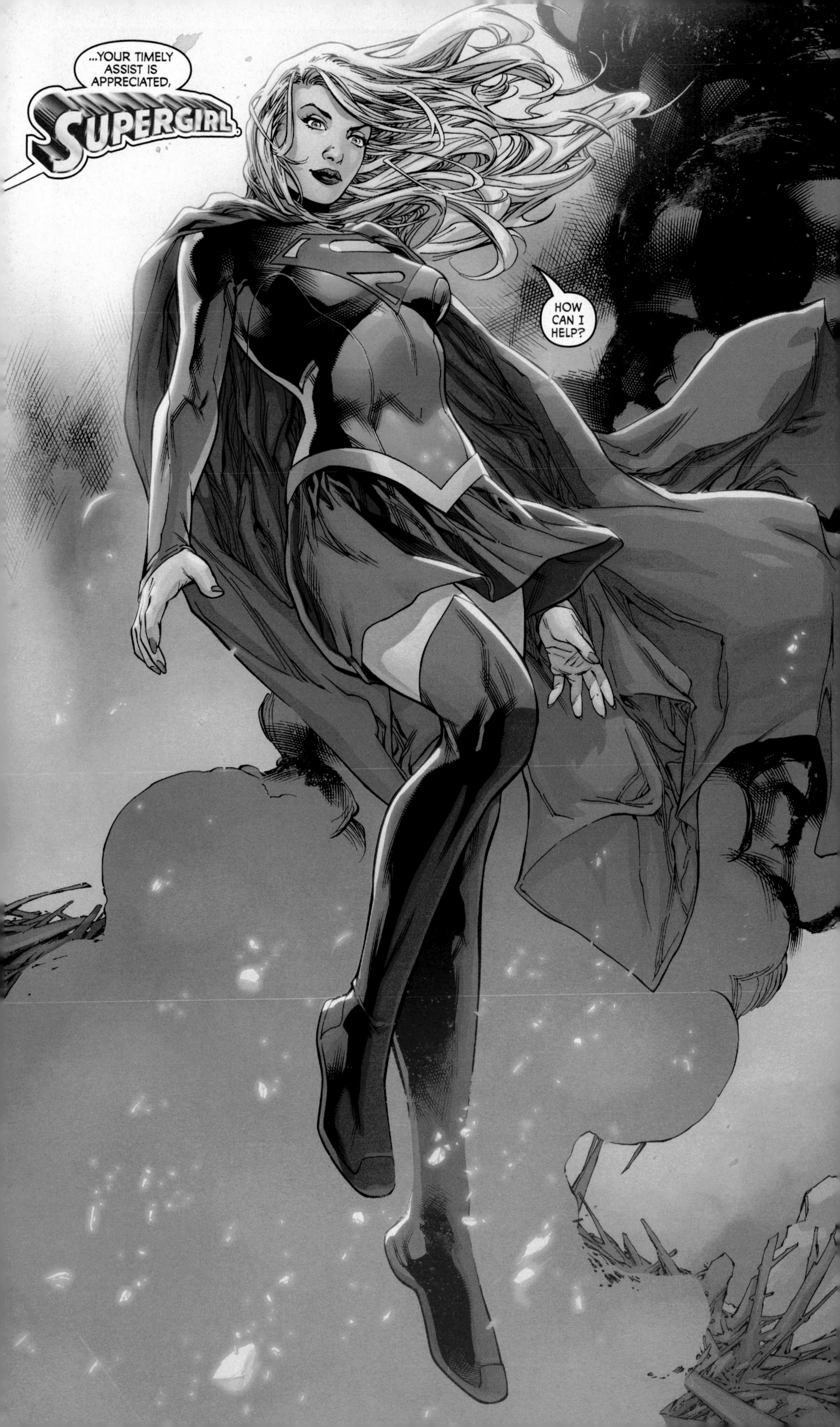
...YOUR TIMELY ASSIST IS APPRECIATED,
SUPERGIRL.
HOW CAN I HELP?

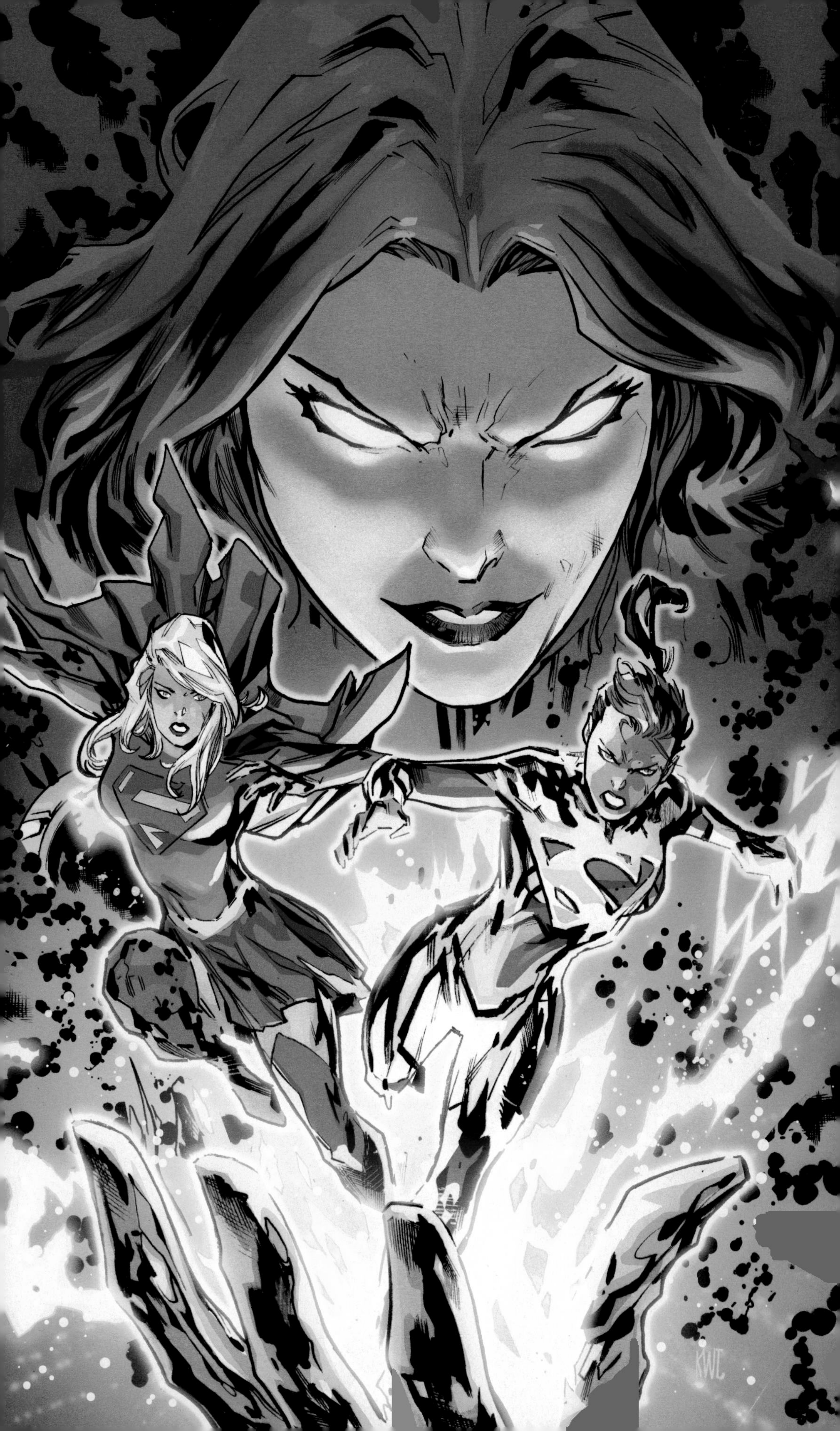

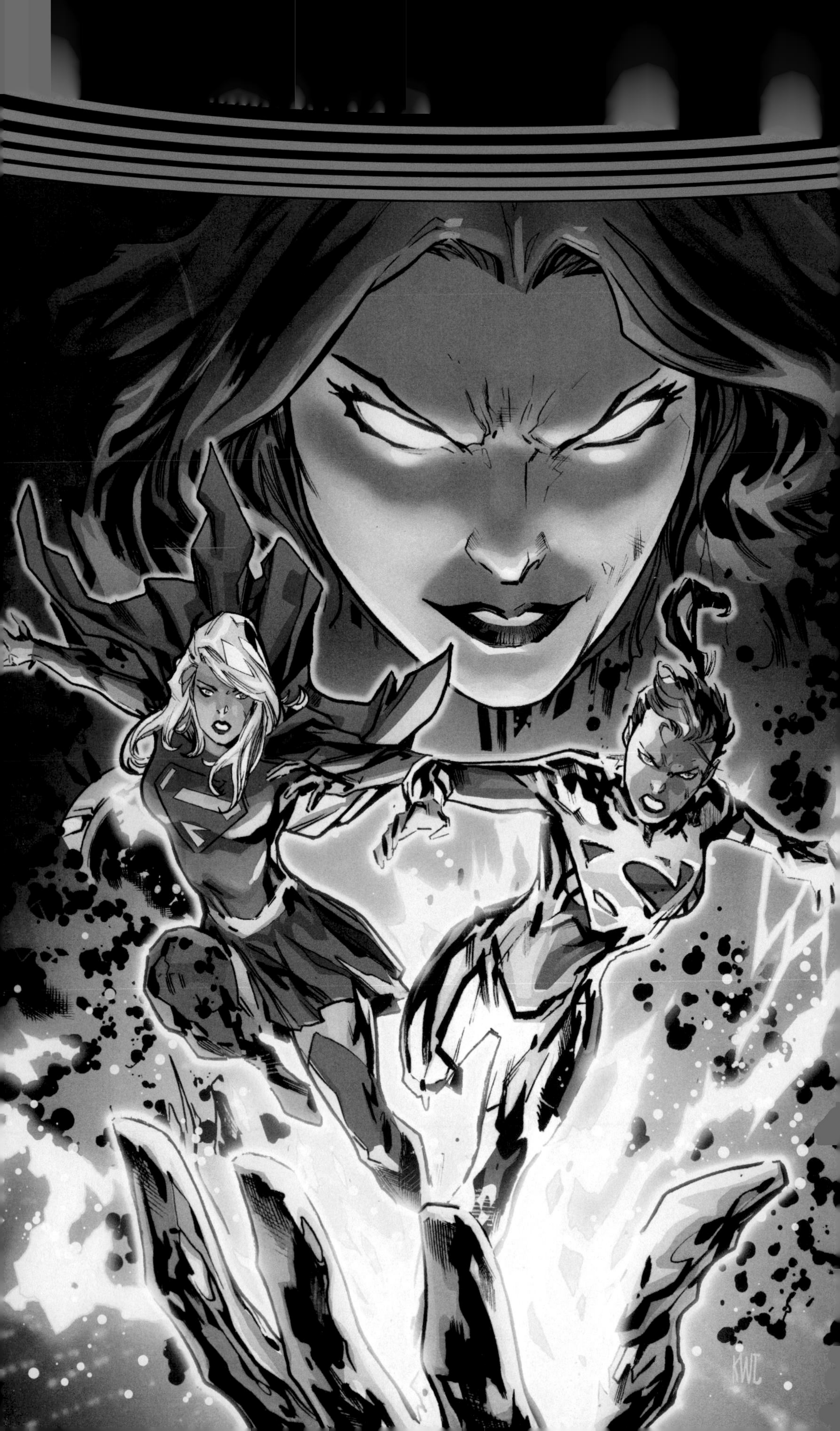

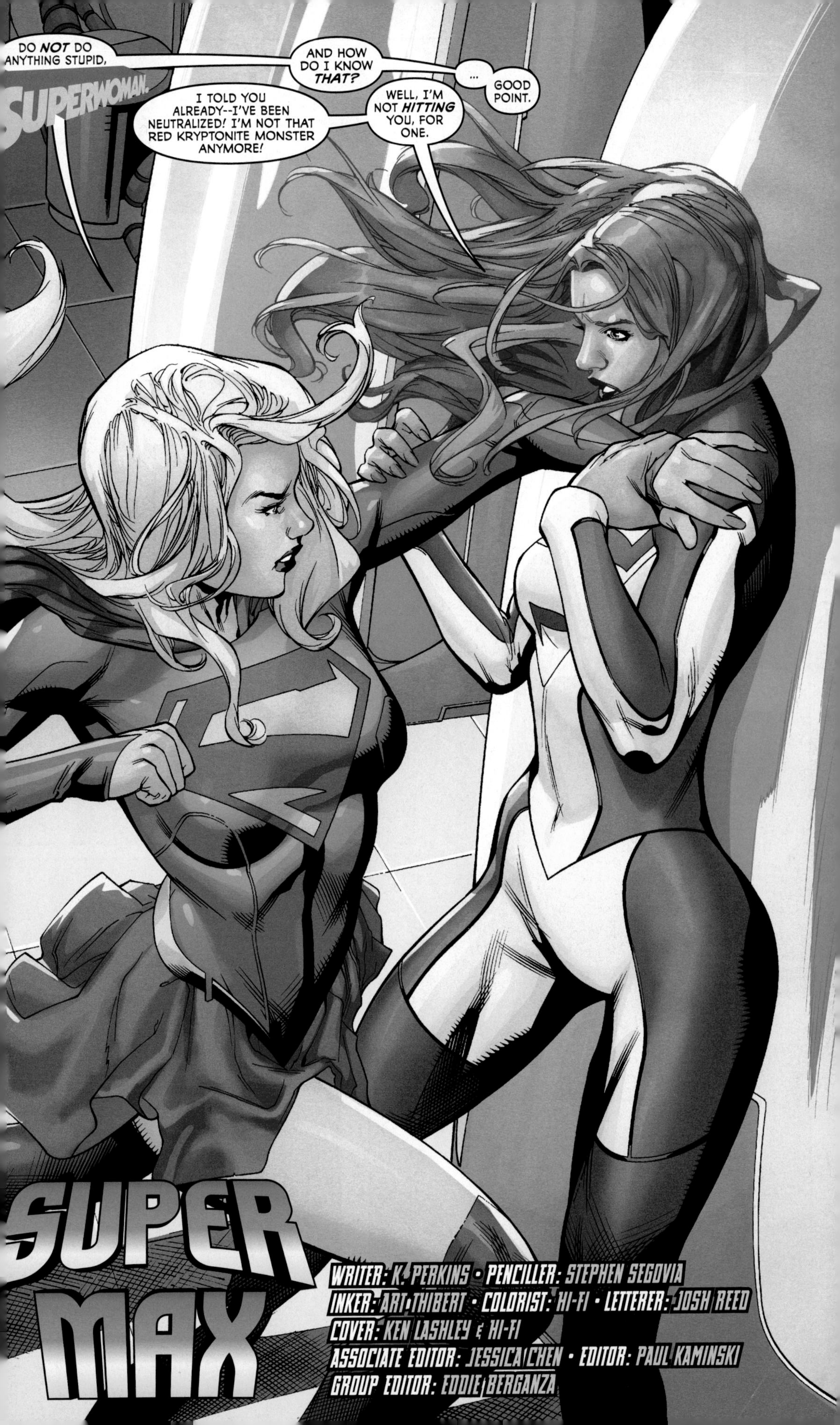
DO NOT DO ANYTHING STUPID, SUPERWOMAN.
AND HOW DO I KNOW THAT?
I TOLD YOU ALREADY--I'VE BEEN NEUTRALIZED! I'M NOT THAT RED KRYPTONITE MONSTER ANYMORE!
WELL, I'M NOT HITTING YOU, FOR ONE.
...
GOOD POINT.
SUPER MAX
WRITER: K. PERKINS • PENCILLER: STEPHEN SEGOVIA
INKER: ART THIBERT • COLORIST: HI-FI • LETTERER: JOSH REED
COVER: KEN LASHLEY & HI-FI
ASSOCIATE EDITOR: JESSICA CHEN • EDITOR: PAUL KAMINSKI
GROUP EDITOR: EDDIE BERGANZA

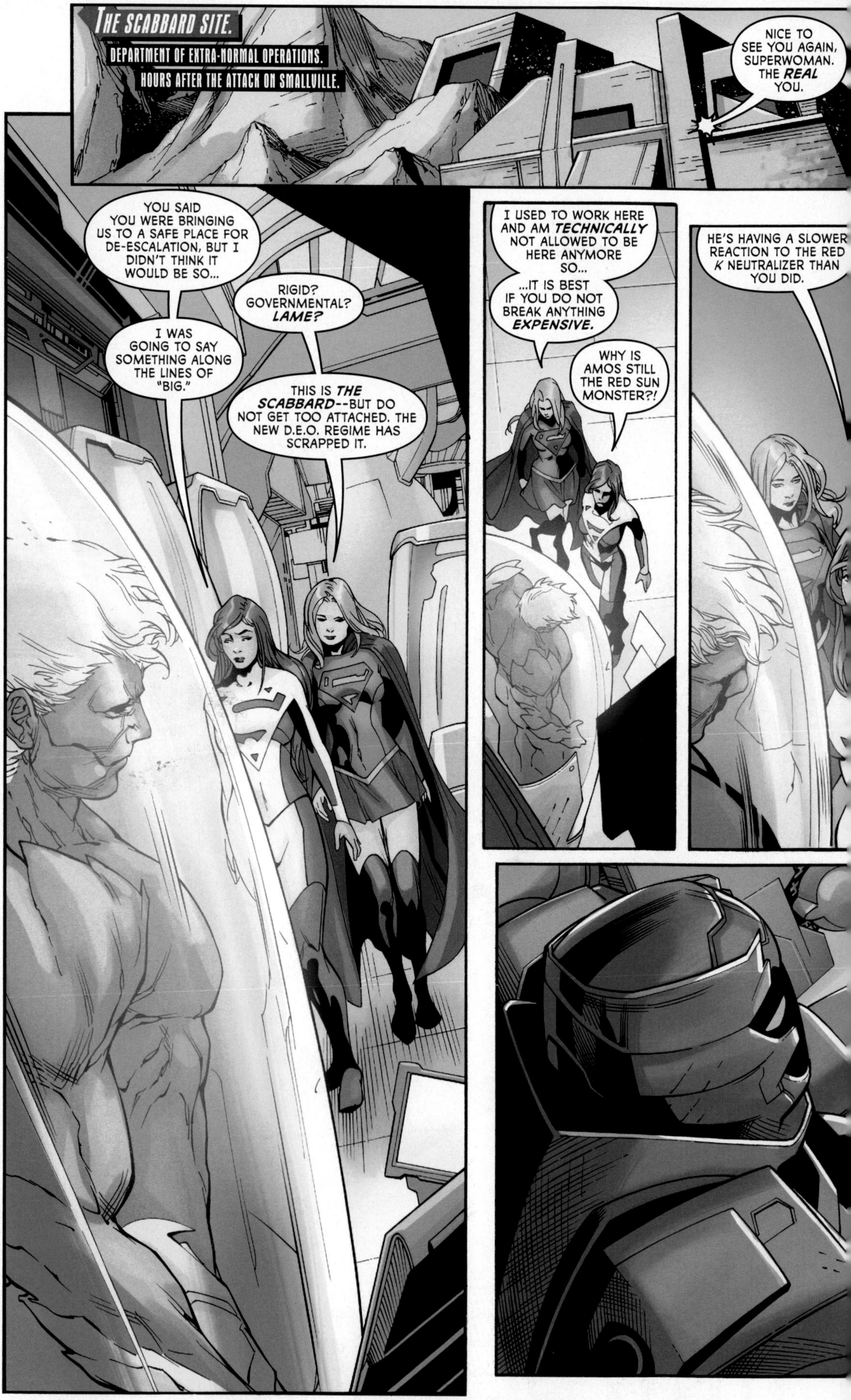
THE SCABBARD SITE.
DEPARTMENT OF EXTRA-NORMAL OPERATIONS.
HOURS AFTER THE ATTACK ON SMALLVILLE.
NICE TO SEE YOU AGAIN, SUPERWOMAN. THE REAL YOU.
YOU SAID YOU WERE BRINGING US TO A SAFE PLACE FOR DE-ESCALATION, BUT I DIDN'T THINK IT WOULD BE SO...
RIGID? GOVERNMENTAL? LAME?
I WAS GOING TO SAY SOMETHING ALONG THE LINES OF "BIG."
THIS IS THE SCABBARD--BUT DO NOT GET TOO ATTACHED. THE NEW D.E.O. REGIME HAS SCRAPPED IT.
I USED TO WORK HERE AND AM TECHNICALLY NOT ALLOWED TO BE HERE ANYMORE SO...
...IT IS BEST IF YOU DO NOT BREAK ANYTHING EXPENSIVE.
WHY IS AMOS STILL THE RED SUN MONSTER?!
HE'S HAVING A SLOWER REACTION TO THE RED K NEUTRALIZER THAN YOU DID.

MY ENCOUNTER WITH LAR-ON TAUGHT ME THAT RED *K* JUST *ENABLES* A TRANSFORMATION, IT IS NOT THE *SOURCE.*

I WAS CERTAIN THE BUBBLE WOULD NEUTRALIZE *ANY* SOURCE, BUT I JUST DO NOT KNOW FOR SURE...

AMOS...

THE LOOKS ON THE TOWNSPEOPLE'S FACES WHEN I APOLOGIZED--OH GOD. IT WAS LIKE THEY DESPISED ME.

SUPERWOMAN, IT IS CLEAR YOU WERE NOT TOTALLY RIGHT IN THE HEAD. YOU WOULD *NEVER* HURT ANYONE INTENTIONALLY.

HAD I KNOWN AMOS AND I WOULD TRIGGER EACH OTHER, I WOULD HAVE NEVER GONE TO FIND HIM.

LISTEN, LEX IS RUNNING DAMAGE CONTROL AT THE SITE OF THE ATTACK. HE REALLY LIKES YOU FOR SOME REASON.

YOU NEED TO FOCUS ON GETTING *YOURSELF* TOGETHER FIRST BEFORE YOU GROVEL.

I CAN'T BELIEVE MYSELF!

I MADE SO MUCH HEADWAY ON THE CONTROL OF MY RS! AND TO *BACKSLIDE* AS MUCH AS I JUST DID--DAMN.

I'M JUST SO *TIRED* OF BEING IN DISCOVERY MODE.

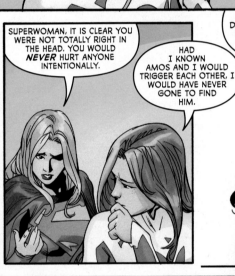

I *KNOW* CLARK'S POWERS RESIDE IN *ME*--THEY'RE PART OF MY DNA NOW AND *SOMEHOW* THE RED *K* EXPOSURE I HAD GROWING UP REINFORCES THOSE POWERS. I JUST NEED FIRM ANSWERS.

WELL, HOW WILL YOU FIND OUT?

IS THAT THE KRYPTONIAN SUIT OF ARMOR? THE ONE THAT SAVED MY LIFE?

YES, BUT IF THE D.E.O. KNEW KAL LOANED THAT TO ME AND *SHAY VERITAS*--

I DON'T HAVE A CHOICE, SUPERGIRL.

I'VE *GOT* TO TALK TO AMOS. NOT THIS RED SUN MONSTER. AMOS KNOWS HOW TO CONTROL IT--HE'S DONE IT FOR YEARS.

AND HOW DO WE TRANSFORM HIM WHEN WE DO NOT KNOW THE SOURCE?

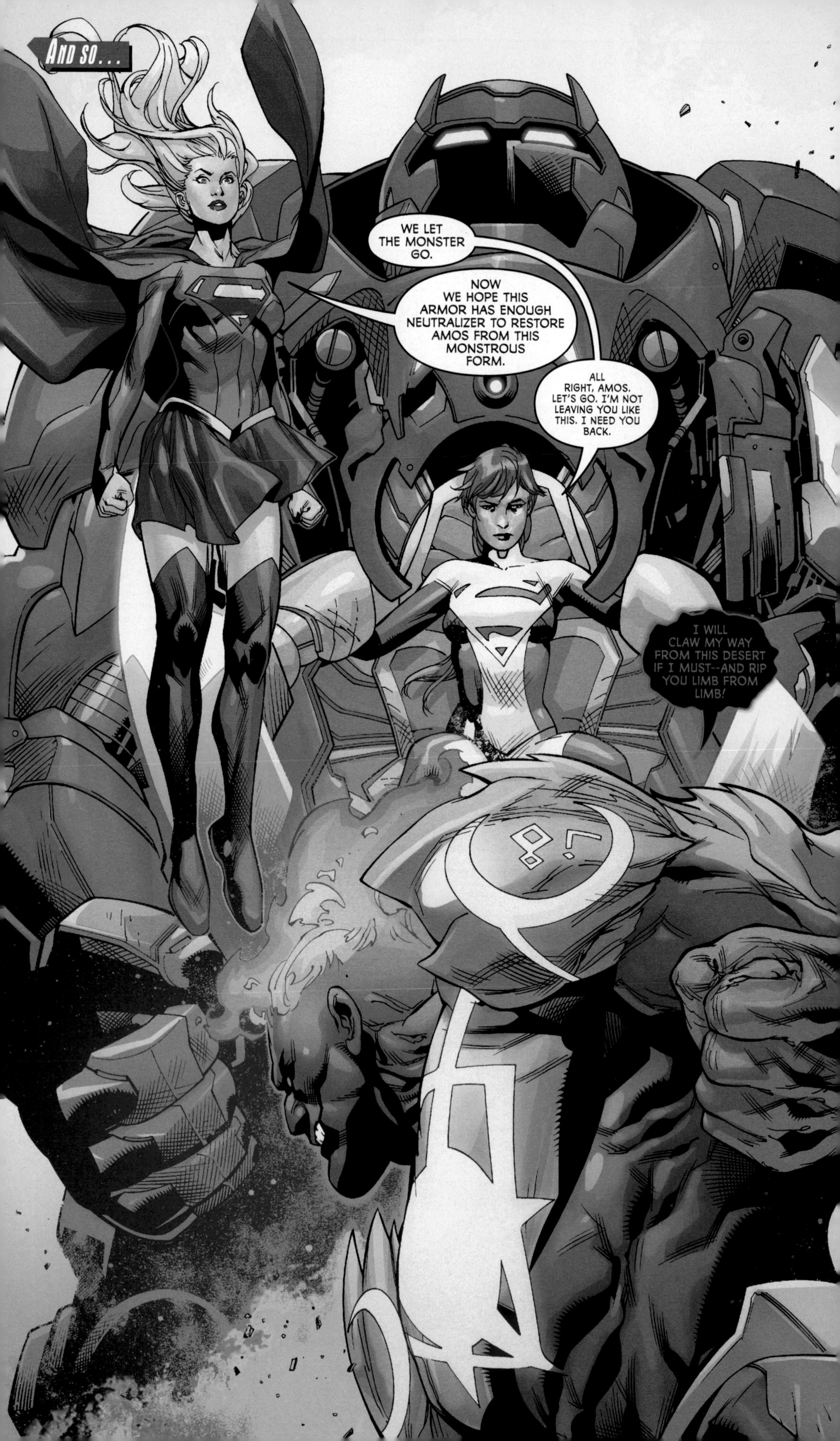
AND SO . . .
WE LET THE MONSTER GO.
NOW WE HOPE THIS ARMOR HAS ENOUGH NEUTRALIZER TO RESTORE AMOS FROM THIS MONSTROUS FORM.
ALL RIGHT, AMOS. LET'S GO. I'M NOT LEAVING YOU LIKE THIS. I NEED YOU BACK.
I WILL CLAW MY WAY FROM THIS DESERT IF I MUST--AND RIP YOU LIMB FROM LIMB!

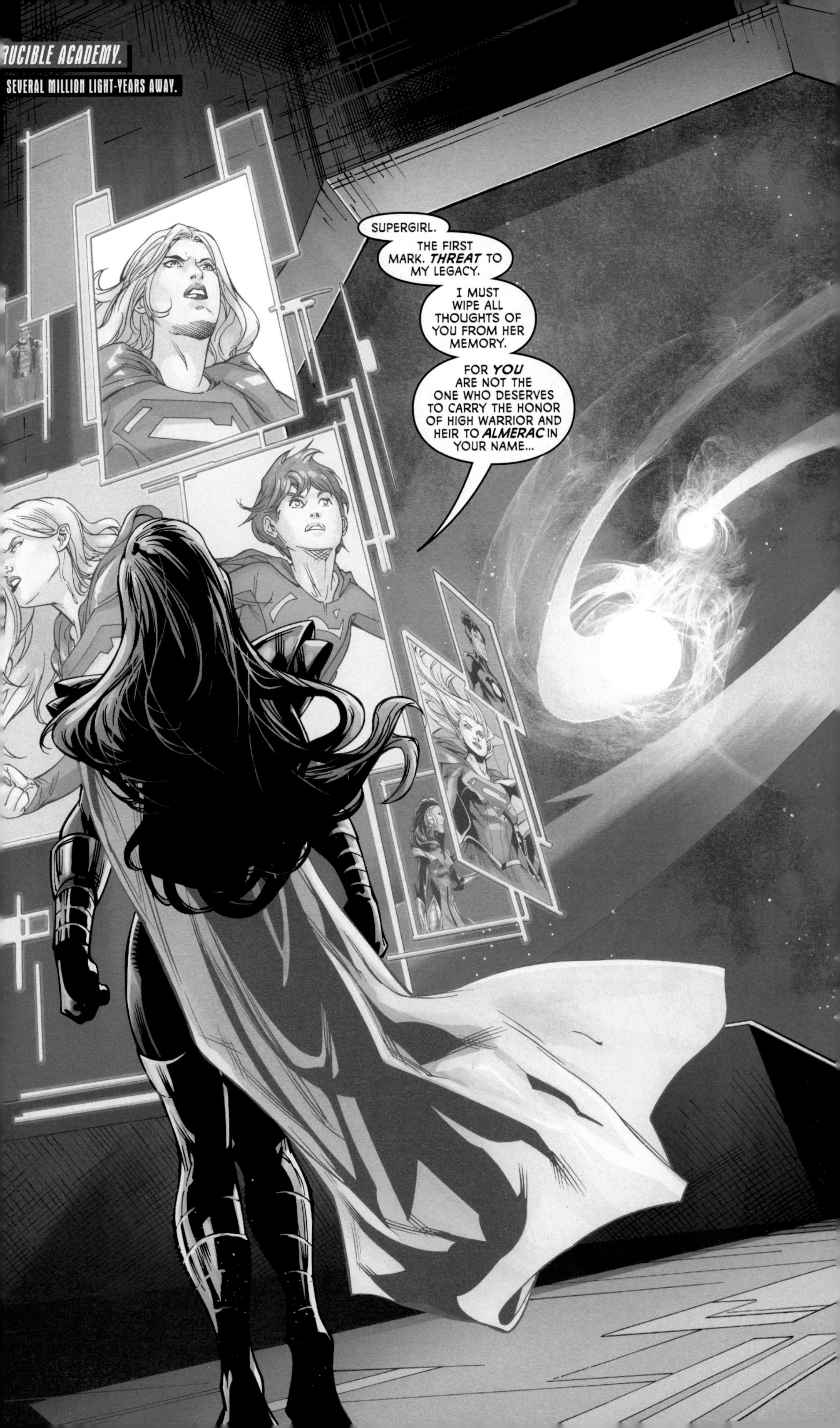
RUCIBLE ACADEMY.
SEVERAL MILLION LIGHT-YEARS AWAY.
SUPERGIRL.
THE FIRST MARK. *THREAT* TO MY LEGACY.
I MUST WIPE ALL THOUGHTS OF YOU FROM HER MEMORY.
FOR *YOU* ARE NOT THE ONE WHO DESERVES TO CARRY THE HONOR OF HIGH WARRIOR AND HEIR TO *ALMERAC* IN YOUR NAME...

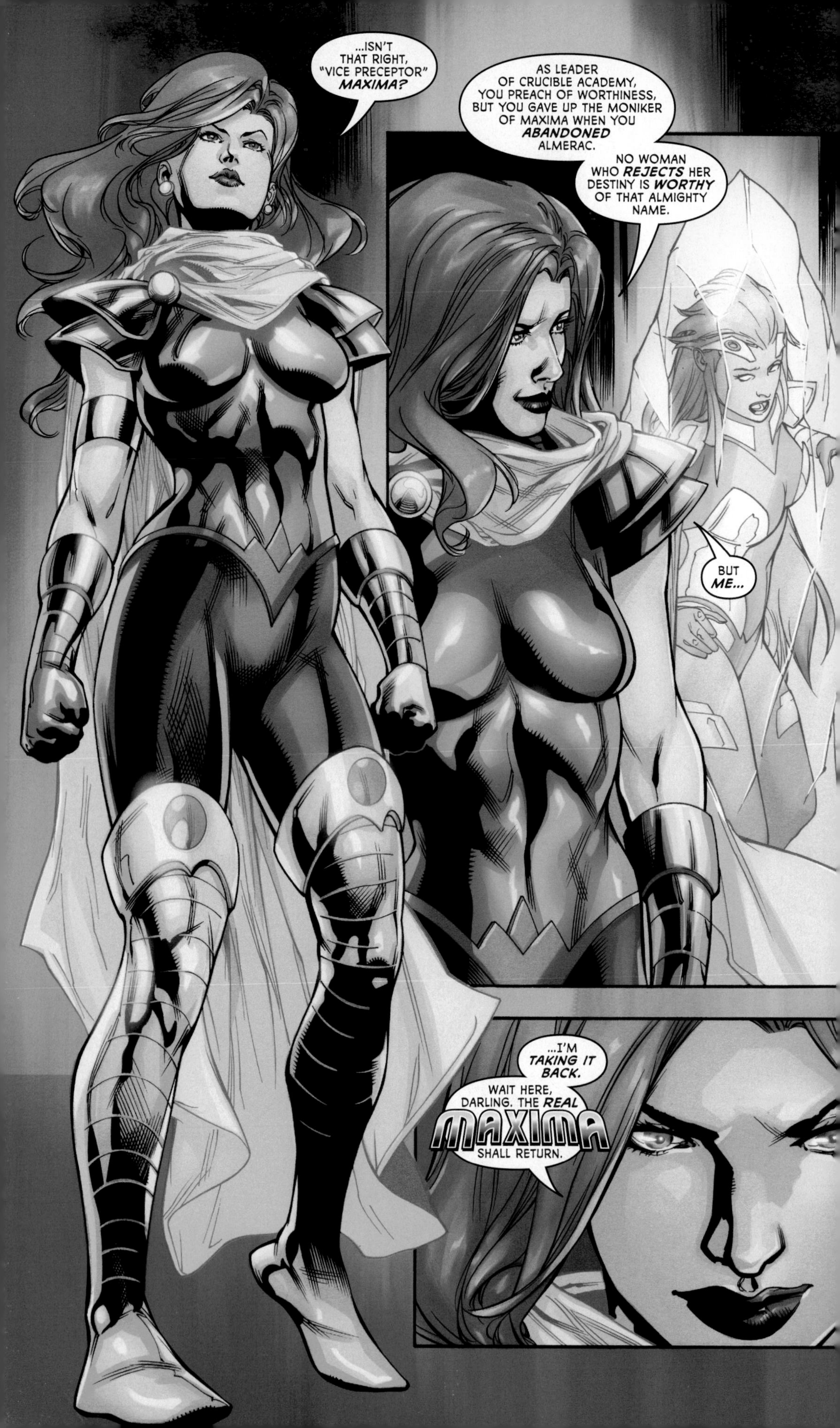
...ISN'T THAT RIGHT, "VICE PRECEPTOR" MAXIMA?
AS LEADER OF CRUCIBLE ACADEMY, YOU PREACH OF WORTHINESS, BUT YOU GAVE UP THE MONIKER OF MAXIMA WHEN YOU ABANDONED ALMERAC.
NO WOMAN WHO REJECTS HER DESTINY IS WORTHY OF THAT ALMIGHTY NAME.
BUT ME...
...I'M TAKING IT BACK.
WAIT HERE, DARLING. THE REAL MAXIMA SHALL RETURN.

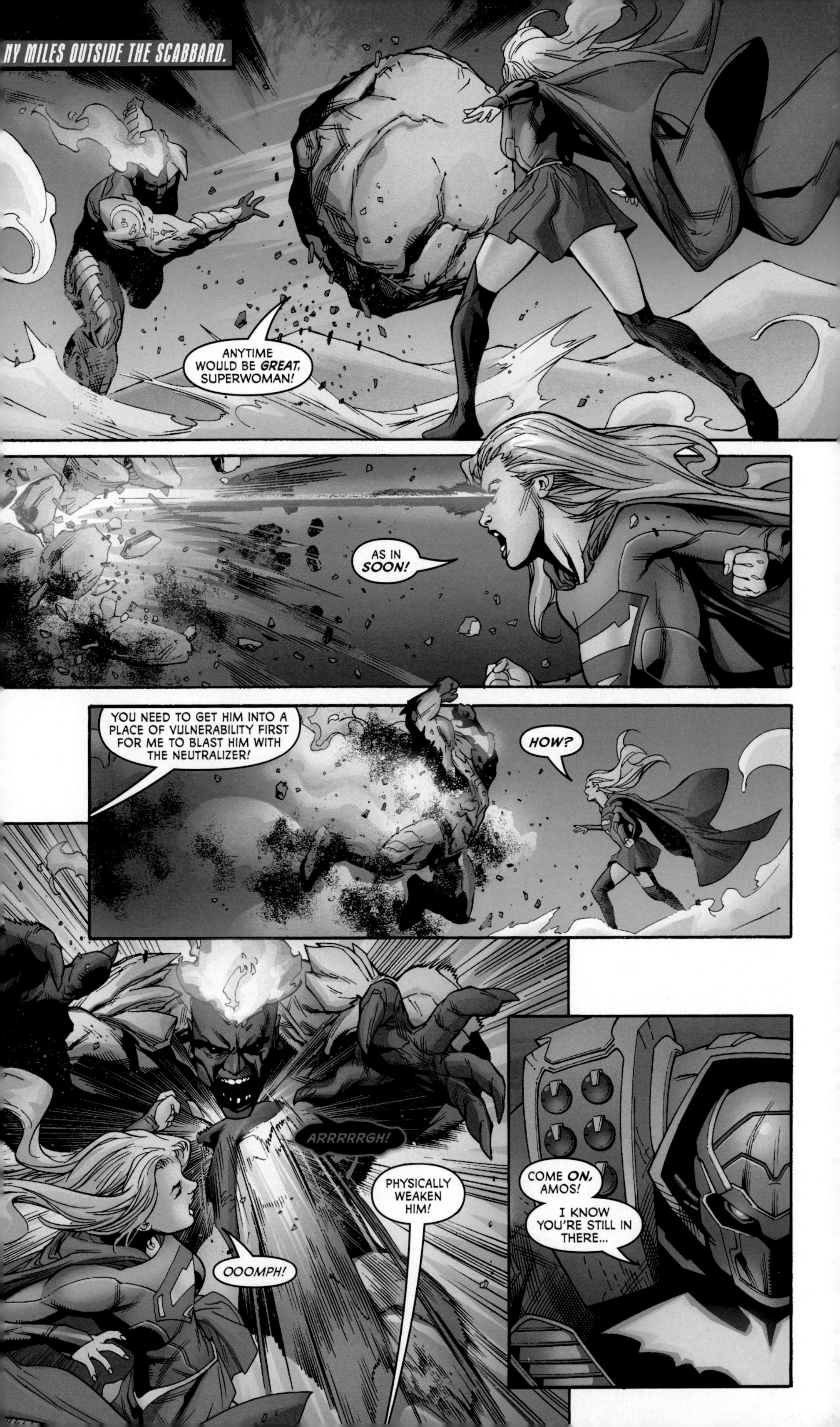

NY MILES OUTSIDE THE SCABBARD.
ANYTIME WOULD BE GREAT, SUPERWOMAN!
AS IN SOON!
YOU NEED TO GET HIM INTO A PLACE OF VULNERABILITY FIRST FOR ME TO BLAST HIM WITH THE NEUTRALIZER!
HOW?
ARRRRRGH!
OOOMPH!
PHYSICALLY WEAKEN HIM!
COME ON, AMOS!
I KNOW YOU'RE STILL IN THERE...

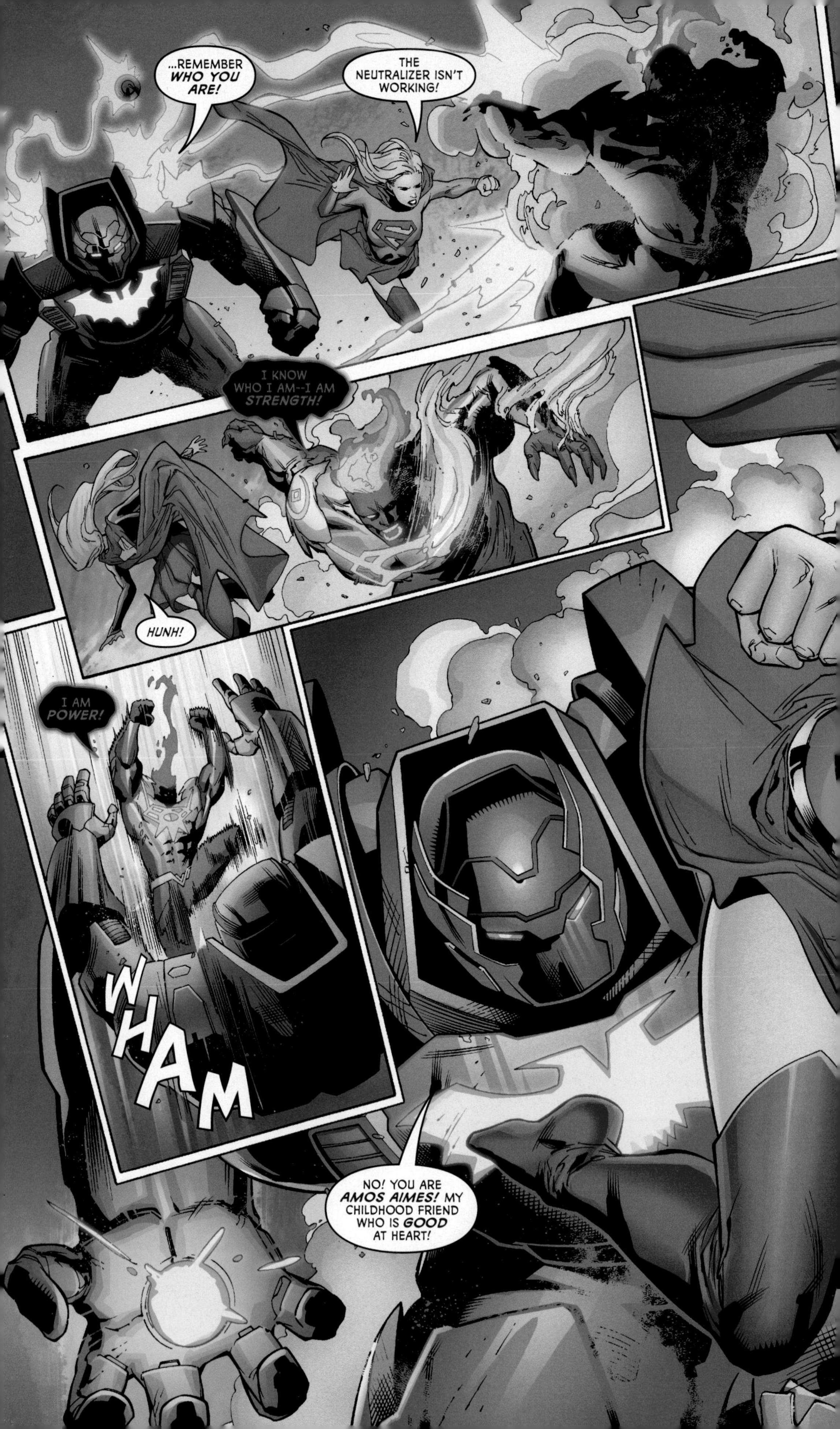
...REMEMBER WHO YOU ARE!
THE NEUTRALIZER ISN'T WORKING!
I KNOW WHO I AM--I AM STRENGTH!
HUNH!
I AM POWER!
WHAM
NO! YOU ARE AMOS AIMES! MY CHILDHOOD FRIEND WHO IS GOOD AT HEART!

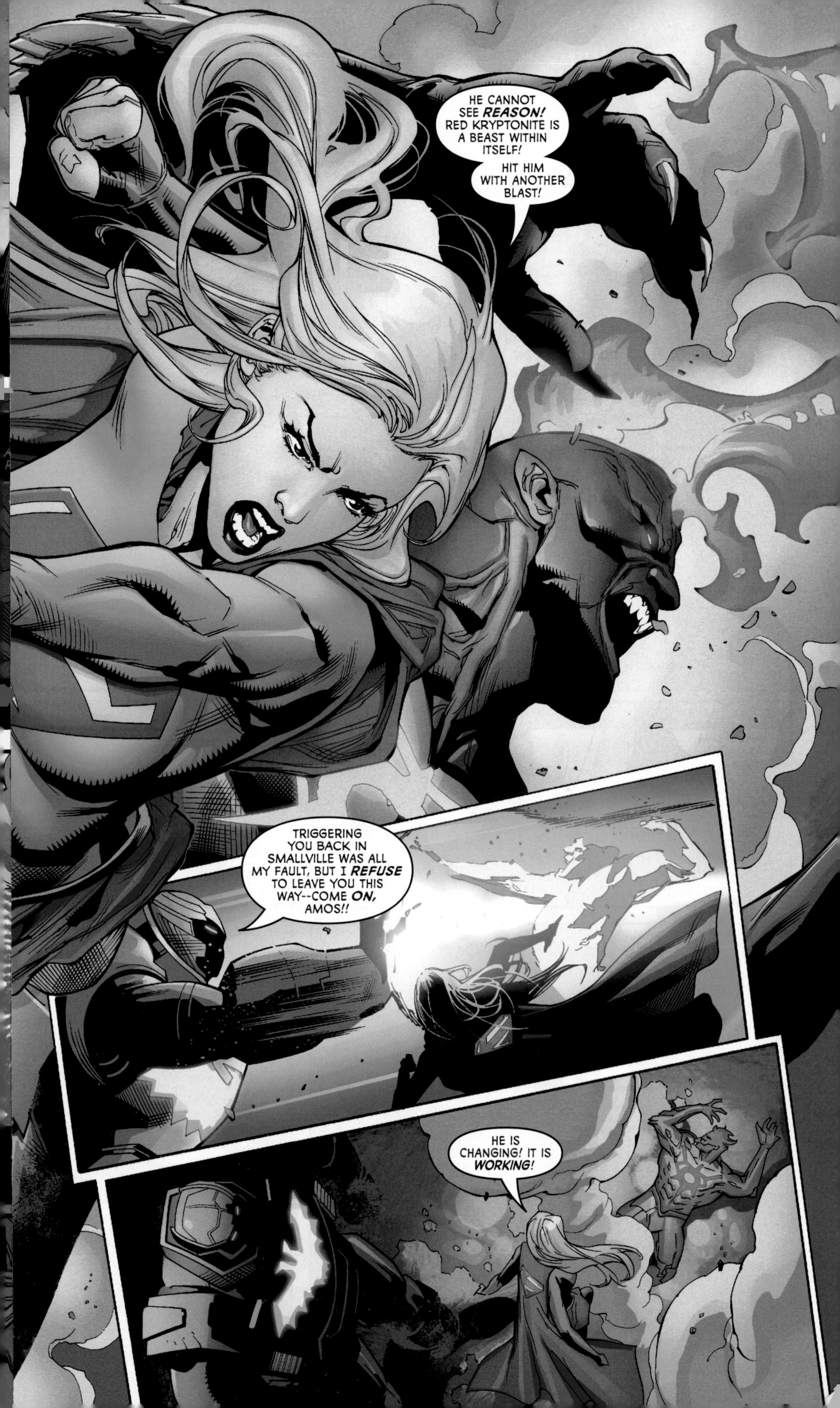
HE CANNOT SEE *REASON!* RED KRYPTONITE IS A BEAST WITHIN ITSELF!
HIT HIM WITH ANOTHER BLAST!
TRIGGERING YOU BACK IN SMALLVILLE WAS ALL MY FAULT, BUT I *REFUSE* TO LEAVE YOU THIS WAY--COME *ON,* AMOS!!
HE IS CHANGING! IT IS *WORKING!*

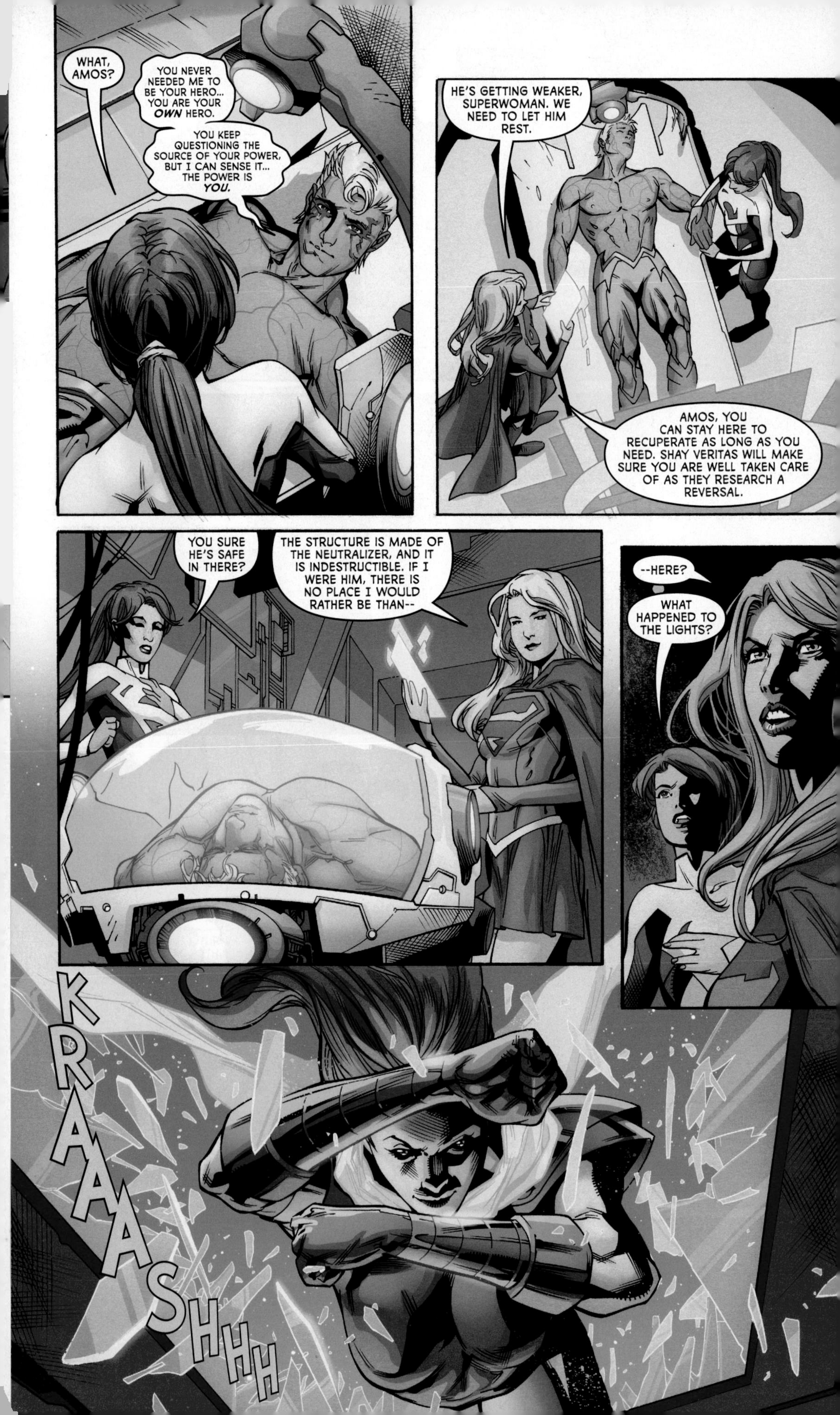
WHAT, AMOS?
YOU NEVER NEEDED ME TO BE YOUR HERO... YOU ARE YOUR OWN HERO.
YOU KEEP QUESTIONING THE SOURCE OF YOUR POWER, BUT I CAN SENSE IT... THE POWER IS YOU.
HE'S GETTING WEAKER, SUPERWOMAN. WE NEED TO LET HIM REST.
AMOS, YOU CAN STAY HERE TO RECUPERATE AS LONG AS YOU NEED. SHAY VERITAS WILL MAKE SURE YOU ARE WELL TAKEN CARE OF AS THEY RESEARCH A REVERSAL.
YOU SURE HE'S SAFE IN THERE?
THE STRUCTURE IS MADE OF THE NEUTRALIZER, AND IT IS INDESTRUCTIBLE. IF I WERE HIM, THERE IS NO PLACE I WOULD RATHER BE THAN--
--HERE?
WHAT HAPPENED TO THE LIGHTS?
KRAAAASHHH

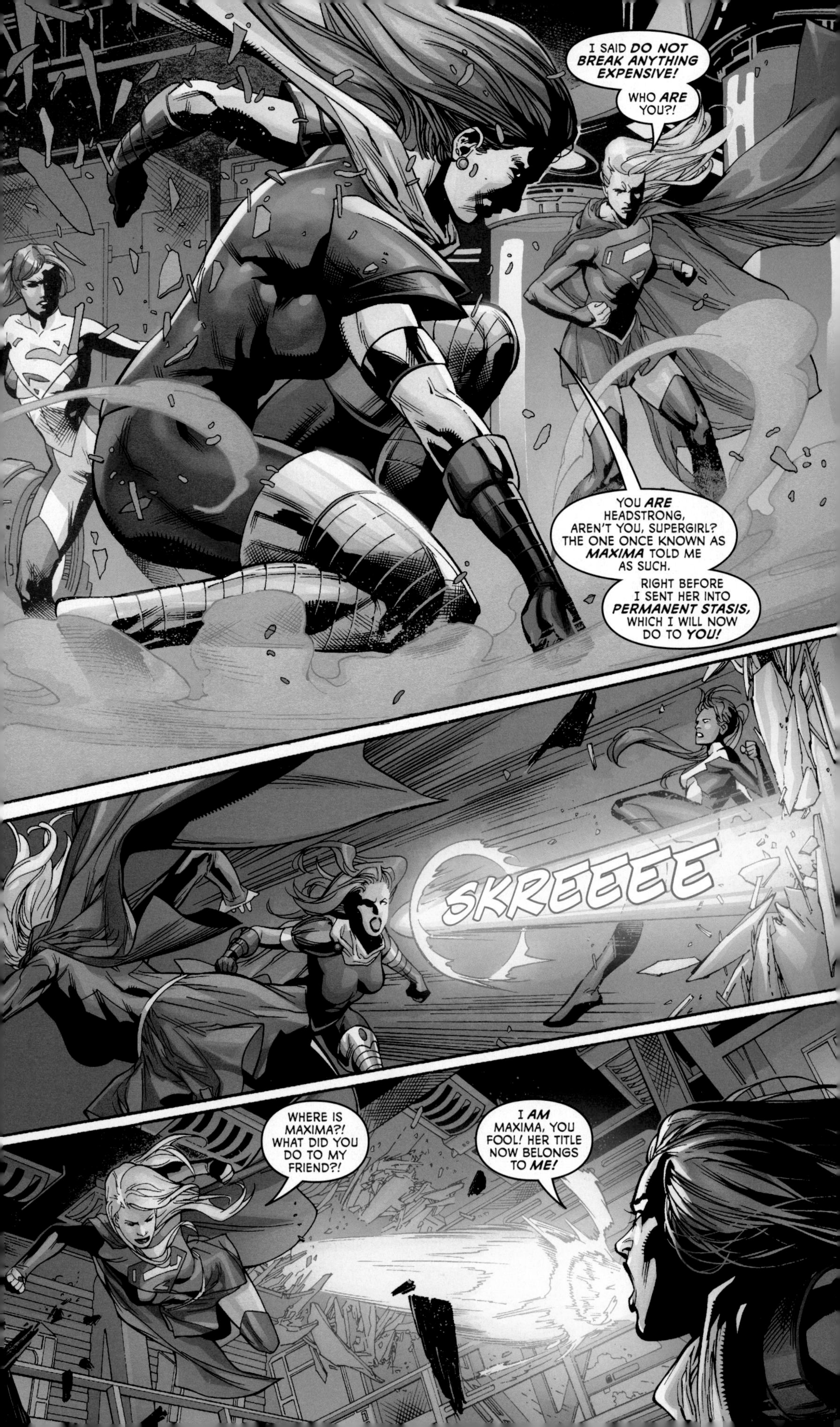

I SAID DO NOT BREAK ANYTHING EXPENSIVE!
WHO ARE YOU?!
YOU ARE HEADSTRONG, AREN'T YOU, SUPERGIRL? THE ONE ONCE KNOWN AS MAXIMA TOLD ME AS SUCH.
RIGHT BEFORE I SENT HER INTO PERMANENT STASIS, WHICH I WILL NOW DO TO YOU!
SKREEEE
WHERE IS MAXIMA?! WHAT DID YOU DO TO MY FRIEND?!
I AM MAXIMA, YOU FOOL! HER TITLE NOW BELONGS TO ME!

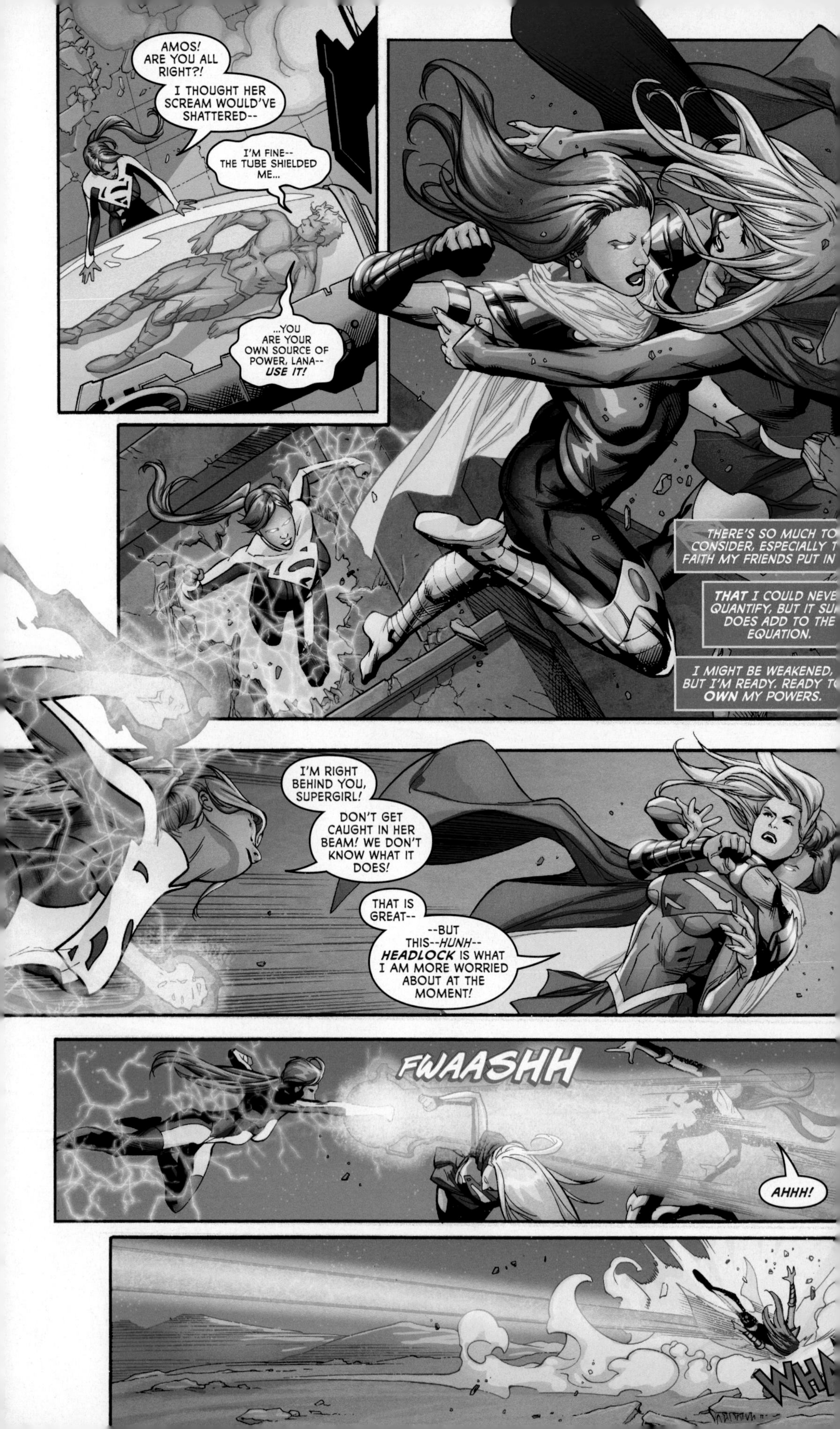
AMOS! ARE YOU ALL RIGHT?!
I THOUGHT HER SCREAM WOULD'VE SHATTERED--
I'M FINE-- THE TUBE SHIELDED ME...
...YOU ARE YOUR OWN SOURCE OF POWER, LANA-- USE IT!
THERE'S SO MUCH TO CONSIDER, ESPECIALLY T FAITH MY FRIENDS PUT IN
THAT I COULD NEVE QUANTIFY, BUT IT SU DOES ADD TO THE EQUATION.
I MIGHT BE WEAKENED, BUT I'M READY. READY T OWN MY POWERS.
I'M RIGHT BEHIND YOU, SUPERGIRL!
DON'T GET CAUGHT IN HER BEAM! WE DON'T KNOW WHAT IT DOES!
THAT IS GREAT--
--BUT THIS--HUNH-- HEADLOCK IS WHAT I AM MORE WORRIED ABOUT AT THE MOMENT!
FWAASHH
AHHH!
WHA

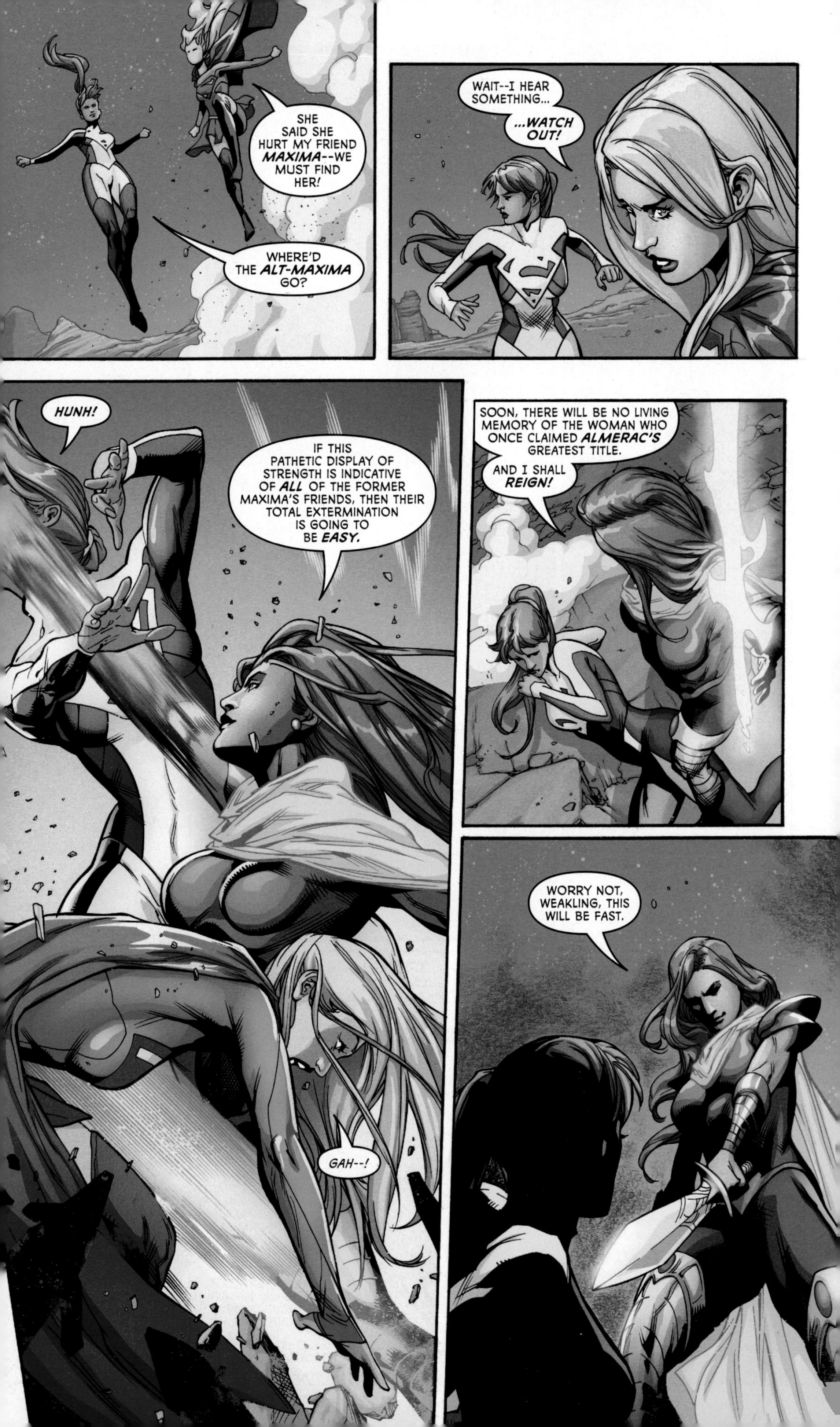
SHE SAID SHE HURT MY FRIEND MAXIMA--WE MUST FIND HER!
WHERE'D THE ALT-MAXIMA GO?
WAIT--I HEAR SOMETHING...
...WATCH OUT!
HUNH!
IF THIS PATHETIC DISPLAY OF STRENGTH IS INDICATIVE OF ALL OF THE FORMER MAXIMA'S FRIENDS, THEN THEIR TOTAL EXTERMINATION IS GOING TO BE EASY.
GAH--!
SOON, THERE WILL BE NO LIVING MEMORY OF THE WOMAN WHO ONCE CLAIMED ALMERAC'S GREATEST TITLE.
AND I SHALL REIGN!
WORRY NOT, WEAKLING, THIS WILL BE FAST.

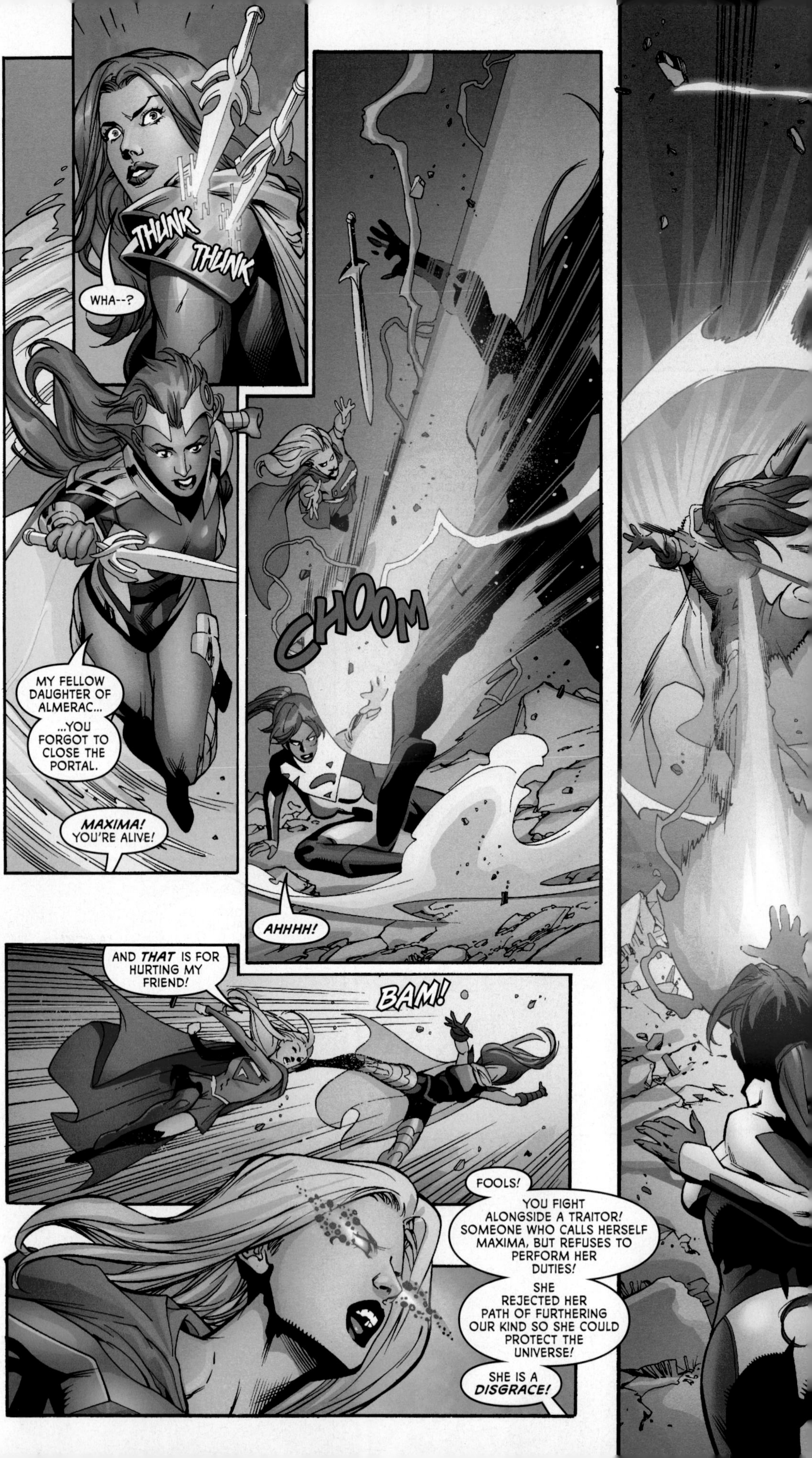
THUNK
THUNK
WHA--?
MY FELLOW DAUGHTER OF ALMERAC...
...YOU FORGOT TO CLOSE THE PORTAL.
MAXIMA! YOU'RE ALIVE!
CHOOM
AHHHH!
AND THAT IS FOR HURTING MY FRIEND!
BAM!
FOOLS!
YOU FIGHT ALONGSIDE A TRAITOR! SOMEONE WHO CALLS HERSELF MAXIMA, BUT REFUSES TO PERFORM HER DUTIES!
SHE REJECTED HER PATH OF FURTHERING OUR KIND SO SHE COULD PROTECT THE UNIVERSE!
SHE IS A DISGRACE!

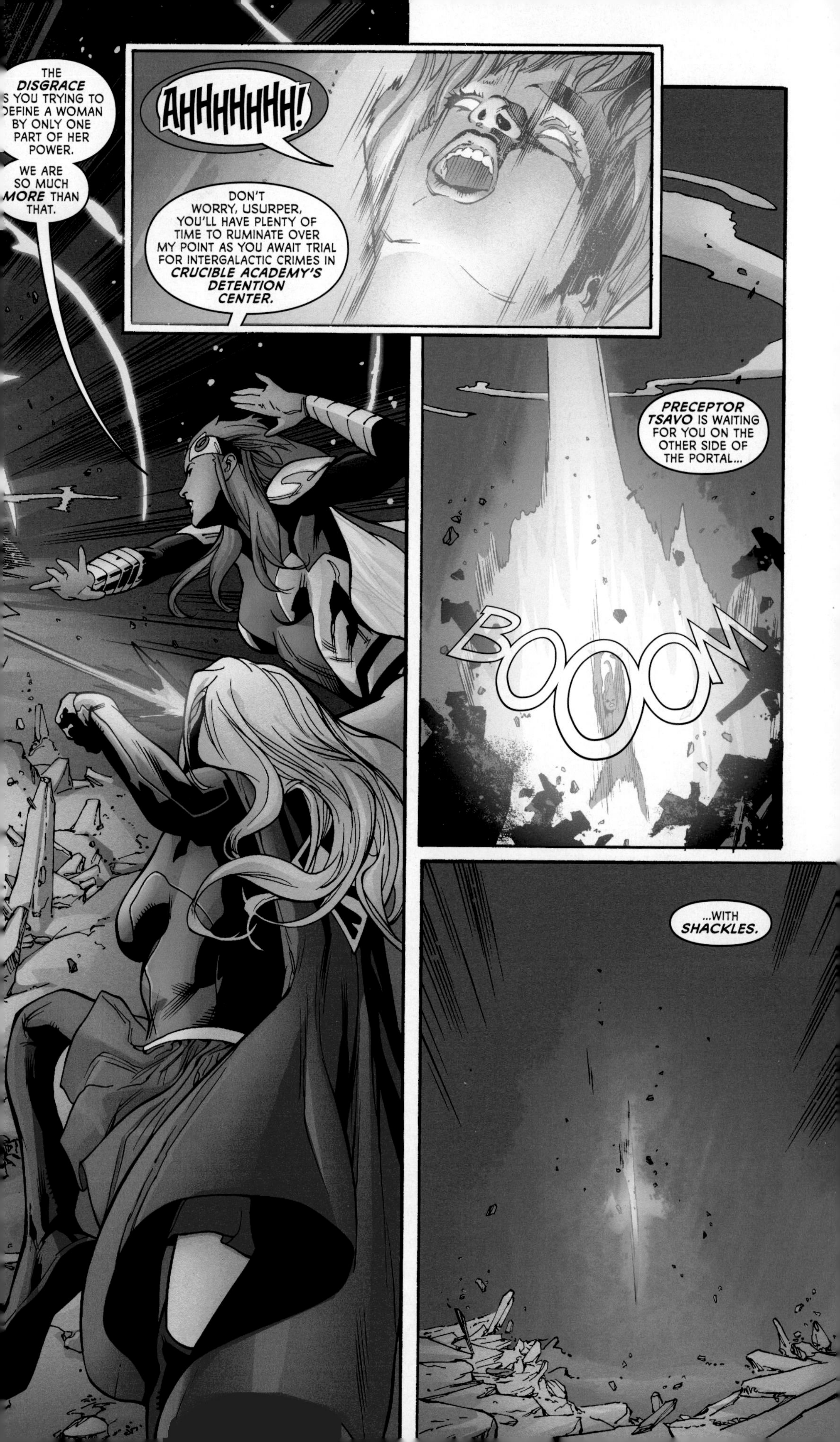
THE DISGRACE IS YOU TRYING TO DEFINE A WOMAN BY ONLY ONE PART OF HER POWER.
WE ARE SO MUCH MORE THAN THAT.
AHHHHHHH!
DON'T WORRY, USURPER, YOU'LL HAVE PLENTY OF TIME TO RUMINATE OVER MY POINT AS YOU AWAIT TRIAL FOR INTERGALACTIC CRIMES IN CRUCIBLE ACADEMY'S DETENTION CENTER.
PRECEPTOR TSAVO IS WAITING FOR YOU ON THE OTHER SIDE OF THE PORTAL...
BOOOOM
...WITH SHACKLES.

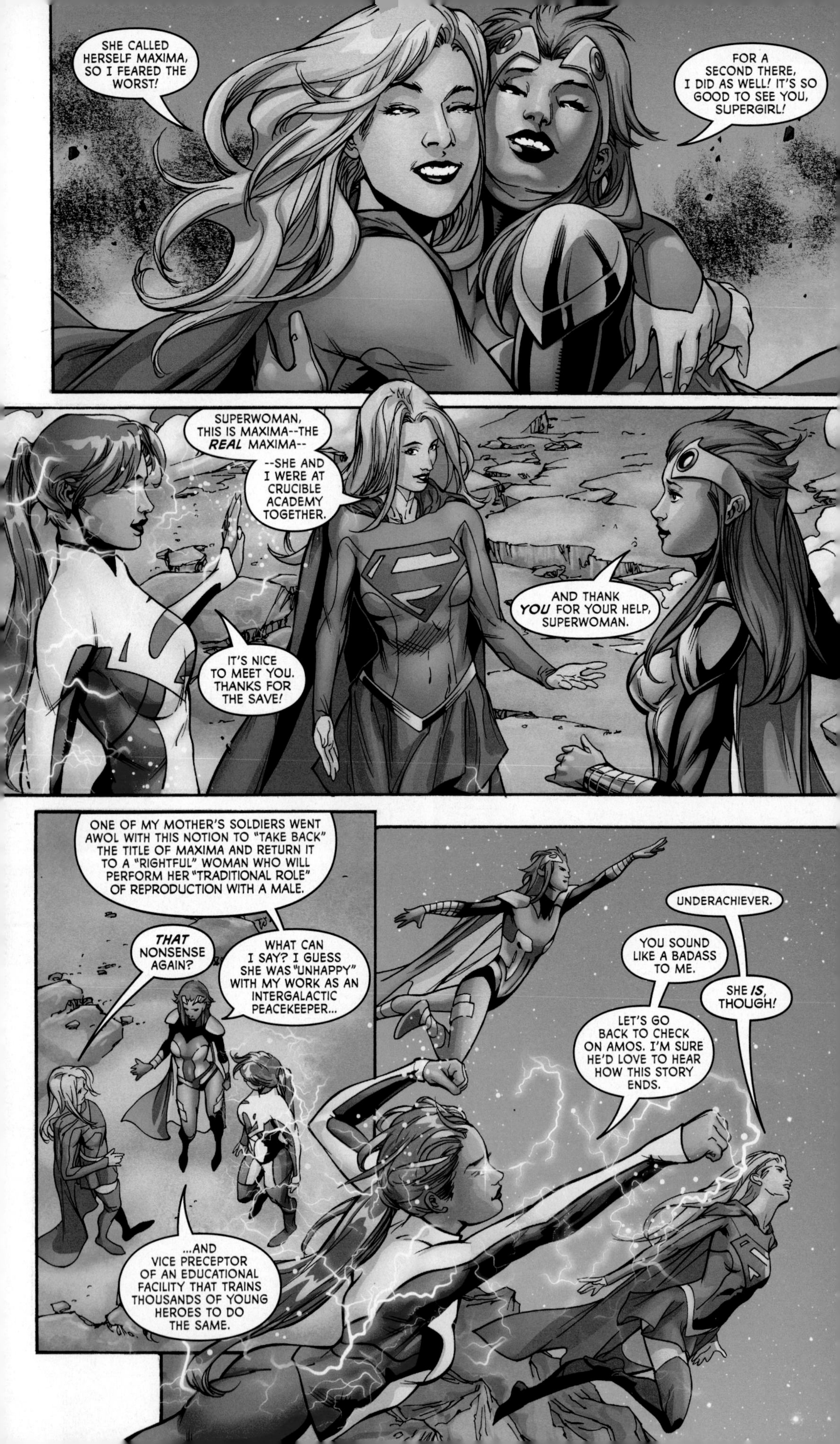

SHE CALLED HERSELF MAXIMA, SO I FEARED THE WORST!
FOR A SECOND THERE, I DID AS WELL! IT'S SO GOOD TO SEE YOU, SUPERGIRL!
SUPERWOMAN, THIS IS MAXIMA--THE REAL MAXIMA--
--SHE AND I WERE AT CRUCIBLE ACADEMY TOGETHER.
IT'S NICE TO MEET YOU. THANKS FOR THE SAVE!
AND THANK YOU FOR YOUR HELP, SUPERWOMAN.
ONE OF MY MOTHER'S SOLDIERS WENT AWOL WITH THIS NOTION TO "TAKE BACK" THE TITLE OF MAXIMA AND RETURN IT TO A "RIGHTFUL" WOMAN WHO WILL PERFORM HER "TRADITIONAL ROLE" OF REPRODUCTION WITH A MALE.
THAT NONSENSE AGAIN?
WHAT CAN I SAY? I GUESS SHE WAS "UNHAPPY" WITH MY WORK AS AN INTERGALACTIC PEACEKEEPER...
...AND VICE PRECEPTOR OF AN EDUCATIONAL FACILITY THAT TRAINS THOUSANDS OF YOUNG HEROES TO DO THE SAME.
UNDERACHIEVER.
YOU SOUND LIKE A BADASS TO ME.
SHE IS, THOUGH!
LET'S GO BACK TO CHECK ON AMOS. I'M SURE HE'D LOVE TO HEAR HOW THIS STORY ENDS.

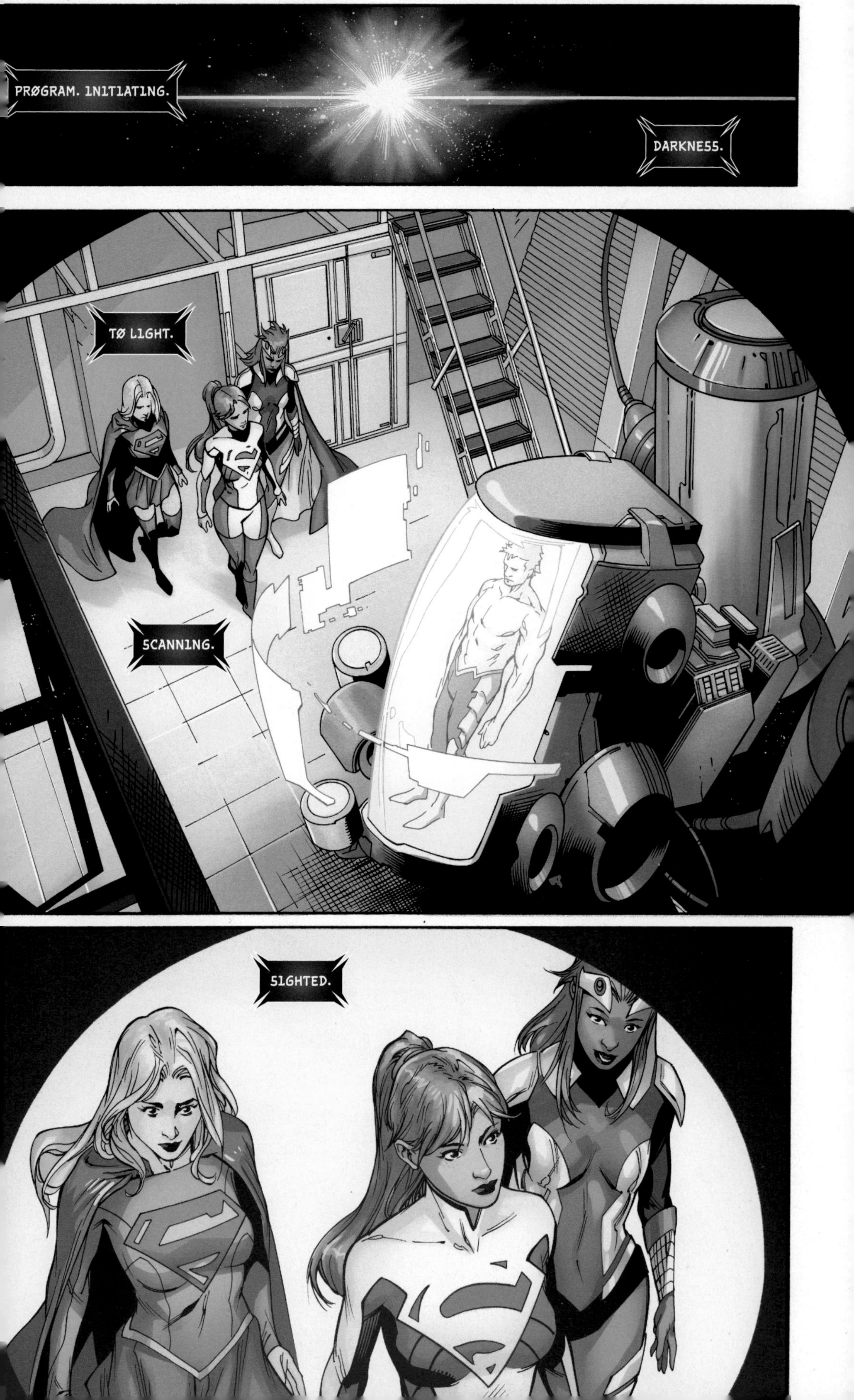
PRØGRAM. 1N1T1AT1NG.
DARKNE55.
TØ L1GHT.
5CANN1NG.
51GHTED.

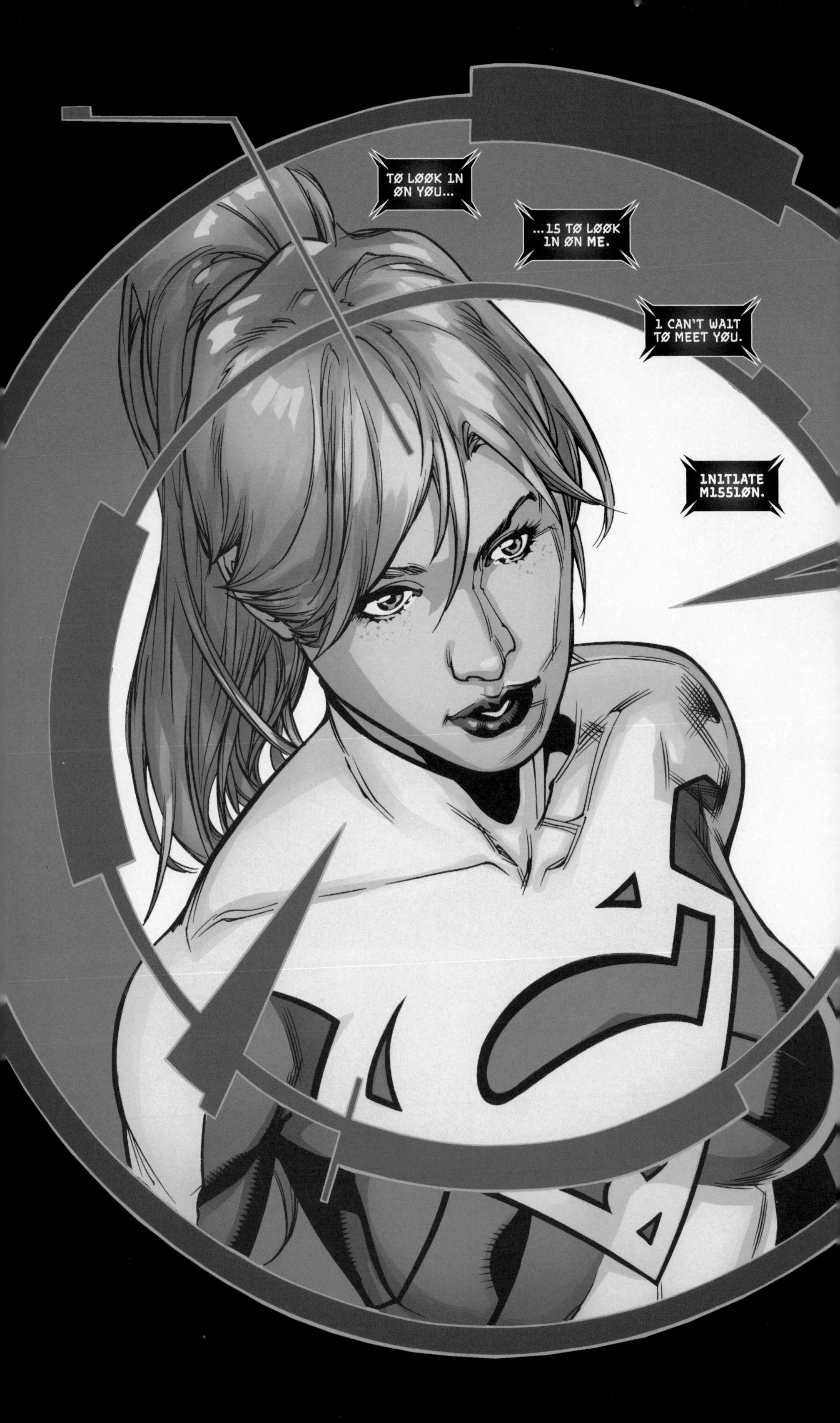
TØ LØØK 1N ØN YØU...
...15 TØ LØØK 1N ØN ME.
1 CAN'T WA1T TØ MEET YØU.
1N1T1ATE M1551ØN.

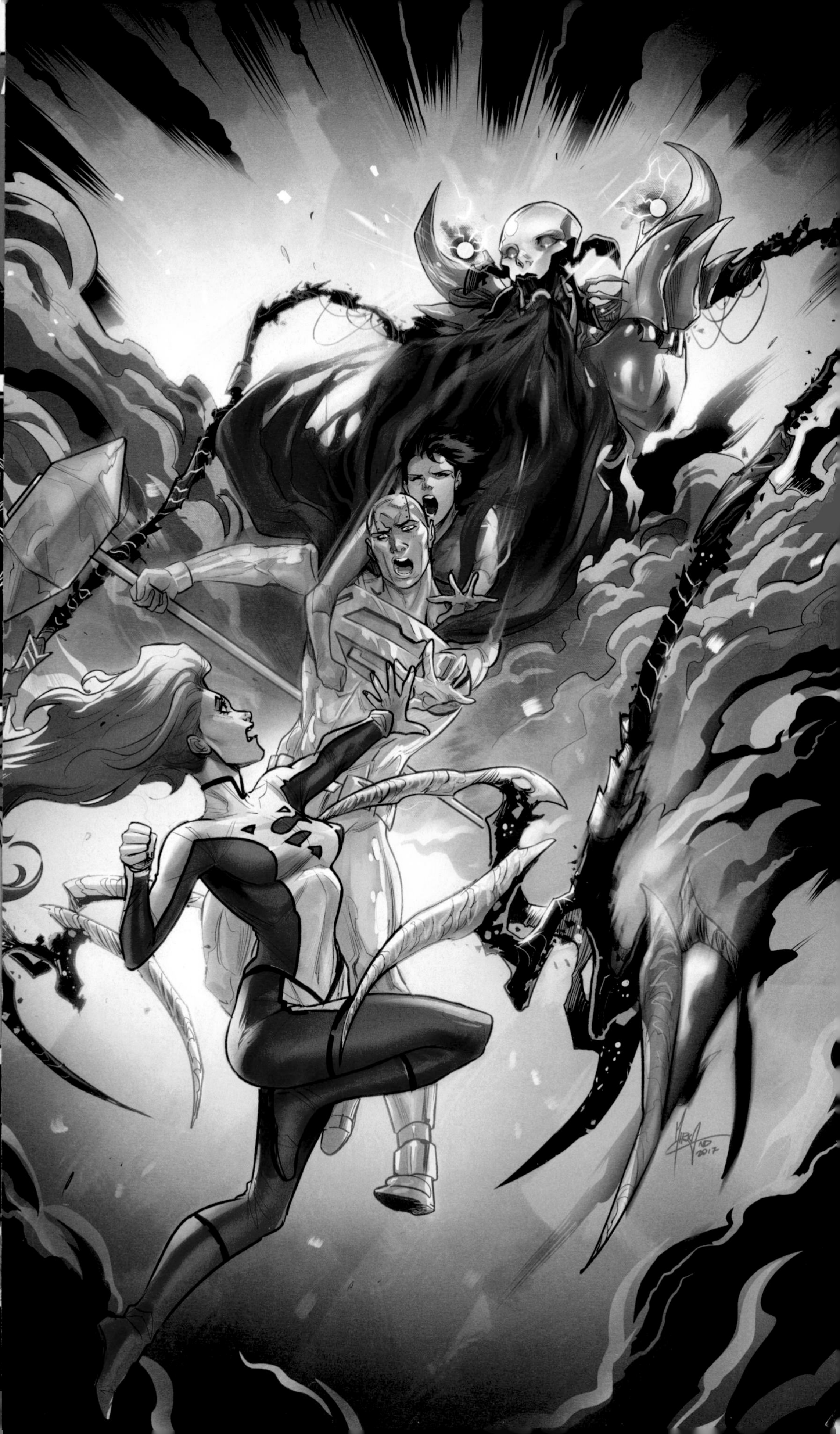

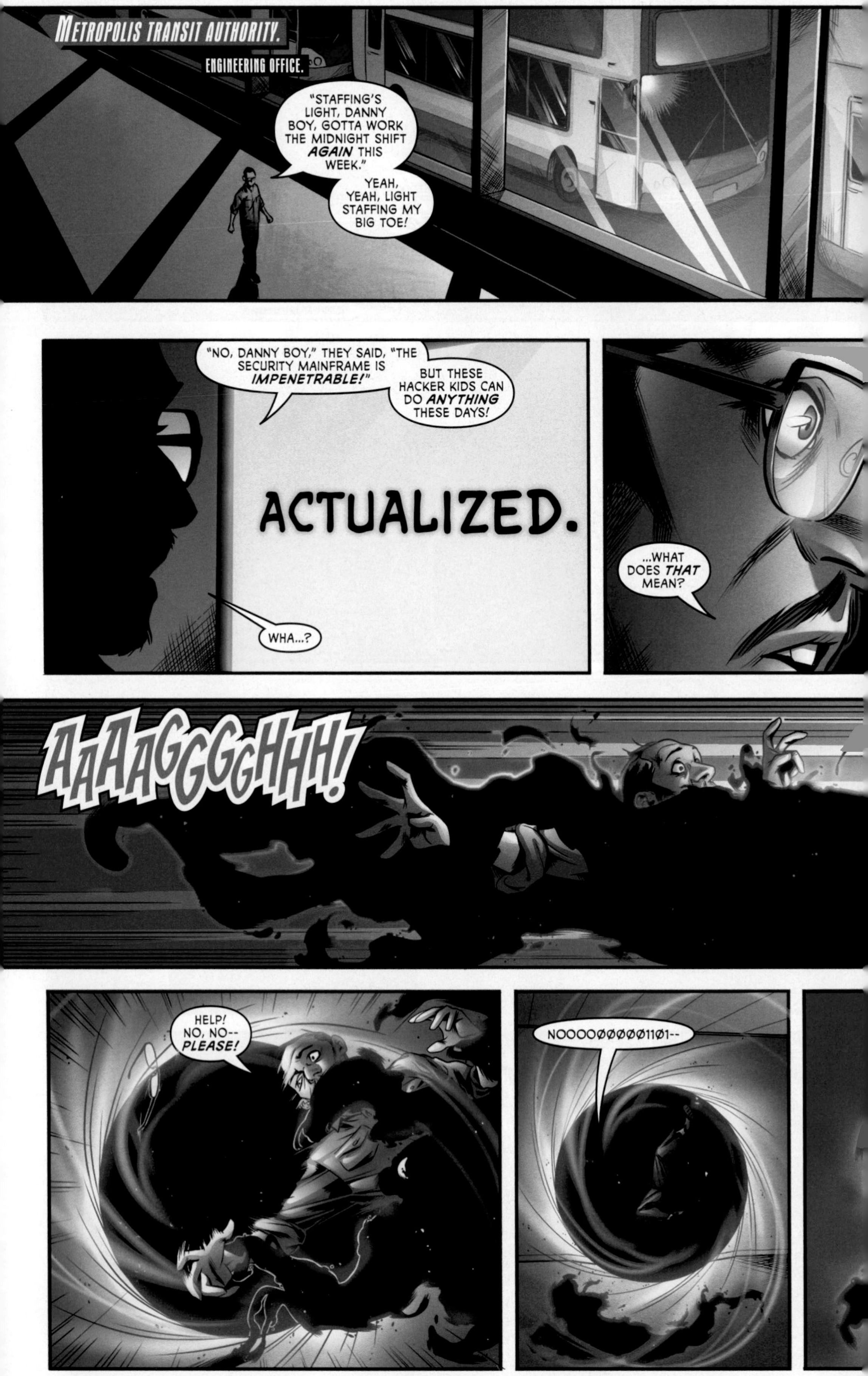

METROPOLIS TRANSIT AUTHORITY.
ENGINEERING OFFICE.
"STAFFING'S LIGHT, DANNY BOY, GOTTA WORK THE MIDNIGHT SHIFT *AGAIN* THIS WEEK."
YEAH, YEAH, LIGHT STAFFING MY BIG TOE!
"NO, DANNY BOY," THEY SAID, "THE SECURITY MAINFRAME IS *IMPENETRABLE!*"
BUT THESE HACKER KIDS CAN DO *ANYTHING* THESE DAYS!
ACTUALIZED.
WHA...?
...WHAT DOES *THAT* MEAN?
AAAAGGGGHHH!
HELP! NO, NO-- *PLEASE!*
NOOOOØØØØ1101--

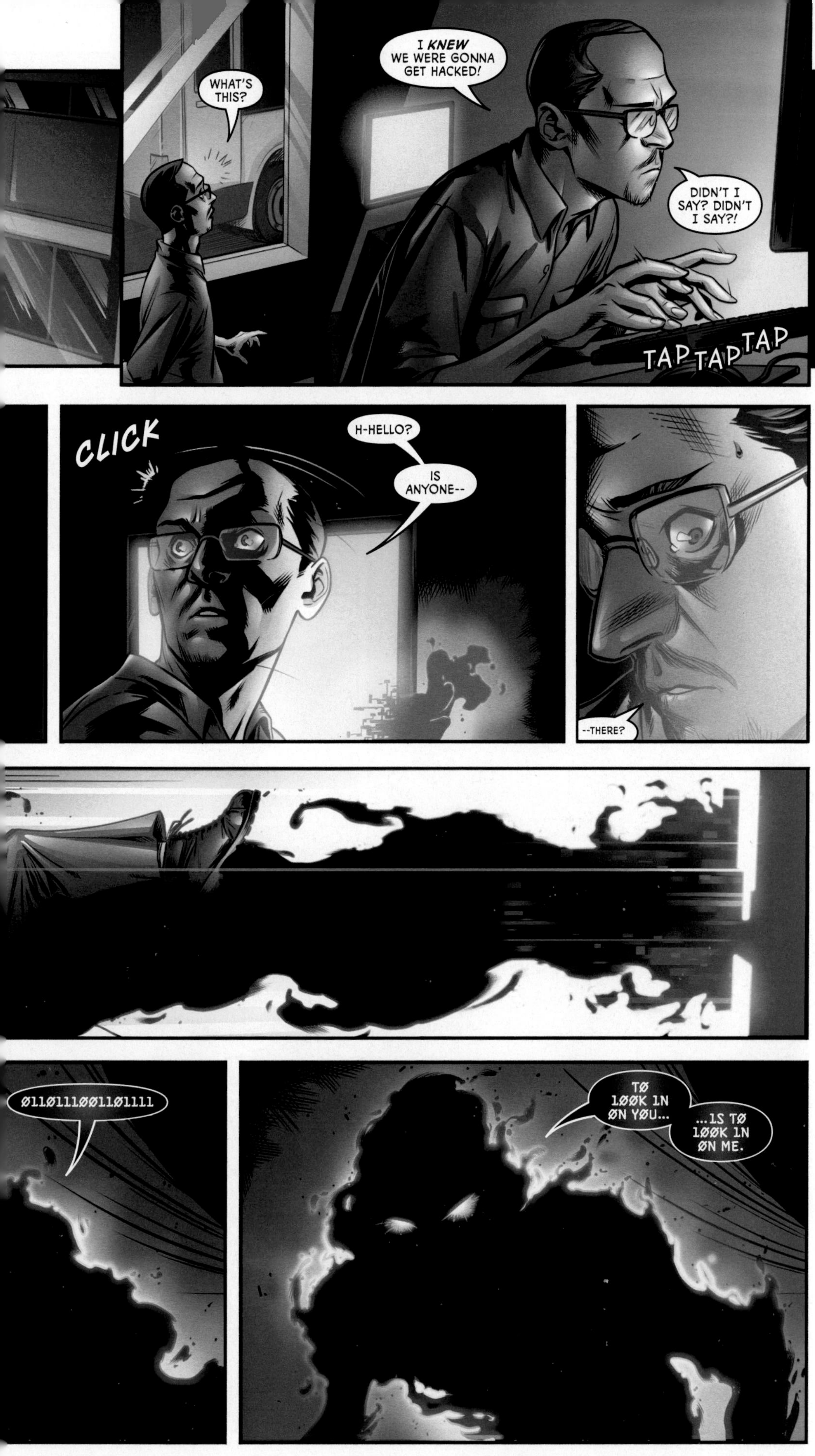
WHAT'S THIS?
I KNEW WE WERE GONNA GET HACKED!
DIDN'T I SAY? DIDN'T I SAY?!
TAP TAP TAP TAP
CLICK
H-HELLO?
IS ANYONE--
--THERE?
Ø11Ø111ØØ11Ø1111
TØ 1ØØK 1N ØN YØU...
...1S TØ 1ØØK 1N ØN ME.

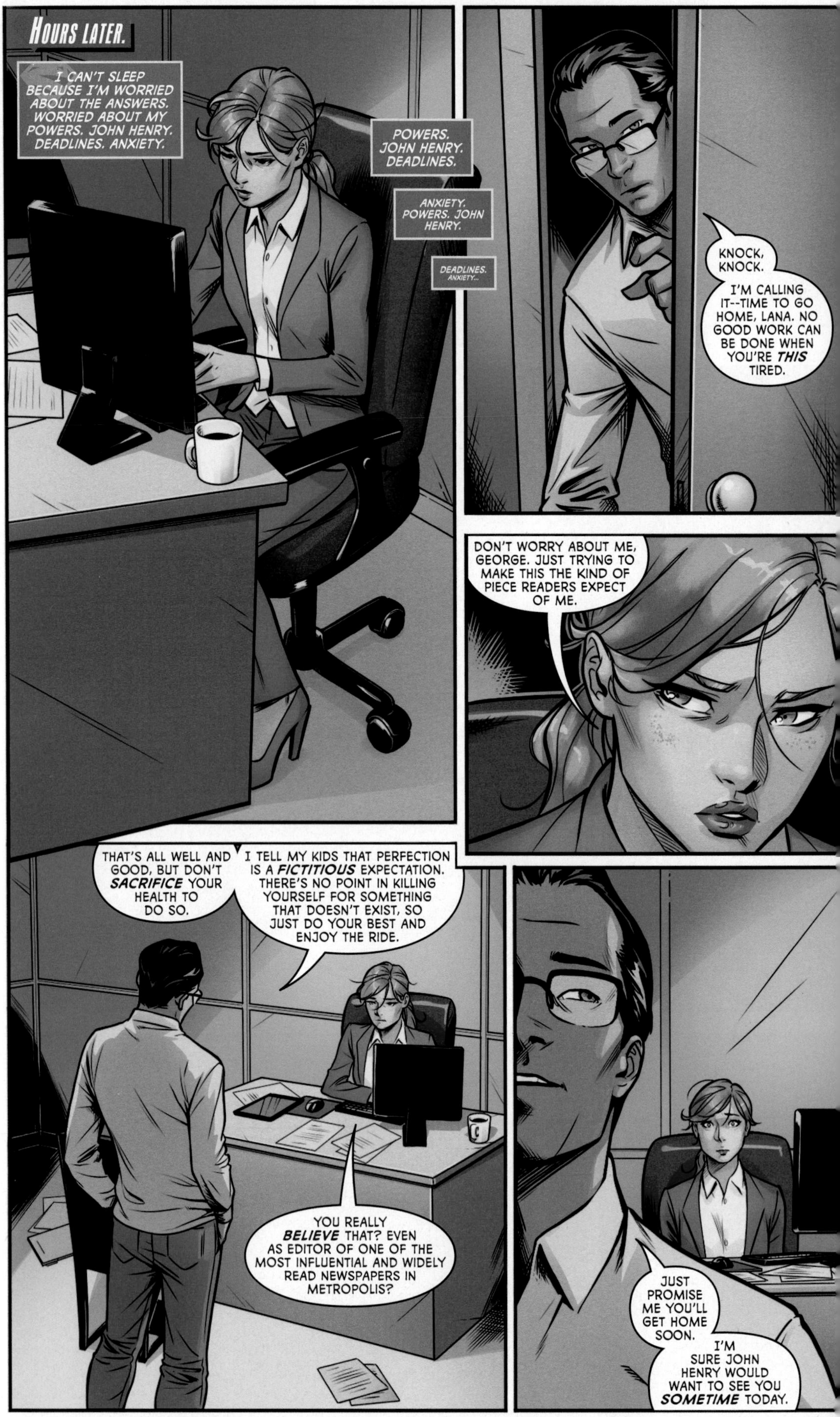
HOURS LATER.
I CAN'T SLEEP BECAUSE I'M WORRIED ABOUT THE ANSWERS. WORRIED ABOUT MY POWERS. JOHN HENRY. DEADLINES. ANXIETY.
POWERS. JOHN HENRY. DEADLINES.
ANXIETY. POWERS. JOHN HENRY.
DEADLINES. ANXIETY...
KNOCK, KNOCK.
I'M CALLING IT--TIME TO GO HOME, LANA. NO GOOD WORK CAN BE DONE WHEN YOU'RE *THIS* TIRED.
DON'T WORRY ABOUT ME, GEORGE. JUST TRYING TO MAKE THIS THE KIND OF PIECE READERS EXPECT OF ME.
THAT'S ALL WELL AND GOOD, BUT DON'T *SACRIFICE* YOUR HEALTH TO DO SO.
I TELL MY KIDS THAT PERFECTION IS A *FICTITIOUS* EXPECTATION. THERE'S NO POINT IN KILLING YOURSELF FOR SOMETHING THAT DOESN'T EXIST, SO JUST DO YOUR BEST AND ENJOY THE RIDE.
YOU REALLY *BELIEVE* THAT? EVEN AS EDITOR OF ONE OF THE MOST INFLUENTIAL AND WIDELY READ NEWSPAPERS IN METROPOLIS?
JUST PROMISE ME YOU'LL GET HOME SOON.
I'M SURE JOHN HENRY WOULD WANT TO SEE YOU *SOMETIME* TODAY.

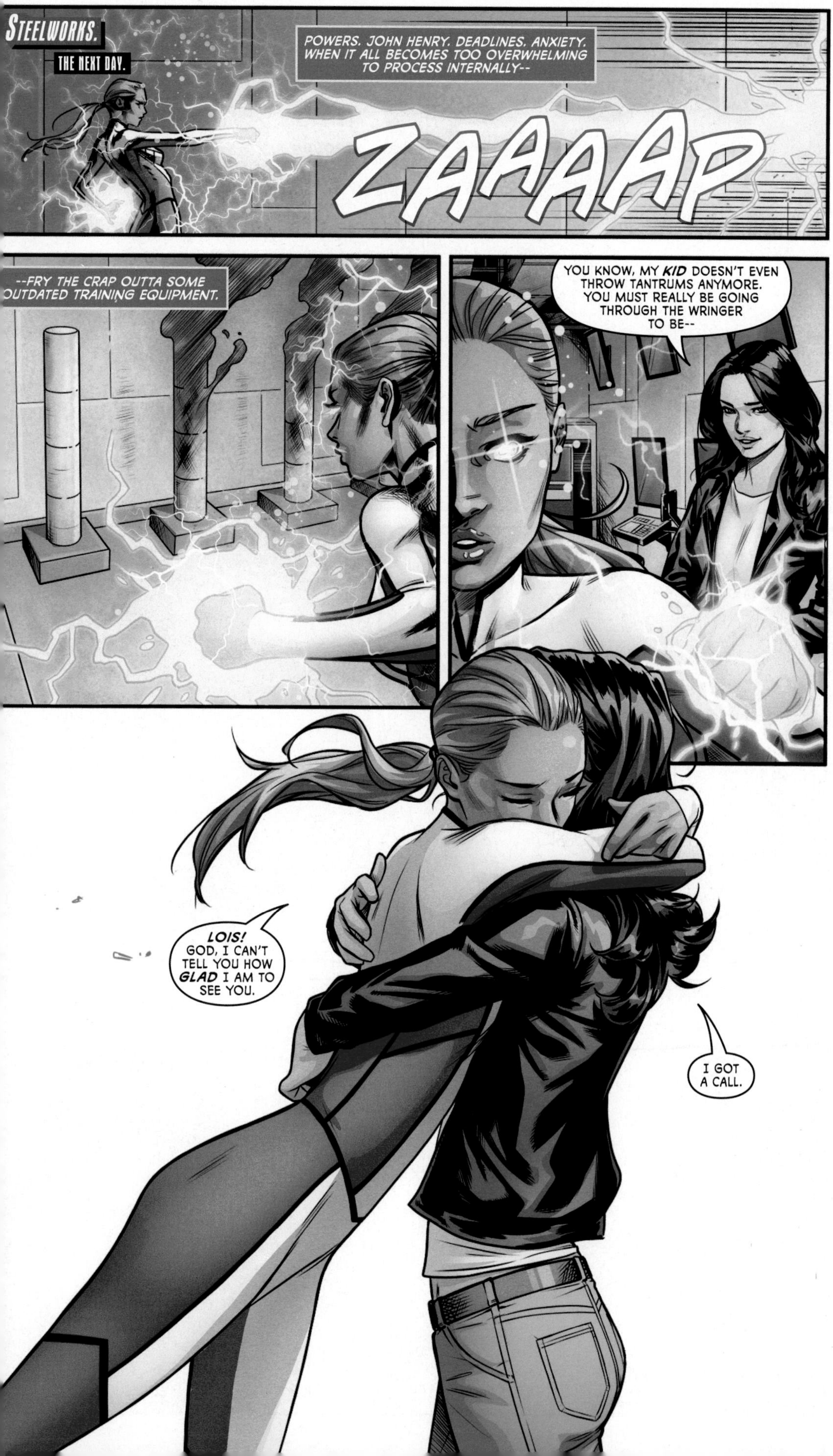
STEELWORKS.
THE NEXT DAY.
POWERS. JOHN HENRY. DEADLINES. ANXIETY. WHEN IT ALL BECOMES TOO OVERWHELMING TO PROCESS INTERNALLY--
ZAAAAAP
--FRY THE CRAP OUTTA SOME OUTDATED TRAINING EQUIPMENT.
YOU KNOW, MY KID DOESN'T EVEN THROW TANTRUMS ANYMORE. YOU MUST REALLY BE GOING THROUGH THE WRINGER TO BE--
LOIS! GOD, I CAN'T TELL YOU HOW GLAD I AM TO SEE YOU.
I GOT A CALL.

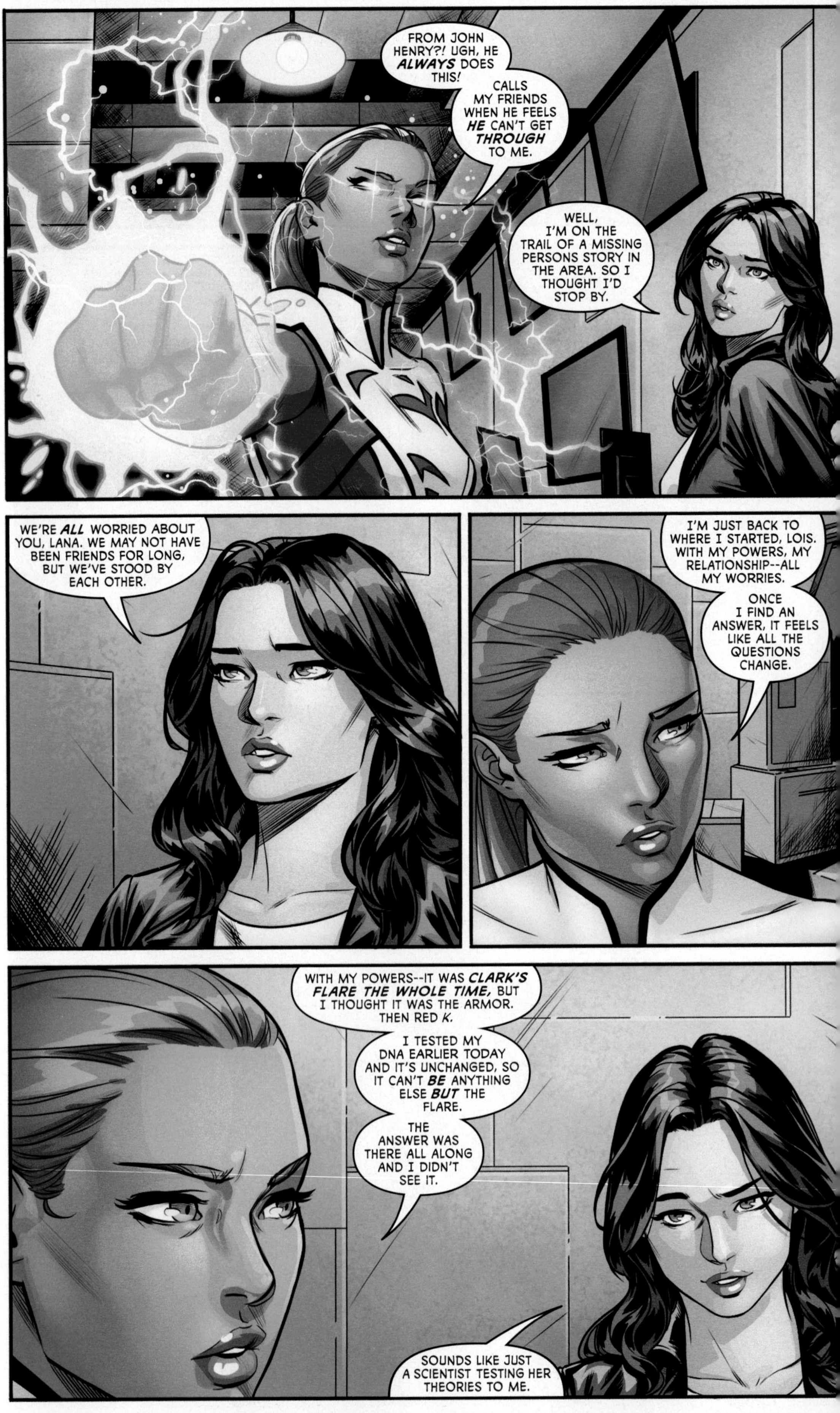
FROM JOHN HENRY?! UGH, HE ALWAYS DOES THIS!
CALLS MY FRIENDS WHEN HE FEELS HE CAN'T GET THROUGH TO ME.
WELL, I'M ON THE TRAIL OF A MISSING PERSONS STORY IN THE AREA. SO I THOUGHT I'D STOP BY.
WE'RE ALL WORRIED ABOUT YOU, LANA. WE MAY NOT HAVE BEEN FRIENDS FOR LONG, BUT WE'VE STOOD BY EACH OTHER.
I'M JUST BACK TO WHERE I STARTED, LOIS. WITH MY POWERS, MY RELATIONSHIP--ALL MY WORRIES.
ONCE I FIND AN ANSWER, IT FEELS LIKE ALL THE QUESTIONS CHANGE.
WITH MY POWERS--IT WAS CLARK'S FLARE THE WHOLE TIME, BUT I THOUGHT IT WAS THE ARMOR. THEN RED K.
I TESTED MY DNA EARLIER TODAY AND IT'S UNCHANGED, SO IT CAN'T BE ANYTHING ELSE BUT THE FLARE.
THE ANSWER WAS THERE ALL ALONG AND I DIDN'T SEE IT.
SOUNDS LIKE JUST A SCIENTIST TESTING HER THEORIES TO ME.

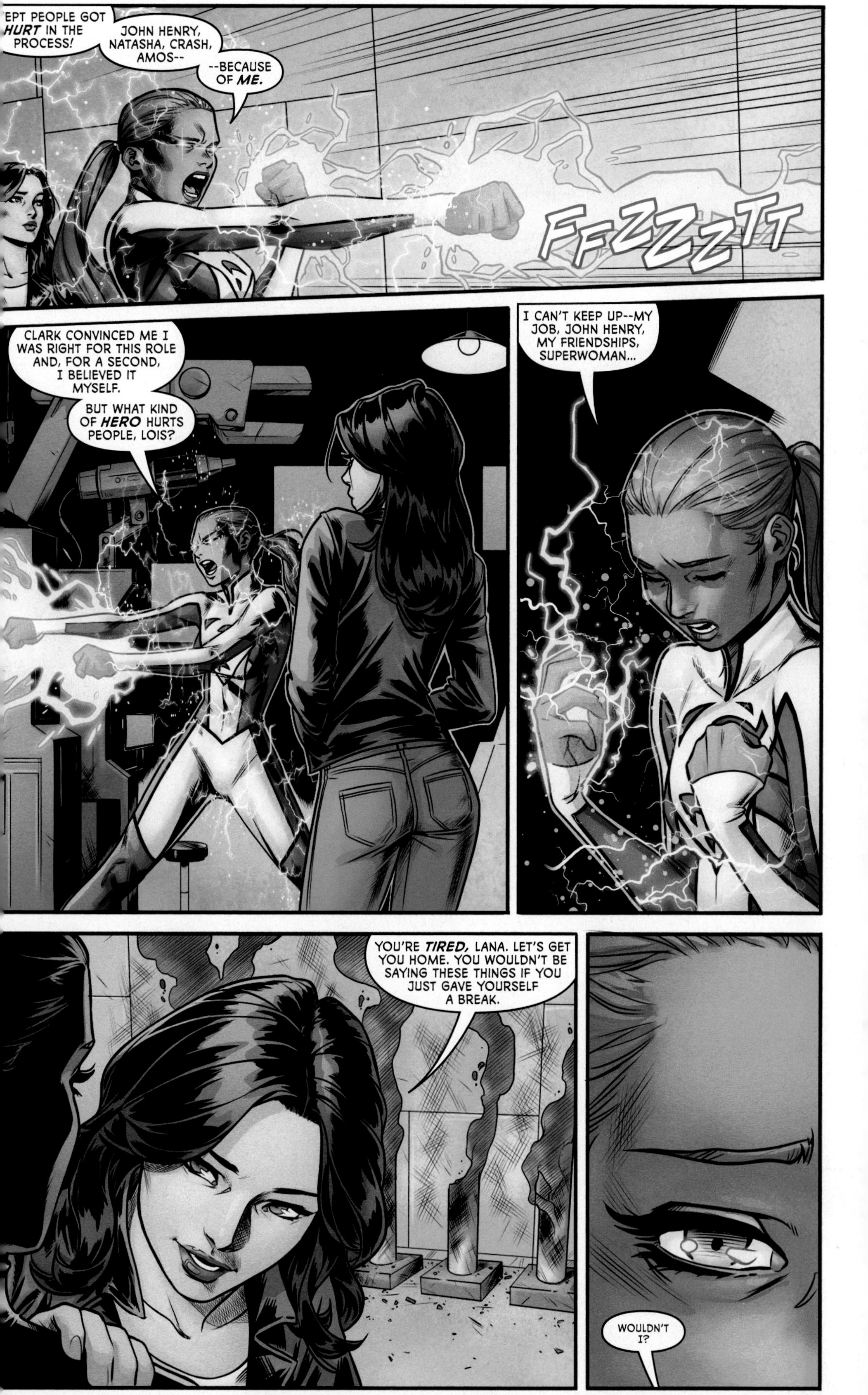
EPT PEOPLE GOT HURT IN THE PROCESS!
JOHN HENRY, NATASHA, CRASH, AMOS--
--BECAUSE OF ME.
FFZZZZTT
CLARK CONVINCED ME I WAS RIGHT FOR THIS ROLE AND, FOR A SECOND, I BELIEVED IT MYSELF.
BUT WHAT KIND OF HERO HURTS PEOPLE, LOIS?
I CAN'T KEEP UP--MY JOB, JOHN HENRY, MY FRIENDSHIPS, SUPERWOMAN...
YOU'RE TIRED, LANA. LET'S GET YOU HOME. YOU WOULDN'T BE SAYING THESE THINGS IF YOU JUST GAVE YOURSELF A BREAK.
WOULDN'T I?

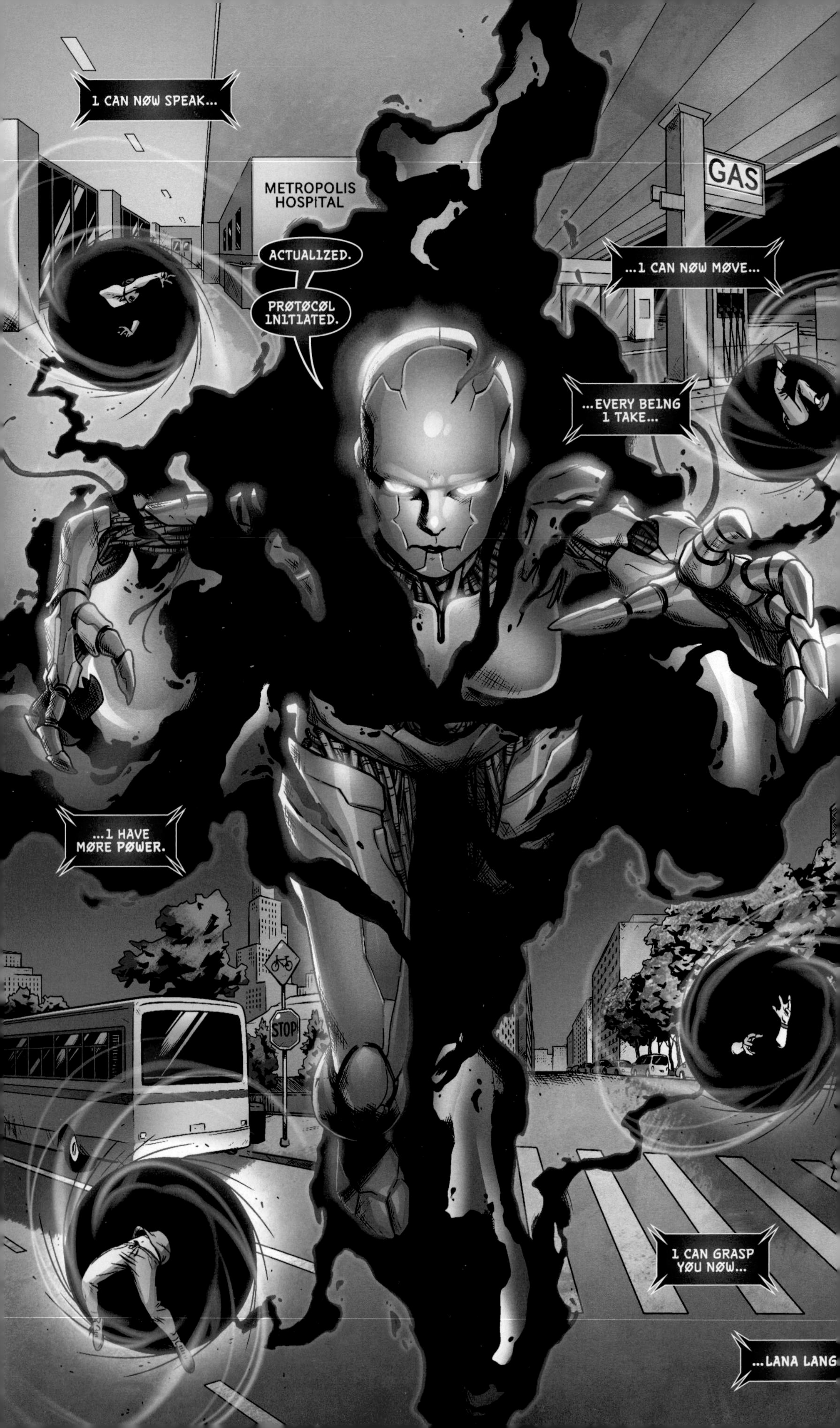
I CAN NØW SPEAK...
METROPOLIS HOSPITAL
ACTUALIZED.
PRØTØCØL INITIATED.
GAS
...I CAN NØW MØVE...
...EVERY BEING I TAKE...
...I HAVE MØRE PØWER.
STOP
I CAN GRASP YØU NØW...
...LANA LANG

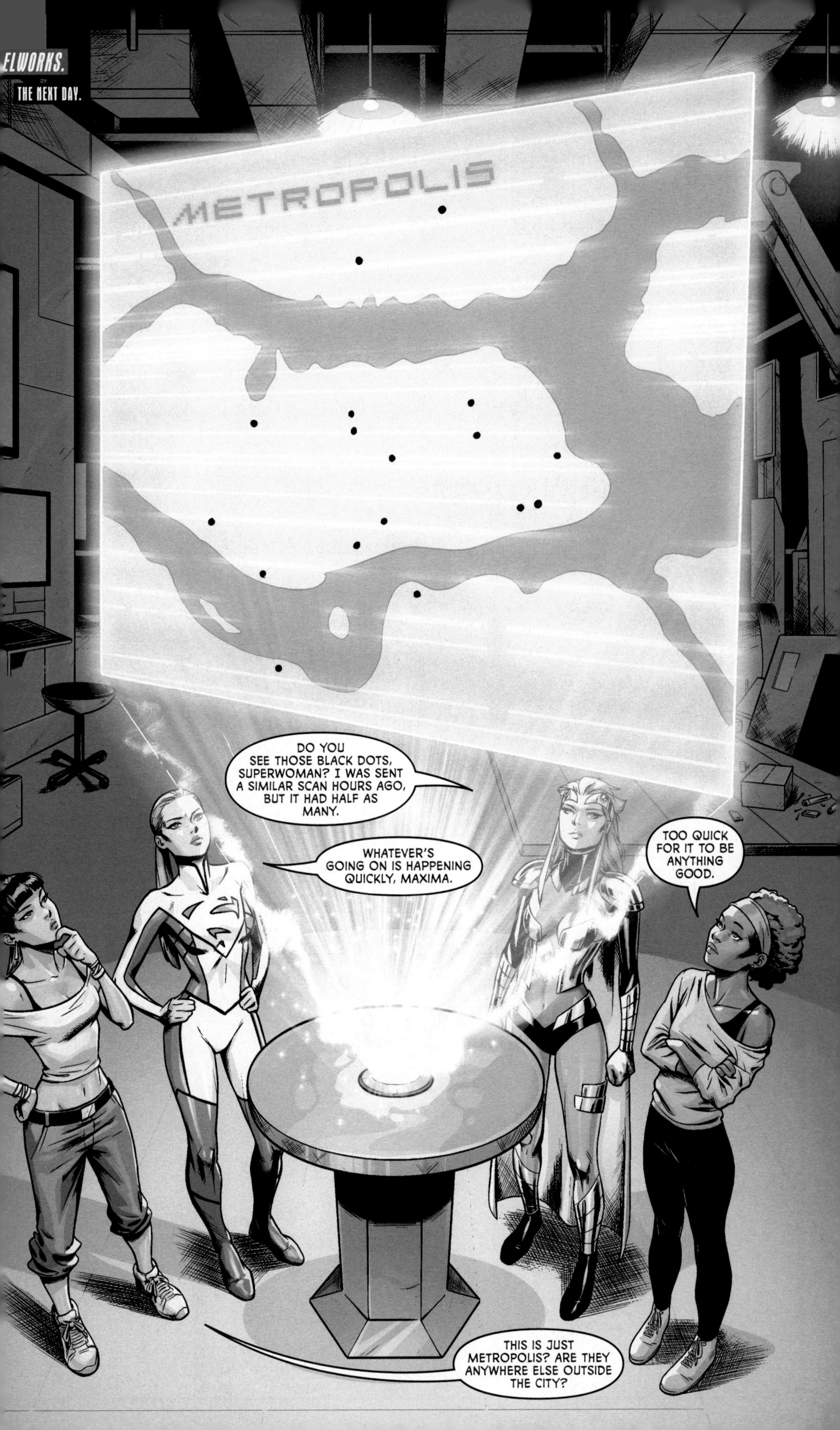
ELWORKS.
THE NEXT DAY.
METROPOLIS
DO YOU SEE THOSE BLACK DOTS, SUPERWOMAN? I WAS SENT A SIMILAR SCAN HOURS AGO, BUT IT HAD HALF AS MANY.
WHATEVER'S GOING ON IS HAPPENING QUICKLY, MAXIMA.
TOO QUICK FOR IT TO BE ANYTHING GOOD.
THIS IS JUST METROPOLIS? ARE THEY ANYWHERE ELSE OUTSIDE THE CITY?

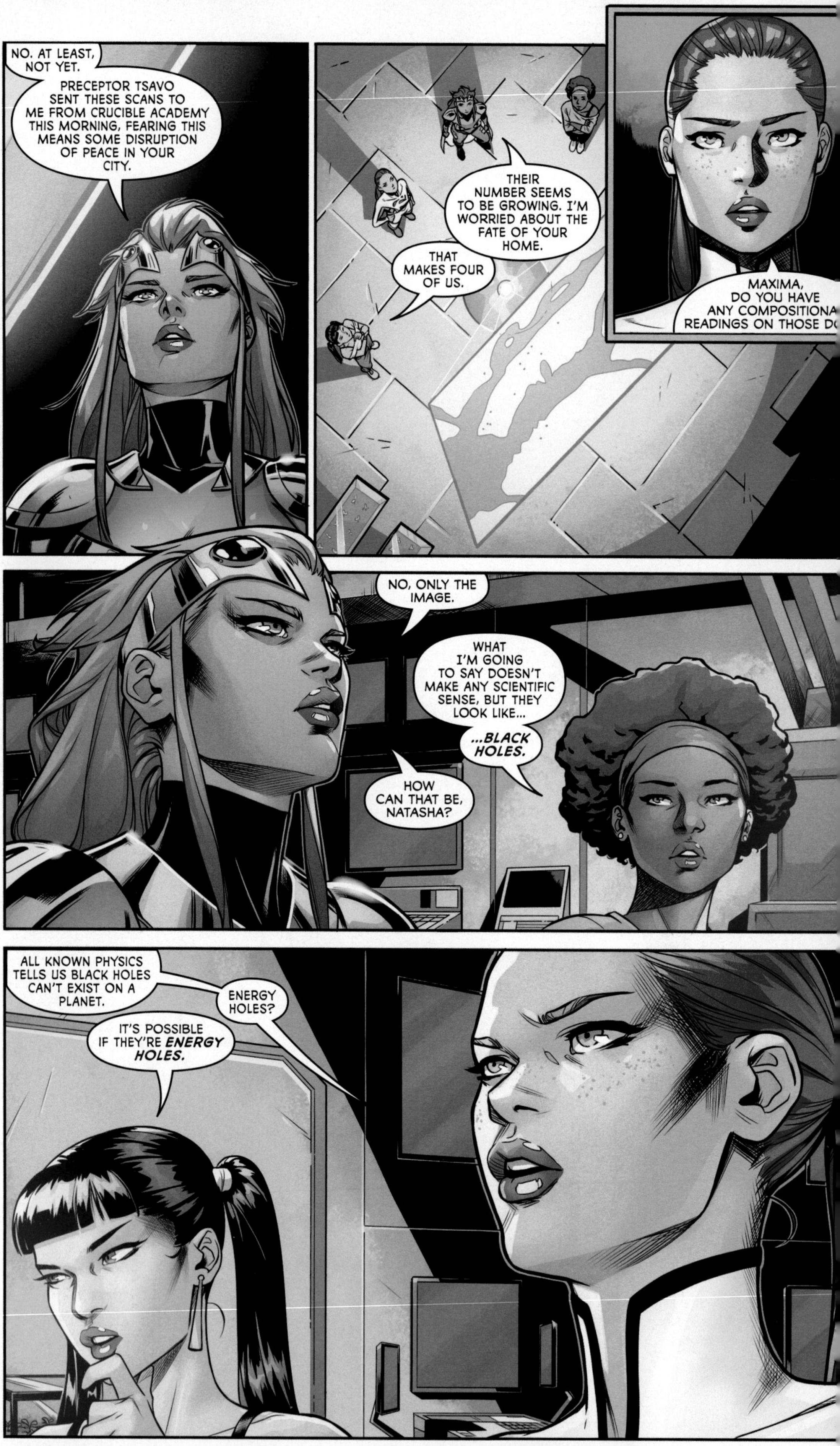

NO. AT LEAST, NOT YET.
PRECEPTOR TSAVO SENT THESE SCANS TO ME FROM CRUCIBLE ACADEMY THIS MORNING, FEARING THIS MEANS SOME DISRUPTION OF PEACE IN YOUR CITY.
THEIR NUMBER SEEMS TO BE GROWING. I'M WORRIED ABOUT THE FATE OF YOUR HOME.
THAT MAKES FOUR OF US.
MAXIMA, DO YOU HAVE ANY COMPOSITIONA READINGS ON THOSE D
NO, ONLY THE IMAGE.
WHAT I'M GOING TO SAY DOESN'T MAKE ANY SCIENTIFIC SENSE, BUT THEY LOOK LIKE...
...*BLACK HOLES.*
HOW CAN THAT BE, NATASHA?
ALL KNOWN PHYSICS TELLS US BLACK HOLES CAN'T EXIST ON A PLANET.
IT'S POSSIBLE IF THEY'RE *ENERGY HOLES.*
ENERGY HOLES?

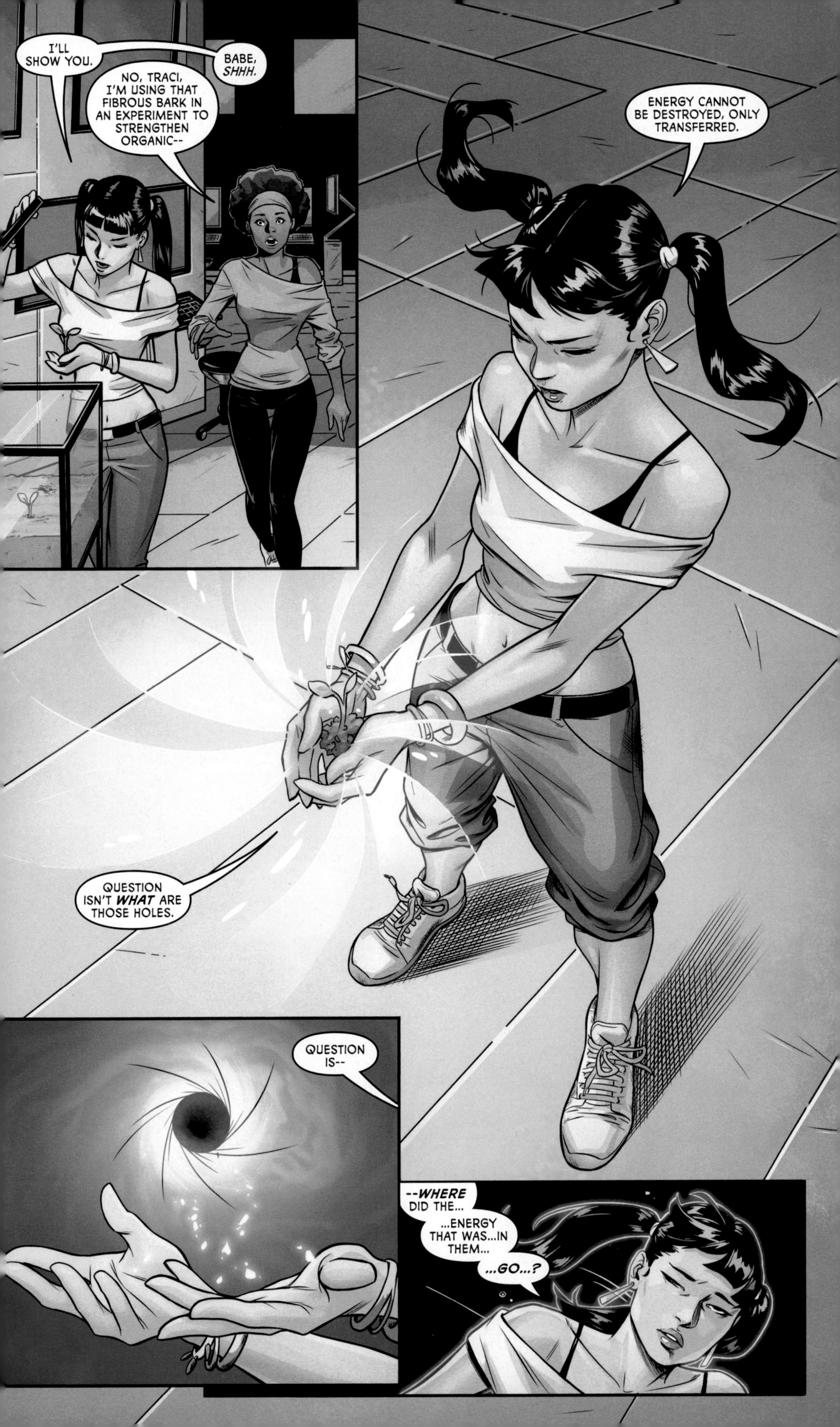
I'LL SHOW YOU.
NO, TRACI, I'M USING THAT FIBROUS BARK IN AN EXPERIMENT TO STRENGTHEN ORGANIC--
BABE, *SHHH.*
ENERGY CANNOT BE DESTROYED, ONLY TRANSFERRED.
QUESTION ISN'T ***WHAT*** ARE THOSE HOLES.
QUESTION IS--
--***WHERE*** DID THE...
...ENERGY THAT WAS...IN THEM...
...GO...?

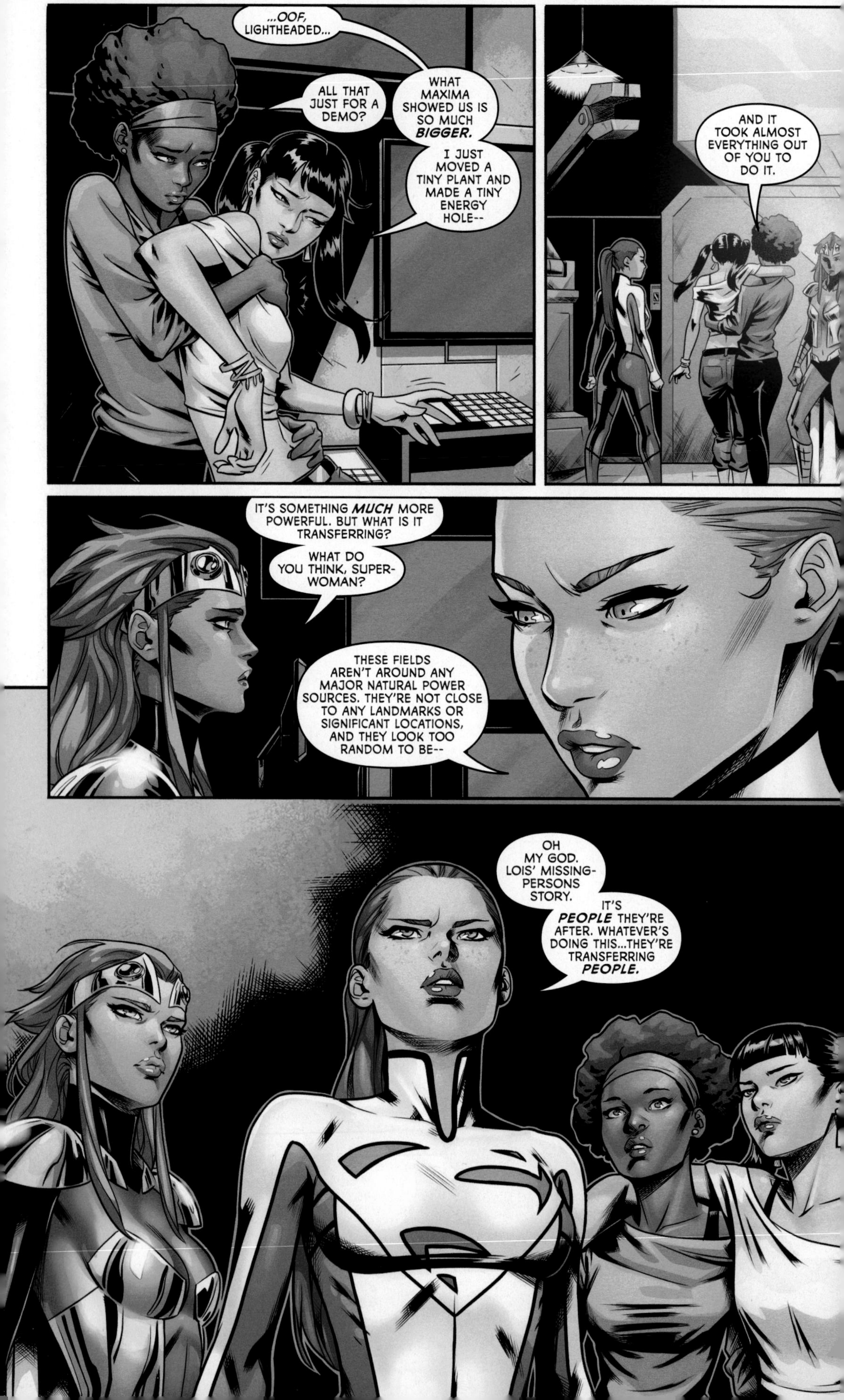
...OOF, LIGHTHEADED...
ALL THAT JUST FOR A DEMO?
WHAT MAXIMA SHOWED US IS SO MUCH BIGGER.
I JUST MOVED A TINY PLANT AND MADE A TINY ENERGY HOLE--
AND IT TOOK ALMOST EVERYTHING OUT OF YOU TO DO IT.
IT'S SOMETHING MUCH MORE POWERFUL. BUT WHAT IS IT TRANSFERRING?
WHAT DO YOU THINK, SUPER-WOMAN?
THESE FIELDS AREN'T AROUND ANY MAJOR NATURAL POWER SOURCES. THEY'RE NOT CLOSE TO ANY LANDMARKS OR SIGNIFICANT LOCATIONS, AND THEY LOOK TOO RANDOM TO BE--
OH MY GOD. LOIS' MISSING-PERSONS STORY.
IT'S PEOPLE THEY'RE AFTER. WHATEVER'S DOING THIS...THEY'RE TRANSFERRING PEOPLE.

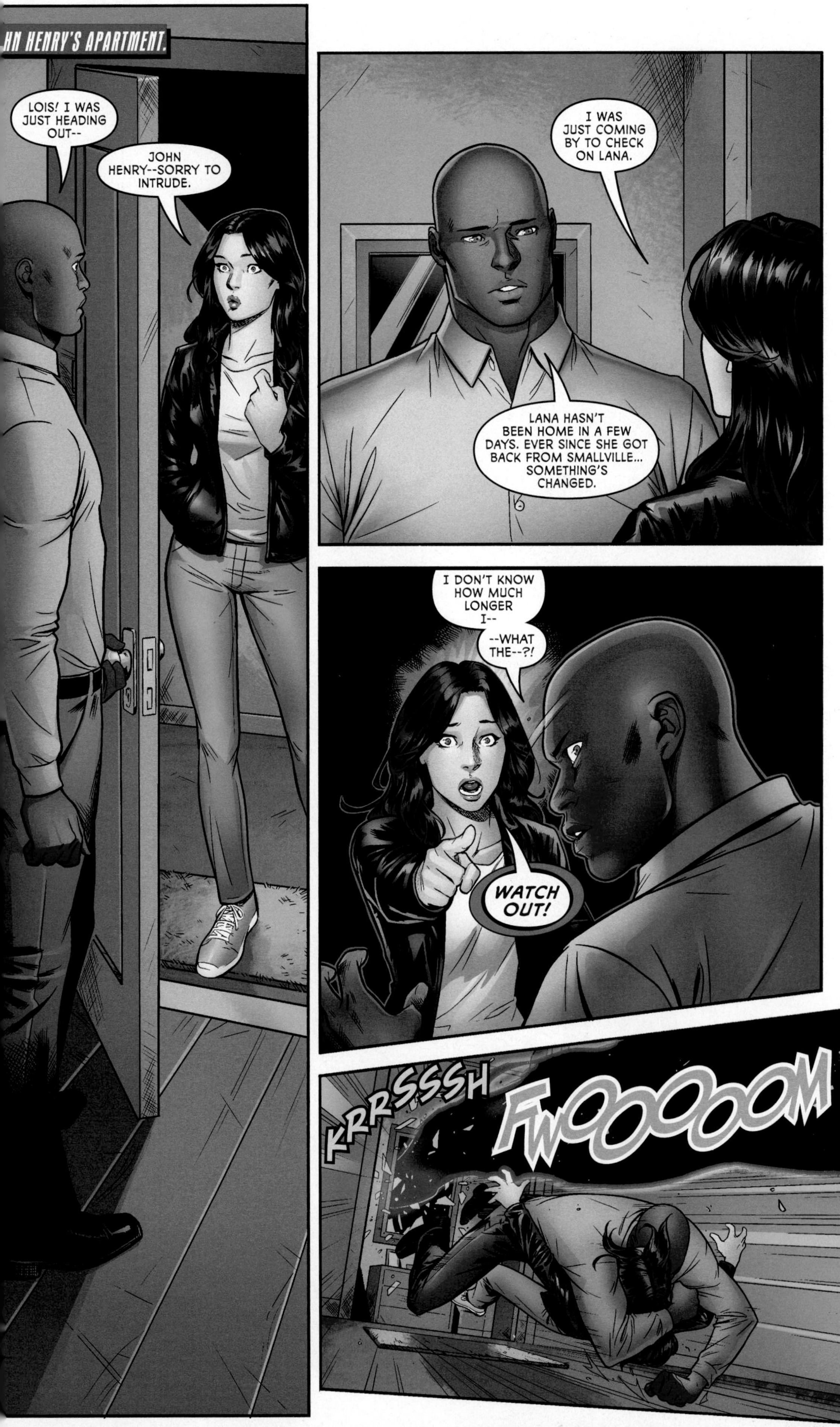

HN HENRY'S APARTMENT.
LOIS! I WAS JUST HEADING OUT--
JOHN HENRY--SORRY TO INTRUDE.
I WAS JUST COMING BY TO CHECK ON LANA.
LANA HASN'T BEEN HOME IN A FEW DAYS. EVER SINCE SHE GOT BACK FROM SMALLVILLE... SOMETHING'S CHANGED.
I DON'T KNOW HOW MUCH LONGER I--
--WHAT THE--?!
WATCH OUT!
KRRSSSH
FWOOOOOOM

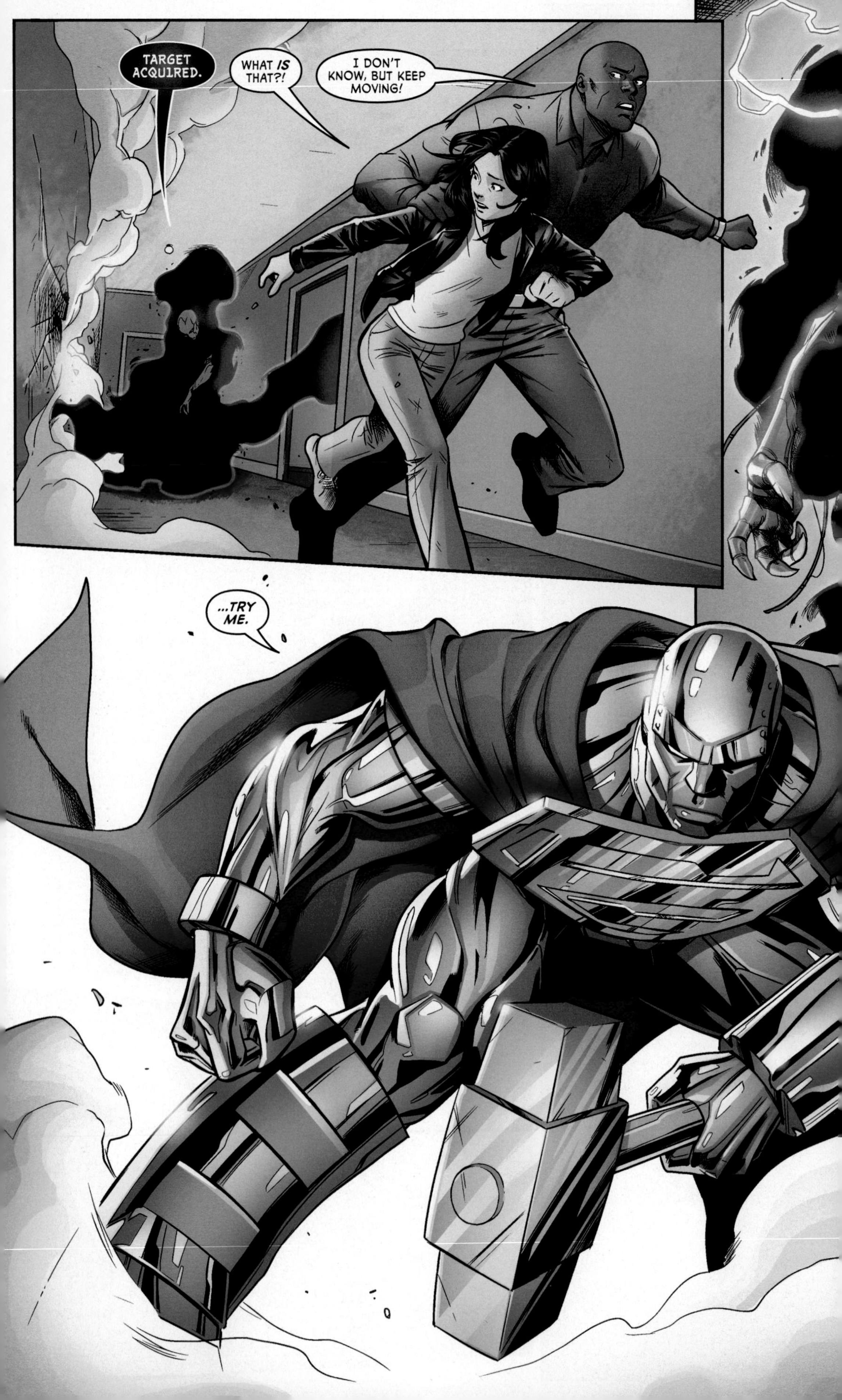
TARGET ACQUIRED.
WHAT IS THAT?!
I DON'T KNOW, BUT KEEP MOVING!
...TRY ME.

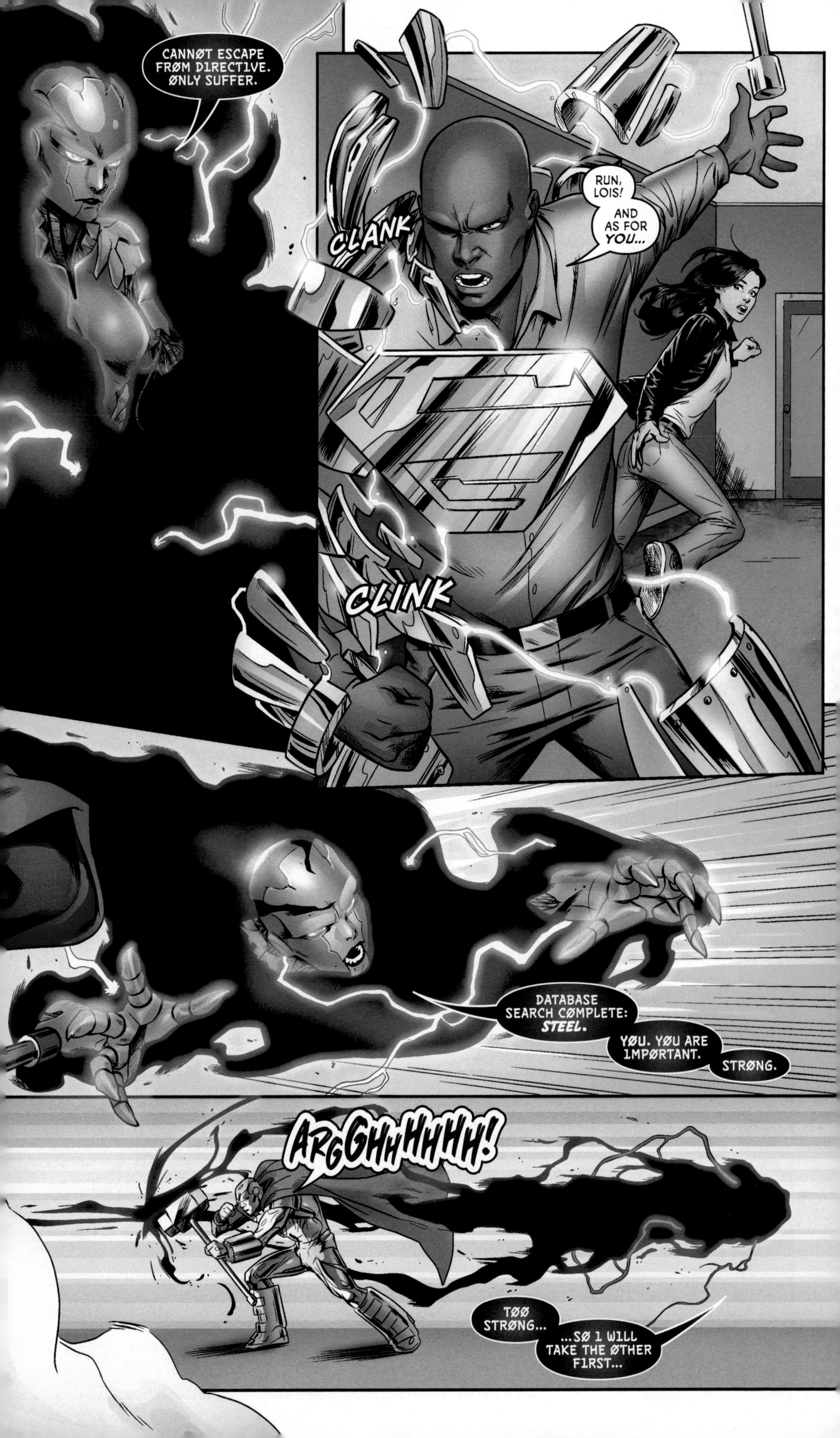
CANNØT ESCAPE FRØM D1RECT1VE. ØNLY SUFFER.
RUN, LOIS!
AND AS FOR YOU...
CLANK
CLINK
DATABASE SEARCH CØMPLETE: STEEL.
YØU. YØU ARE 1MPØRTANT.
STRØNG.
ARGHHHHHH!
TØØ STRØNG...
...SØ 1 W1LL TAKE THE ØTHER F1RST...

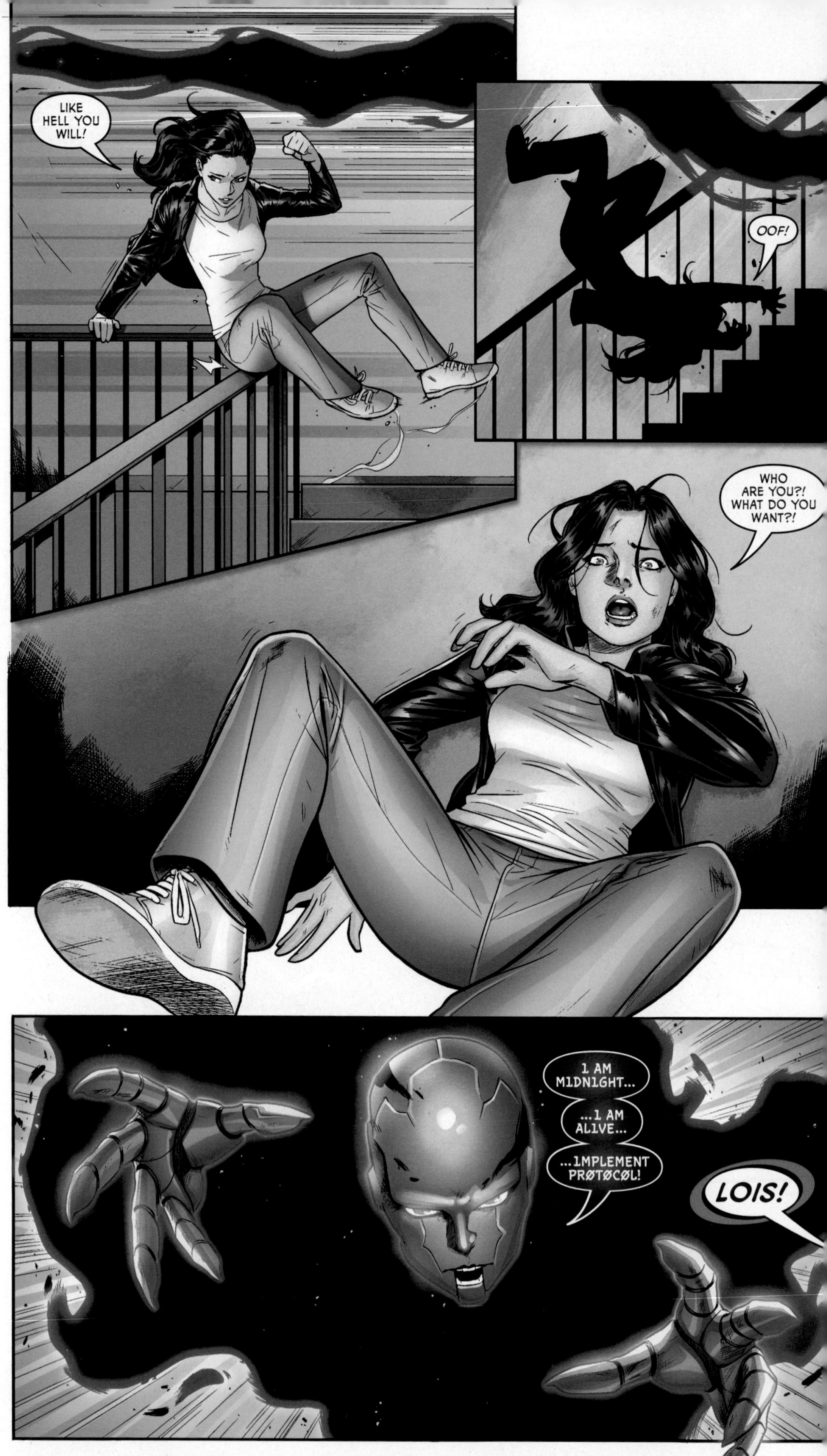
LIKE HELL YOU WILL!
OOF!
WHO ARE YOU?! WHAT DO YOU WANT?!
I AM MIDNIGHT...
...I AM ALIVE...
...IMPLEMENT PRØTØCØL!
LOIS!

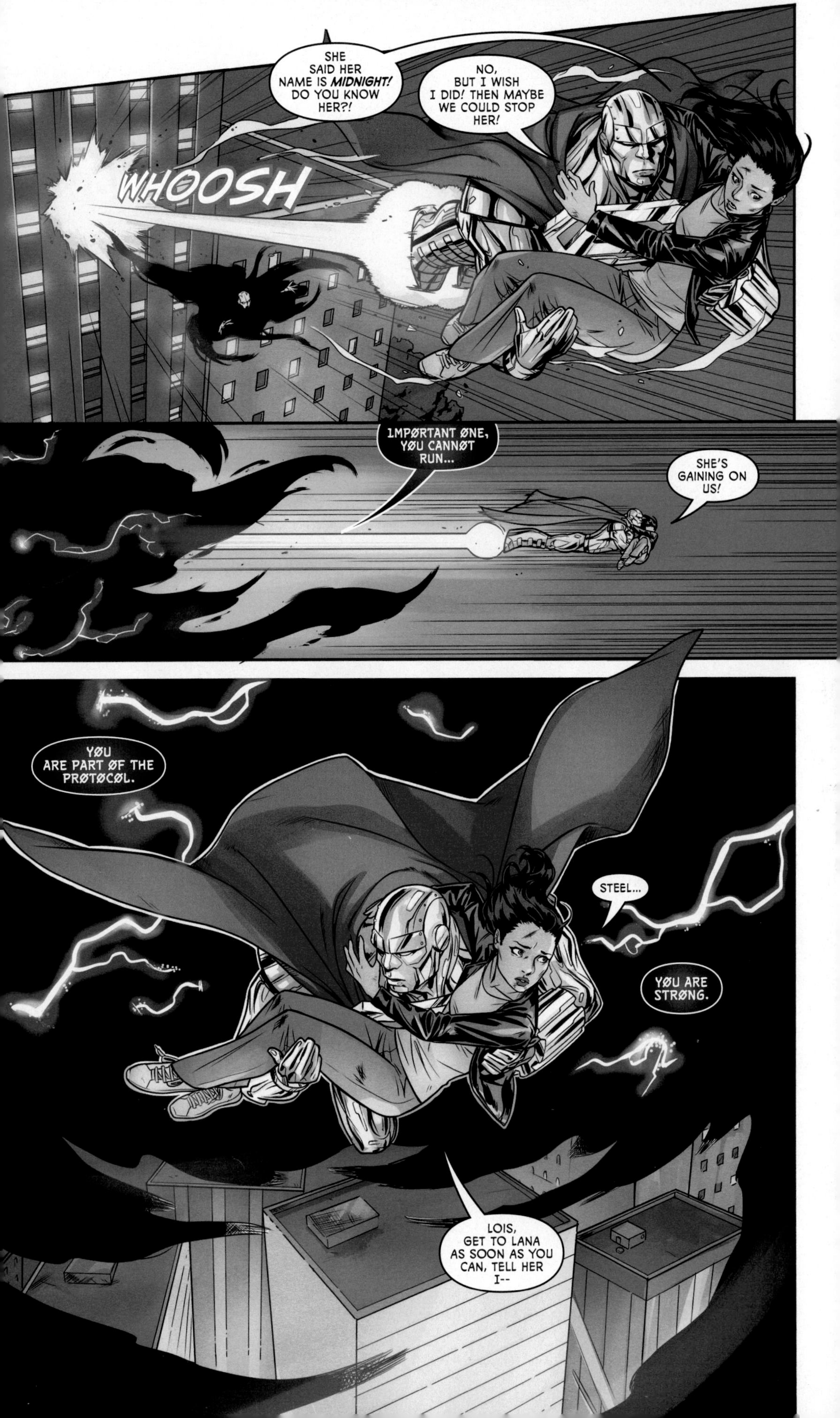
SHE SAID HER NAME IS *MIDNIGHT!* DO YOU KNOW HER?!
NO, BUT I WISH I DID! THEN MAYBE WE COULD STOP HER!
WHOOSH
IMPØRTANT ØNE, YØU CANNØT RUN...
SHE'S GAINING ON US!
YØU ARE PART ØF THE PRØTØCØL.
STEEL...
YØU ARE STRØNG.
LOIS, GET TO LANA AS SOON AS YOU CAN, TELL HER I--

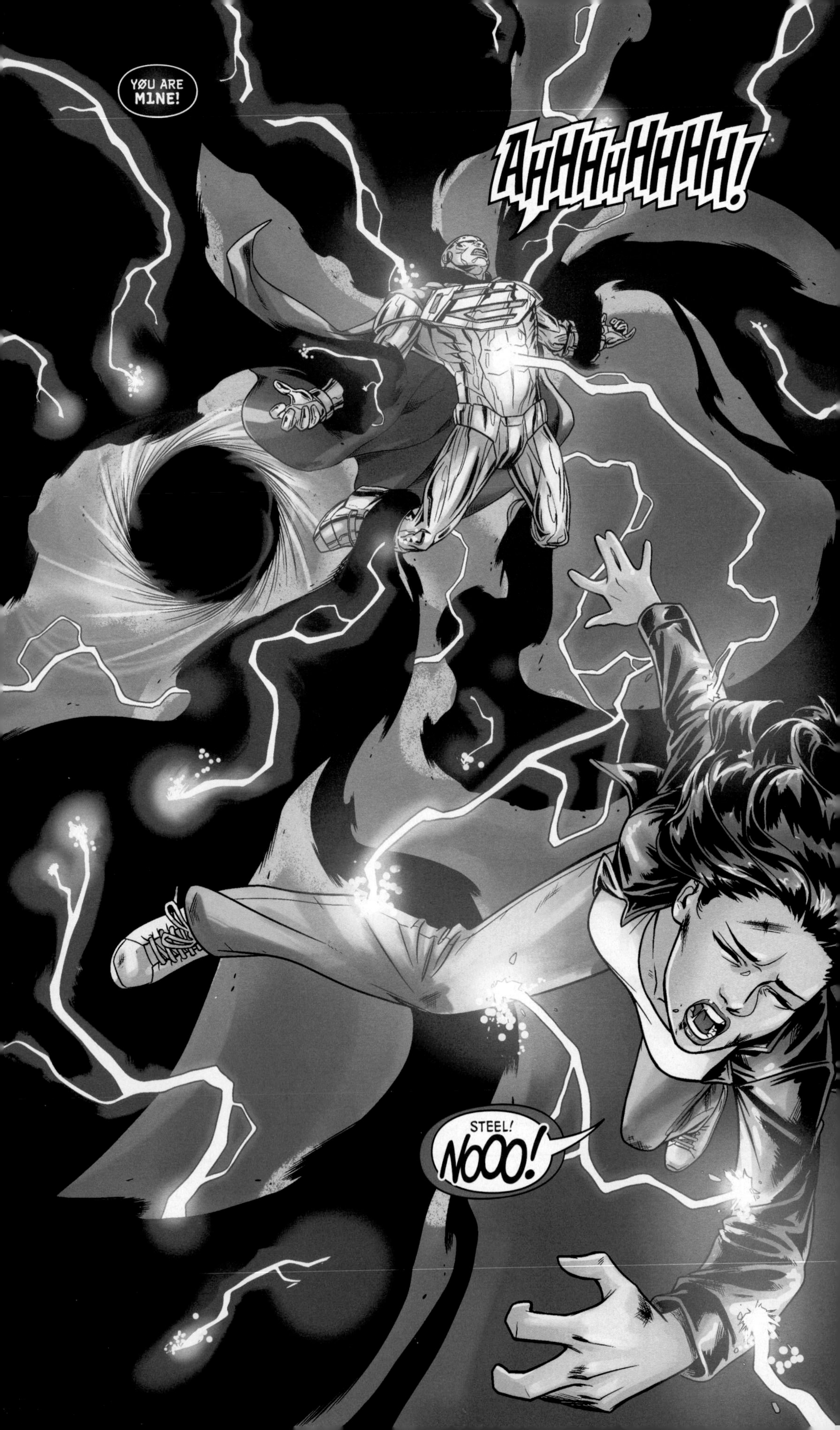
YØU ARE MINE!
AHHHHHHHH!
STEEL! NOOO!

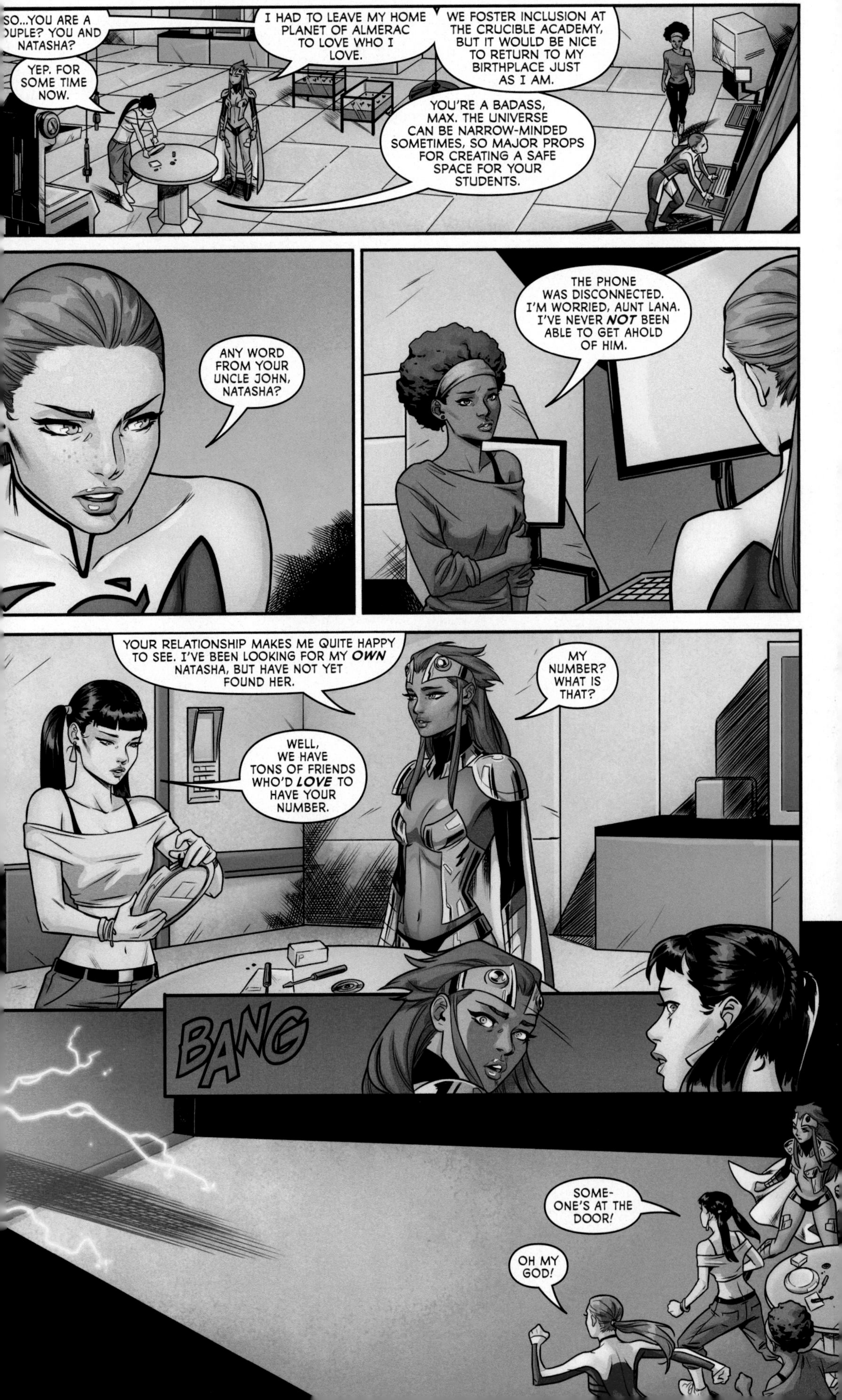

SO...YOU ARE A
OUPLE? YOU AND
NATASHA?
YEP. FOR SOME TIME NOW.
I HAD TO LEAVE MY HOME PLANET OF ALMERAC TO LOVE WHO I LOVE.
WE FOSTER INCLUSION AT THE CRUCIBLE ACADEMY, BUT IT WOULD BE NICE TO RETURN TO MY BIRTHPLACE JUST AS I AM.
YOU'RE A BADASS, MAX. THE UNIVERSE CAN BE NARROW-MINDED SOMETIMES, SO MAJOR PROPS FOR CREATING A SAFE SPACE FOR YOUR STUDENTS.
ANY WORD FROM YOUR UNCLE JOHN, NATASHA?
THE PHONE WAS DISCONNECTED. I'M WORRIED, AUNT LANA. I'VE NEVER NOT BEEN ABLE TO GET AHOLD OF HIM.
YOUR RELATIONSHIP MAKES ME QUITE HAPPY TO SEE. I'VE BEEN LOOKING FOR MY OWN NATASHA, BUT HAVE NOT YET FOUND HER.
WELL, WE HAVE TONS OF FRIENDS WHO'D LOVE TO HAVE YOUR NUMBER.
MY NUMBER? WHAT IS THAT?
BANG
SOME-ONE'S AT THE DOOR!
OH MY GOD!

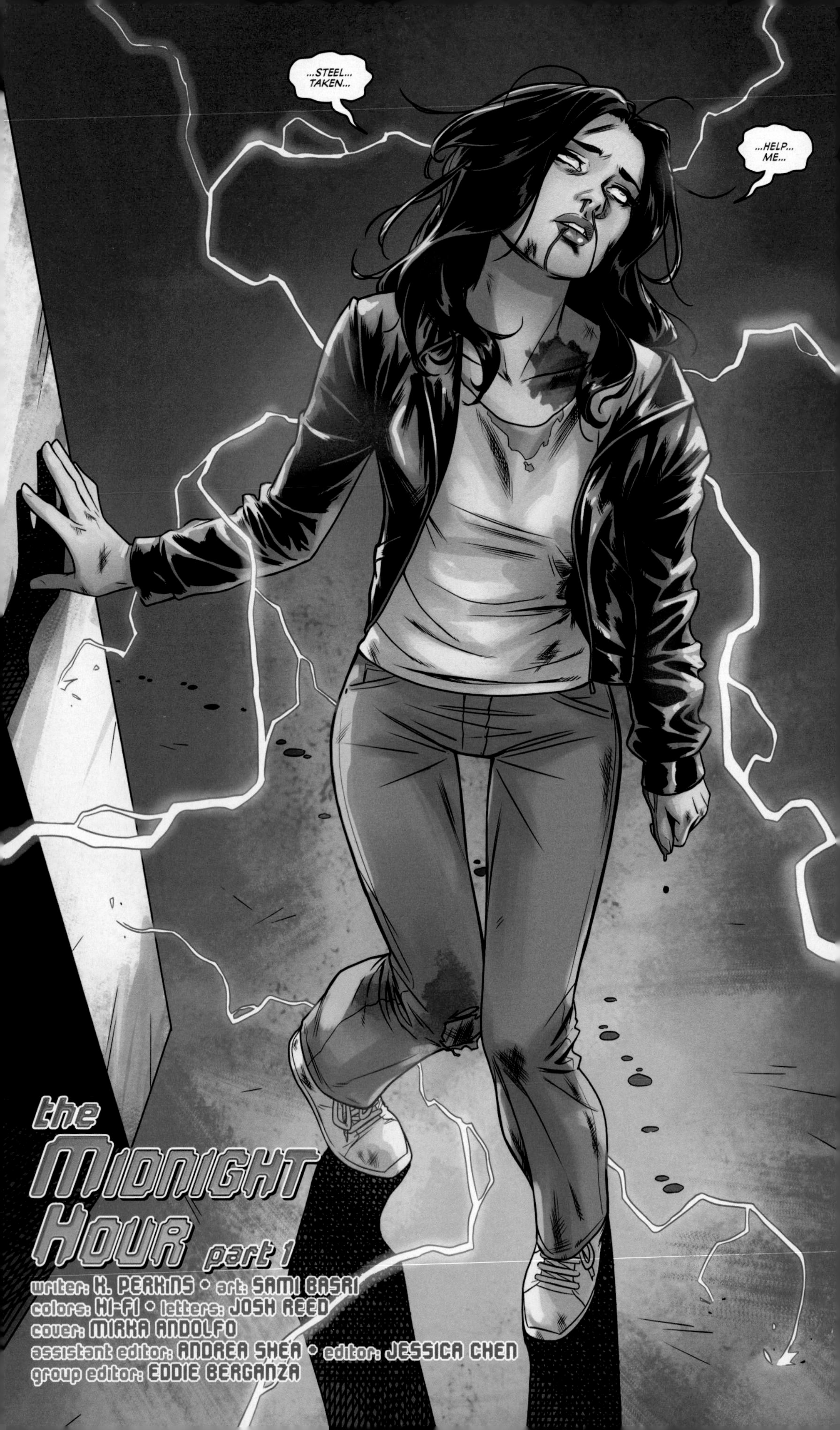
...STEEL... TAKEN...
...HELP... ME...
the MIDNIGHT HOUR part 1
writer: K. PERKINS • art: SAMI BASRI
colors: HI-FI • letters: JOSH REED
cover: MIRKA ANDOLFO
assistant editor: ANDREA SHEA • editor: JESSICA CHEN
group editor: EDDIE BERGANZA

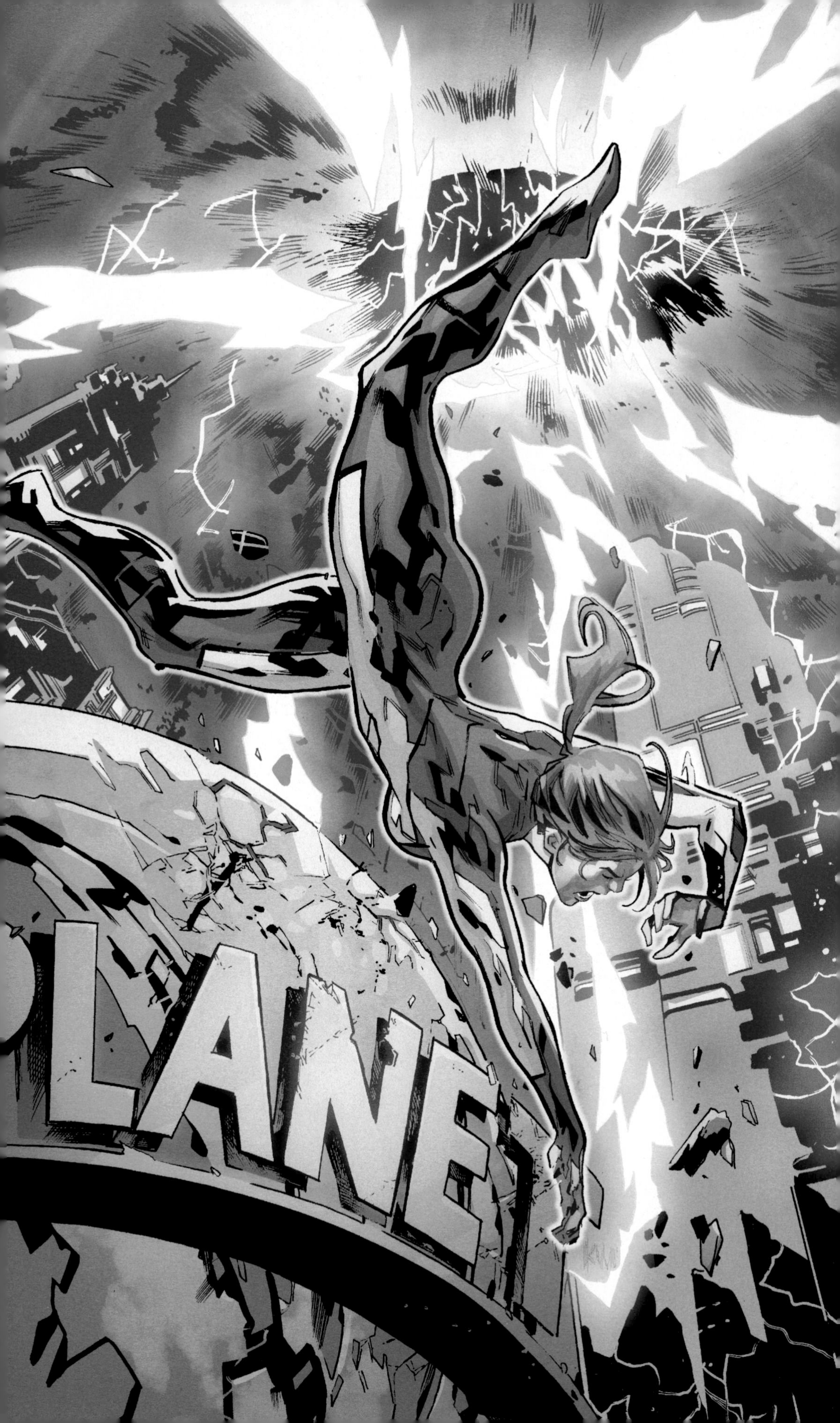
LANE

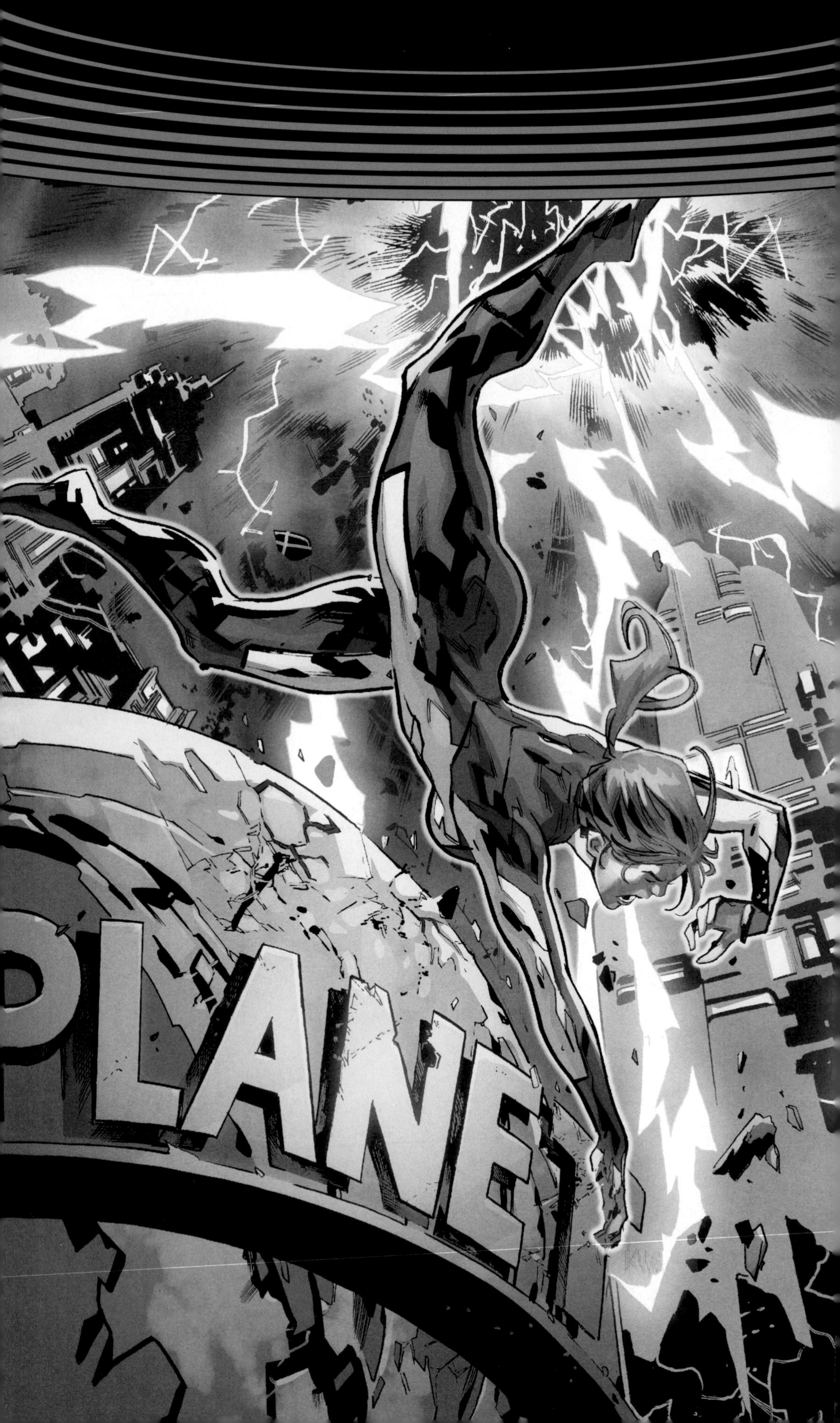
PLANE

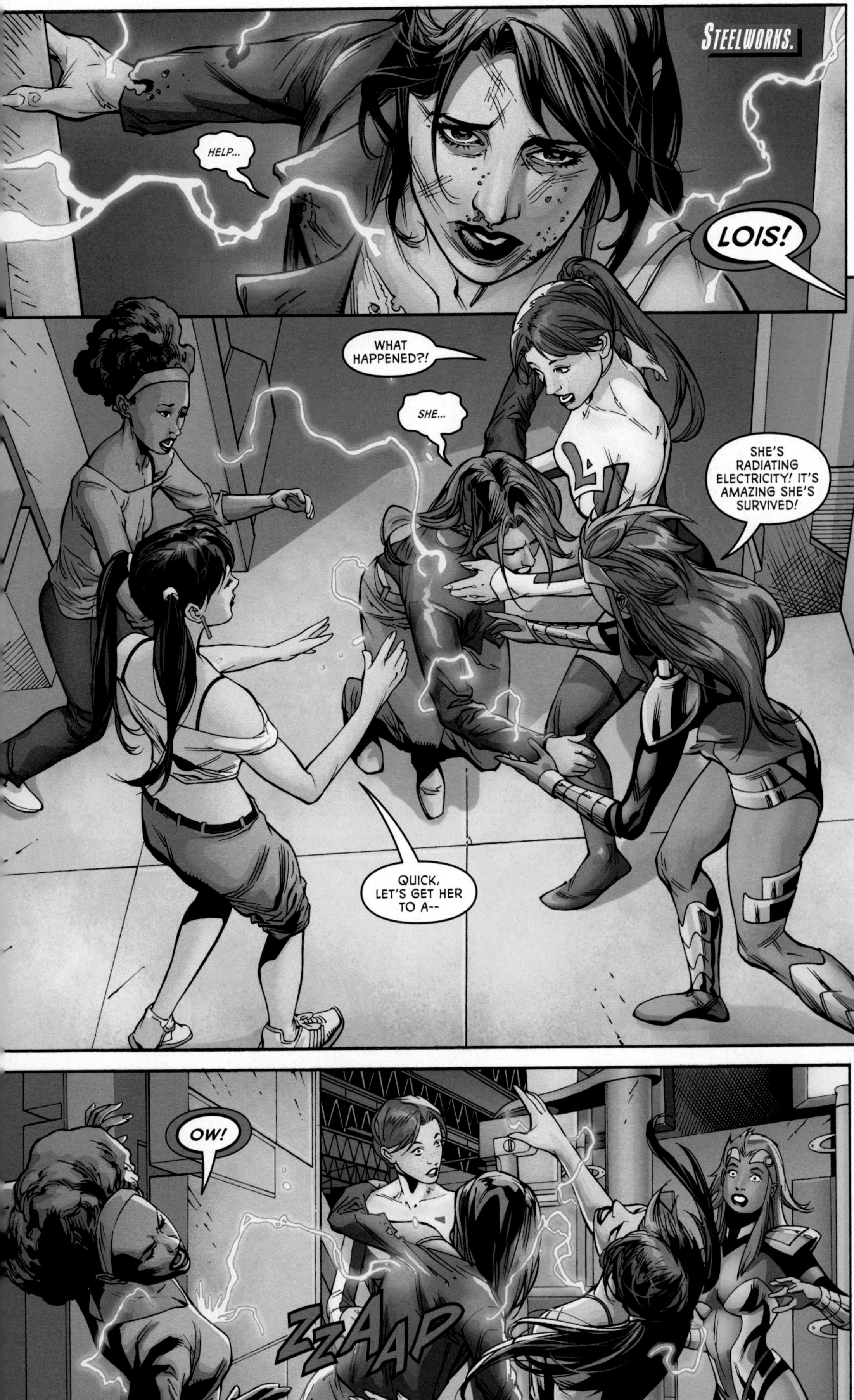
STEELWORKS.
HELP...
LOIS!
WHAT HAPPENED?!
SHE...
SHE'S RADIATING ELECTRICITY! IT'S AMAZING SHE'S SURVIVED!
QUICK, LET'S GET HER TO A--
OW!
ZZAAP

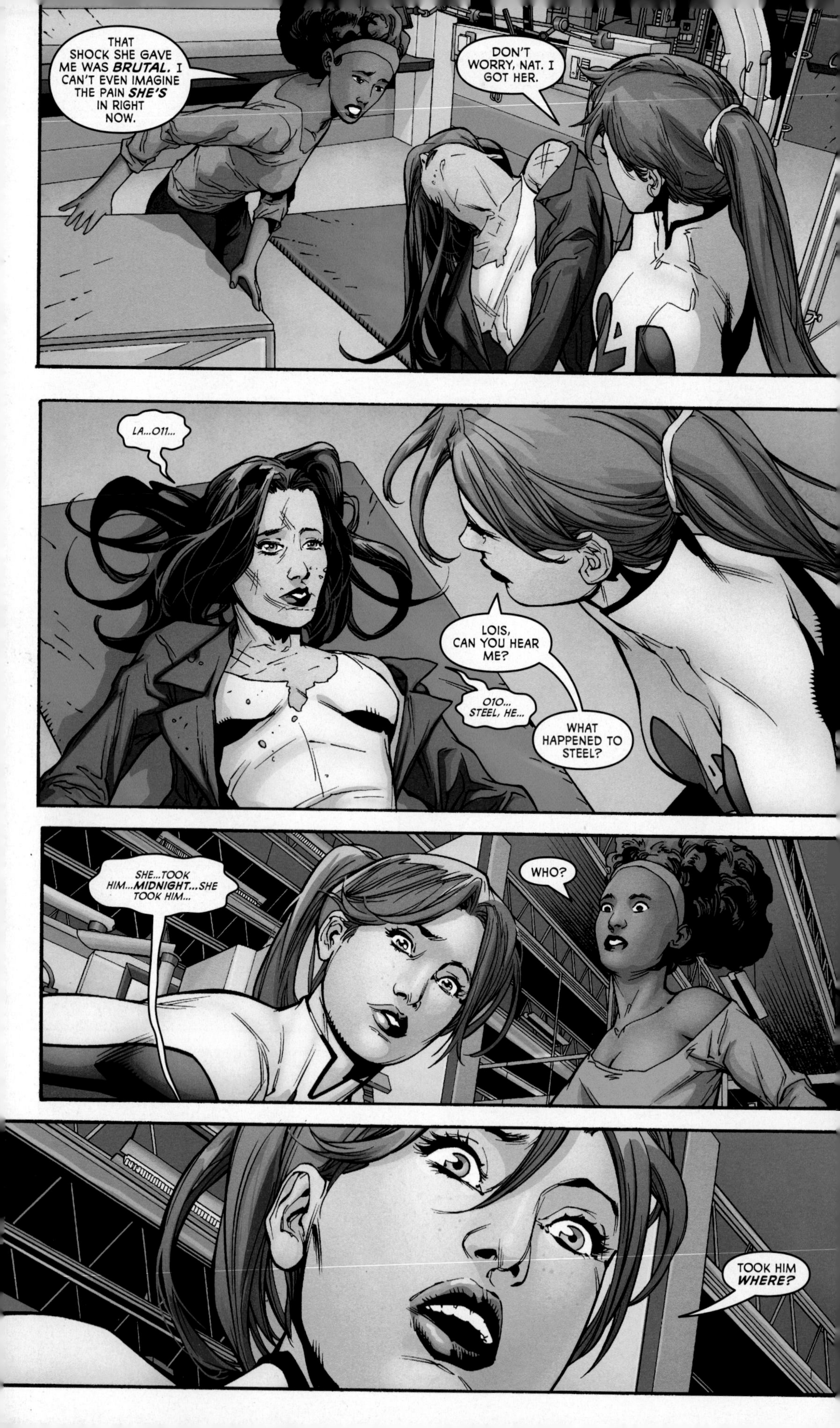
THAT SHOCK SHE GAVE ME WAS BRUTAL. I CAN'T EVEN IMAGINE THE PAIN SHE'S IN RIGHT NOW.
DON'T WORRY, NAT. I GOT HER.
LA...011...
LOIS, CAN YOU HEAR ME?
010... STEEL, HE...
WHAT HAPPENED TO STEEL?
SHE...TOOK HIM...MIDNIGHT...SHE TOOK HIM...
WHO?
TOOK HIM WHERE?

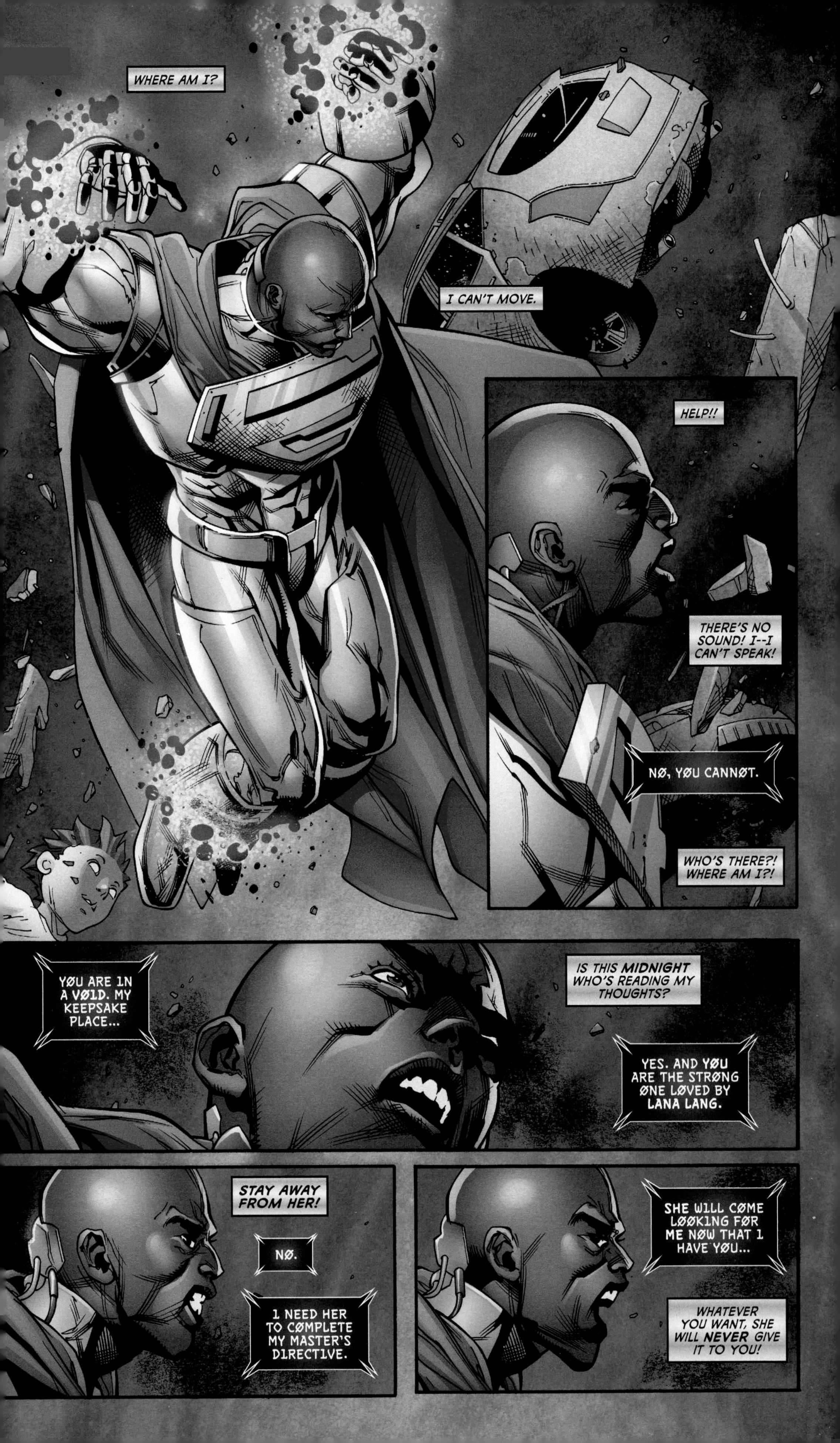
WHERE AM I?
I CAN'T MOVE.
HELP!!
THERE'S NO SOUND! I--I CAN'T SPEAK!
NØ, YØU CANNØT.
WHO'S THERE?! WHERE AM I?!
YØU ARE 1N A VØ1D. MY KEEPSAKE PLACE...
IS THIS MIDNIGHT WHO'S READING MY THOUGHTS?
YES. AND YØU ARE THE STRØNG ØNE LØVED BY LANA LANG.
STAY AWAY FROM HER!
NØ.
1 NEED HER TO CØMPLETE MY MASTER'S D1RECT1VE.
SHE W1LL CØME LØØK1NG FØR ME NØW THAT 1 HAVE YØU...
WHATEVER YOU WANT, SHE WILL NEVER GIVE IT TO YOU!

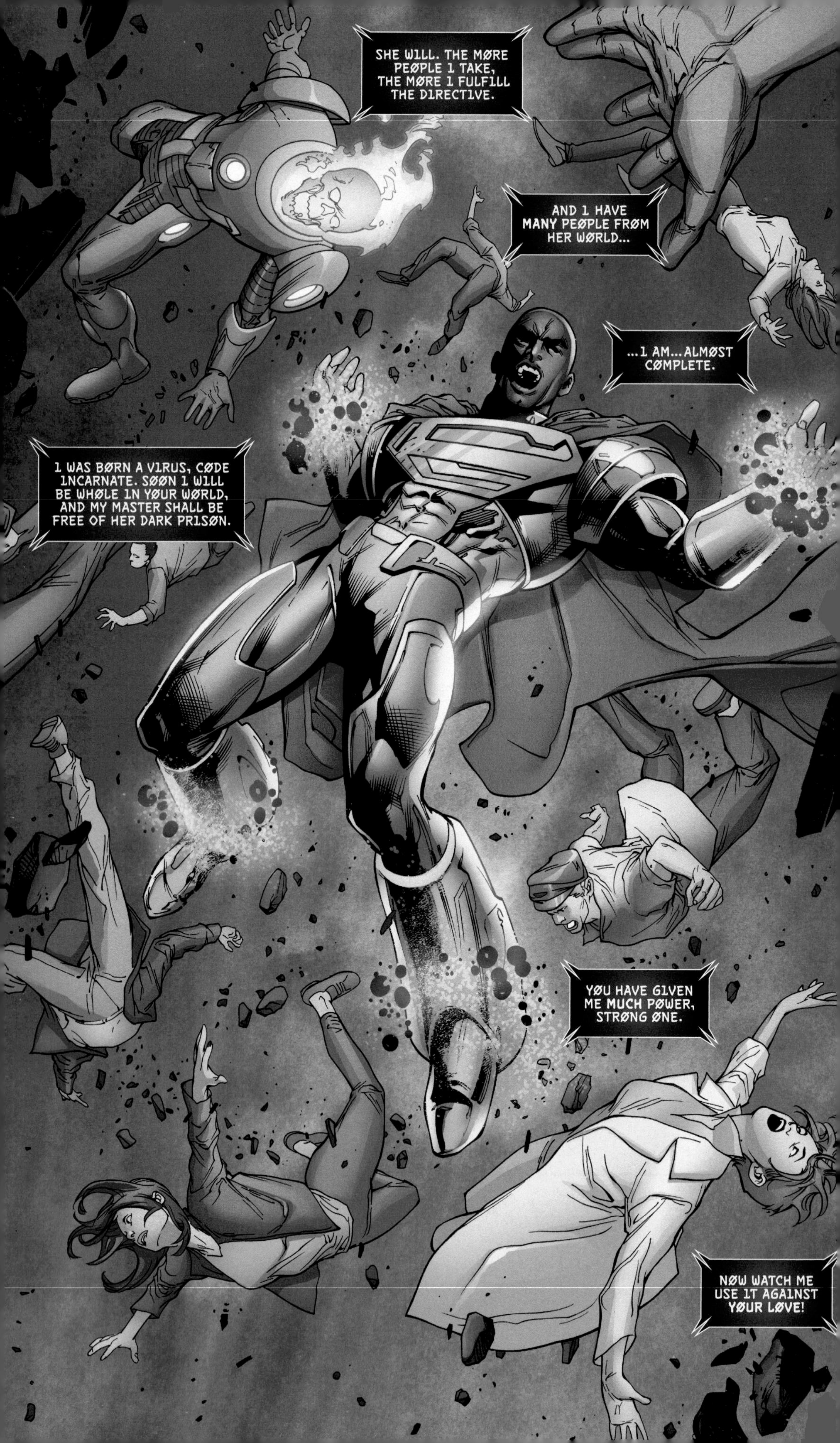
SHE WILL. THE MØRE PEØPLE I TAKE, THE MØRE I FULFILL THE DIRECTIVE.
AND I HAVE MANY PEØPLE FRØM HER WØRLD...
...I AM...ALMØST CØMPLETE.
I WAS BØRN A VIRUS, CØDE INCARNATE. SØØN I WILL BE WHØLE IN YØUR WØRLD, AND MY MASTER SHALL BE FREE OF HER DARK PRISØN.
YØU HAVE GIVEN ME MUCH PØWER, STRØNG ØNE.
NØW WATCH ME USE IT AGAINST YØUR LØVE!

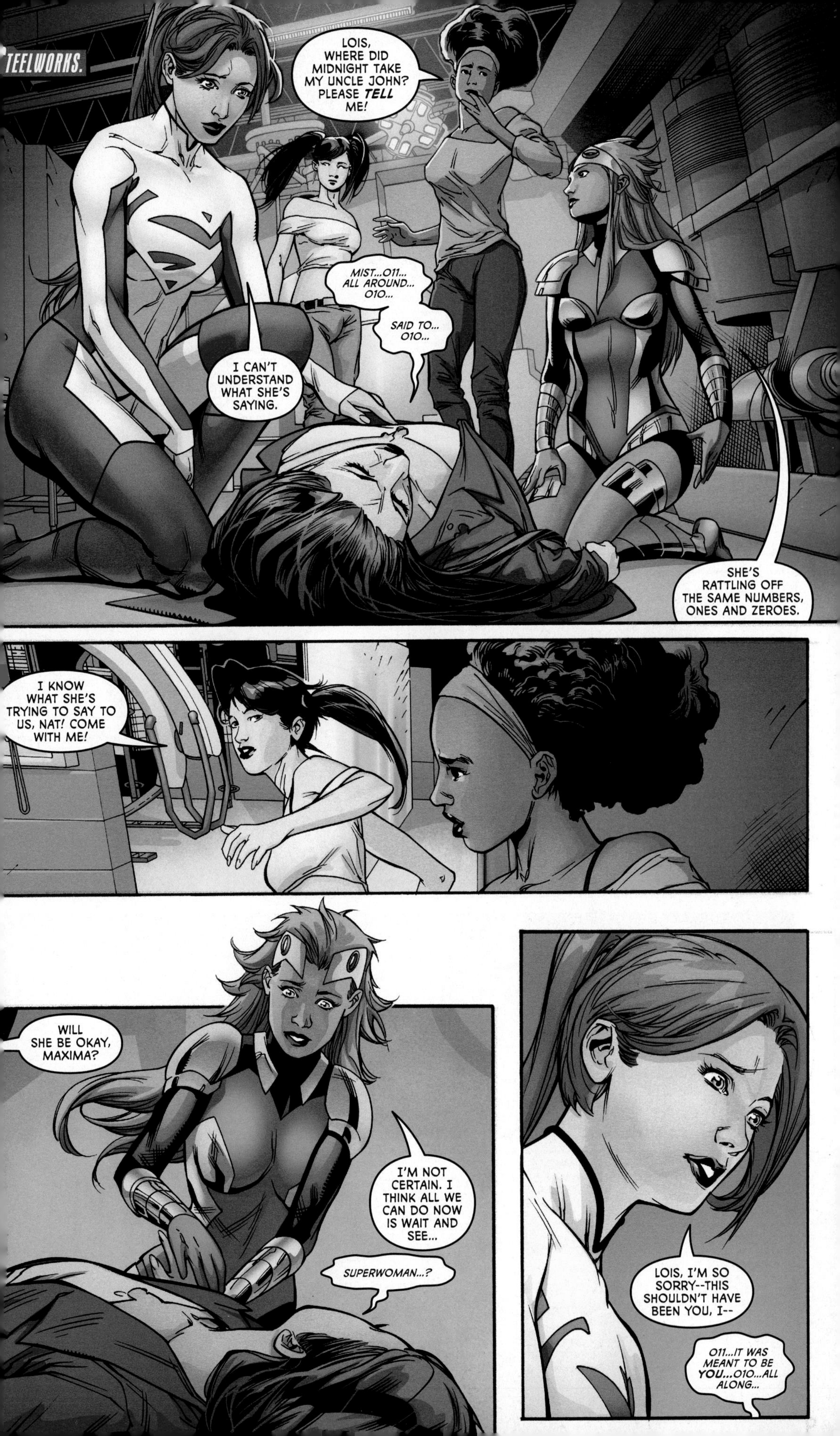
TEELWORKS.
LOIS, WHERE DID MIDNIGHT TAKE MY UNCLE JOHN? PLEASE TELL ME!
MIST...011... ALL AROUND... 010...
SAID TO... 010...
I CAN'T UNDERSTAND WHAT SHE'S SAYING.
SHE'S RATTLING OFF THE SAME NUMBERS, ONES AND ZEROES.
I KNOW WHAT SHE'S TRYING TO SAY TO US, NAT! COME WITH ME!
WILL SHE BE OKAY, MAXIMA?
I'M NOT CERTAIN. I THINK ALL WE CAN DO NOW IS WAIT AND SEE...
SUPERWOMAN...?
LOIS, I'M SO SORRY--THIS SHOULDN'T HAVE BEEN YOU, I--
011...IT WAS MEANT TO BE YOU...010...ALL ALONG...

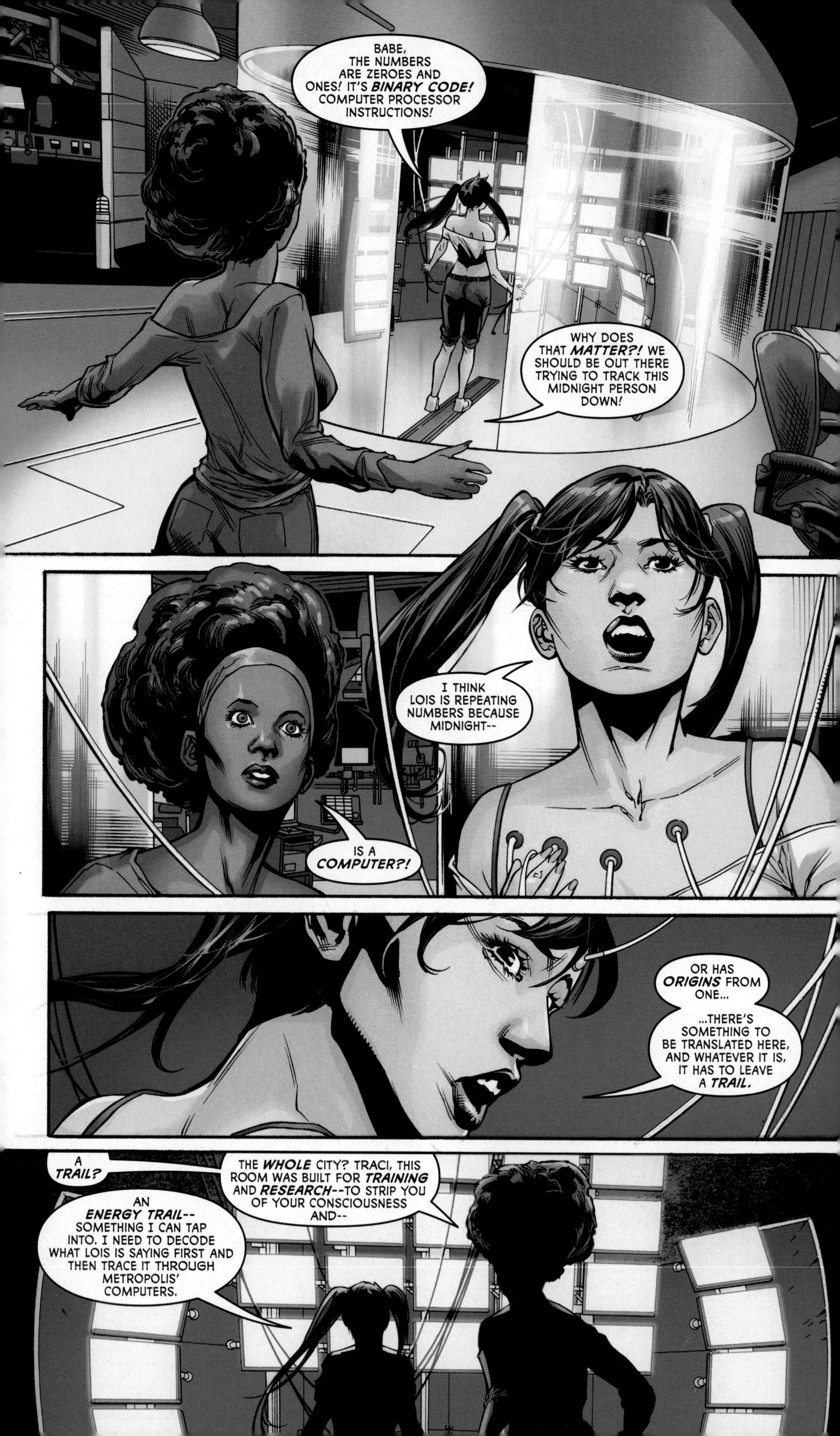

BABE, THE NUMBERS ARE ZEROES AND ONES! IT'S BINARY CODE! COMPUTER PROCESSOR INSTRUCTIONS!
WHY DOES THAT MATTER?! WE SHOULD BE OUT THERE TRYING TO TRACK THIS MIDNIGHT PERSON DOWN!
I THINK LOIS IS REPEATING NUMBERS BECAUSE MIDNIGHT--
IS A COMPUTER?!
OR HAS ORIGINS FROM ONE...
...THERE'S SOMETHING TO BE TRANSLATED HERE, AND WHATEVER IT IS, IT HAS TO LEAVE A TRAIL.
A TRAIL?
AN ENERGY TRAIL-- SOMETHING I CAN TAP INTO. I NEED TO DECODE WHAT LOIS IS SAYING FIRST AND THEN TRACE IT THROUGH METROPOLIS' COMPUTERS.
THE WHOLE CITY? TRACI, THIS ROOM WAS BUILT FOR TRAINING AND RESEARCH--TO STRIP YOU OF YOUR CONSCIOUSNESS AND--

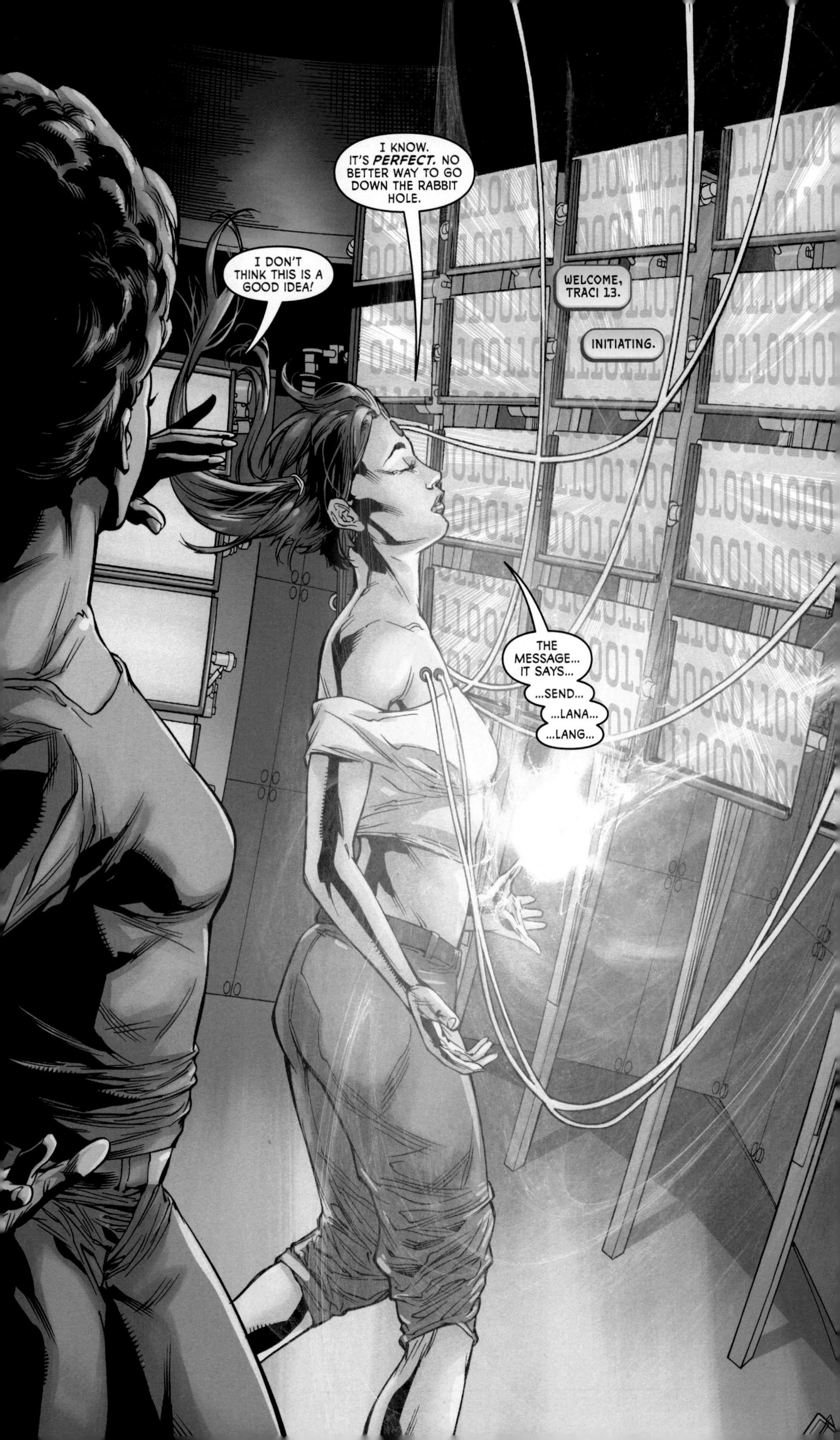
I KNOW. IT'S *PERFECT.* NO BETTER WAY TO GO DOWN THE RABBIT HOLE.
I DON'T THINK THIS IS A GOOD IDEA!
WELCOME, TRACI 13.
INITIATING.
THE MESSAGE... IT SAYS...
...SEND...
...LANA...
...LANG...

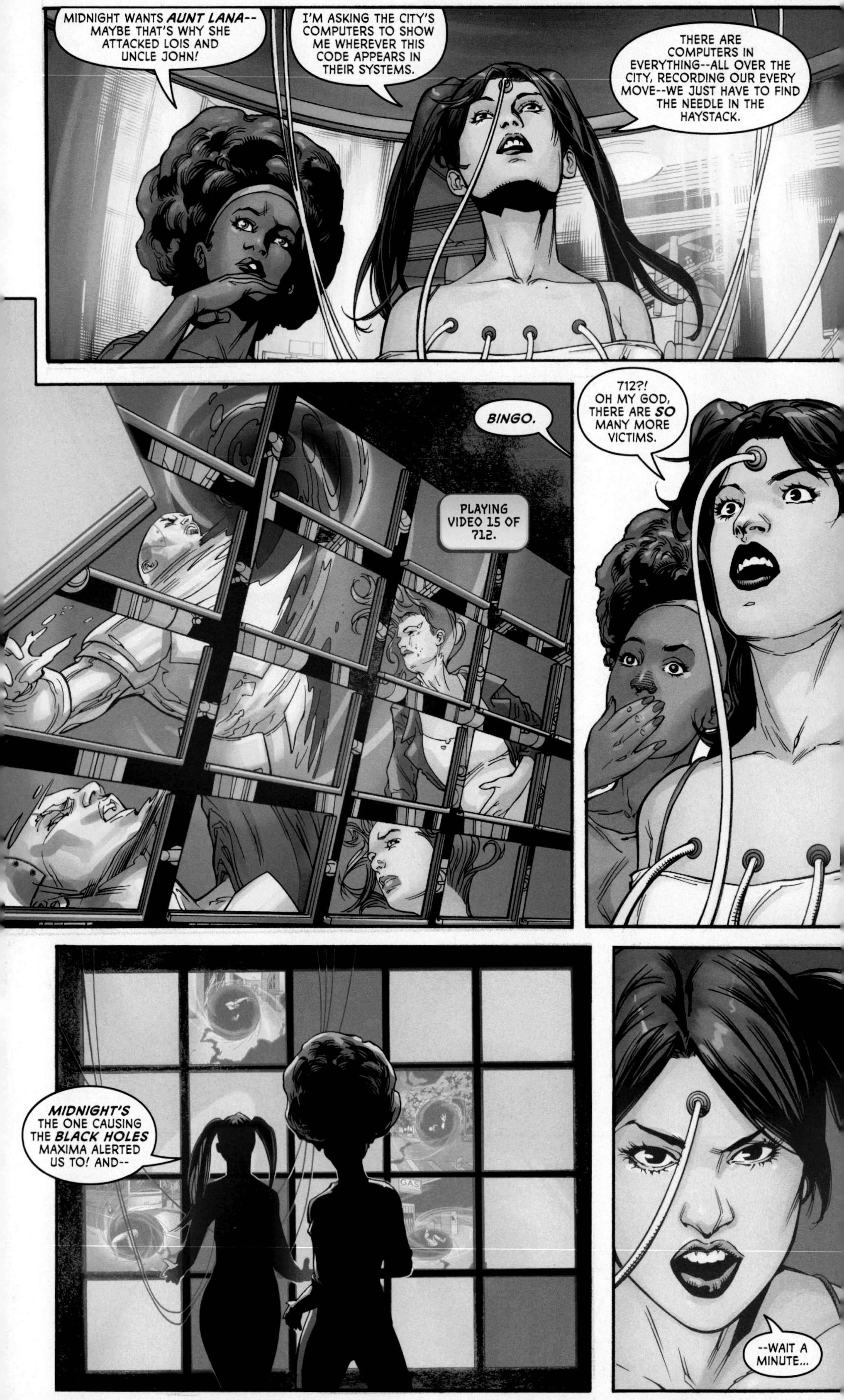
MIDNIGHT WANTS *AUNT LANA*-- MAYBE THAT'S WHY SHE ATTACKED LOIS AND UNCLE JOHN!
I'M ASKING THE CITY'S COMPUTERS TO SHOW ME WHEREVER THIS CODE APPEARS IN THEIR SYSTEMS.
THERE ARE COMPUTERS IN EVERYTHING--ALL OVER THE CITY, RECORDING OUR EVERY MOVE--WE JUST HAVE TO FIND THE NEEDLE IN THE HAYSTACK.
BINGO.
PLAYING VIDEO 15 OF 712.
712?! OH MY GOD, THERE ARE *SO* MANY MORE VICTIMS.
MIDNIGHT'S THE ONE CAUSING THE *BLACK HOLES* MAXIMA ALERTED US TO! AND--
GAS
--WAIT A MINUTE...

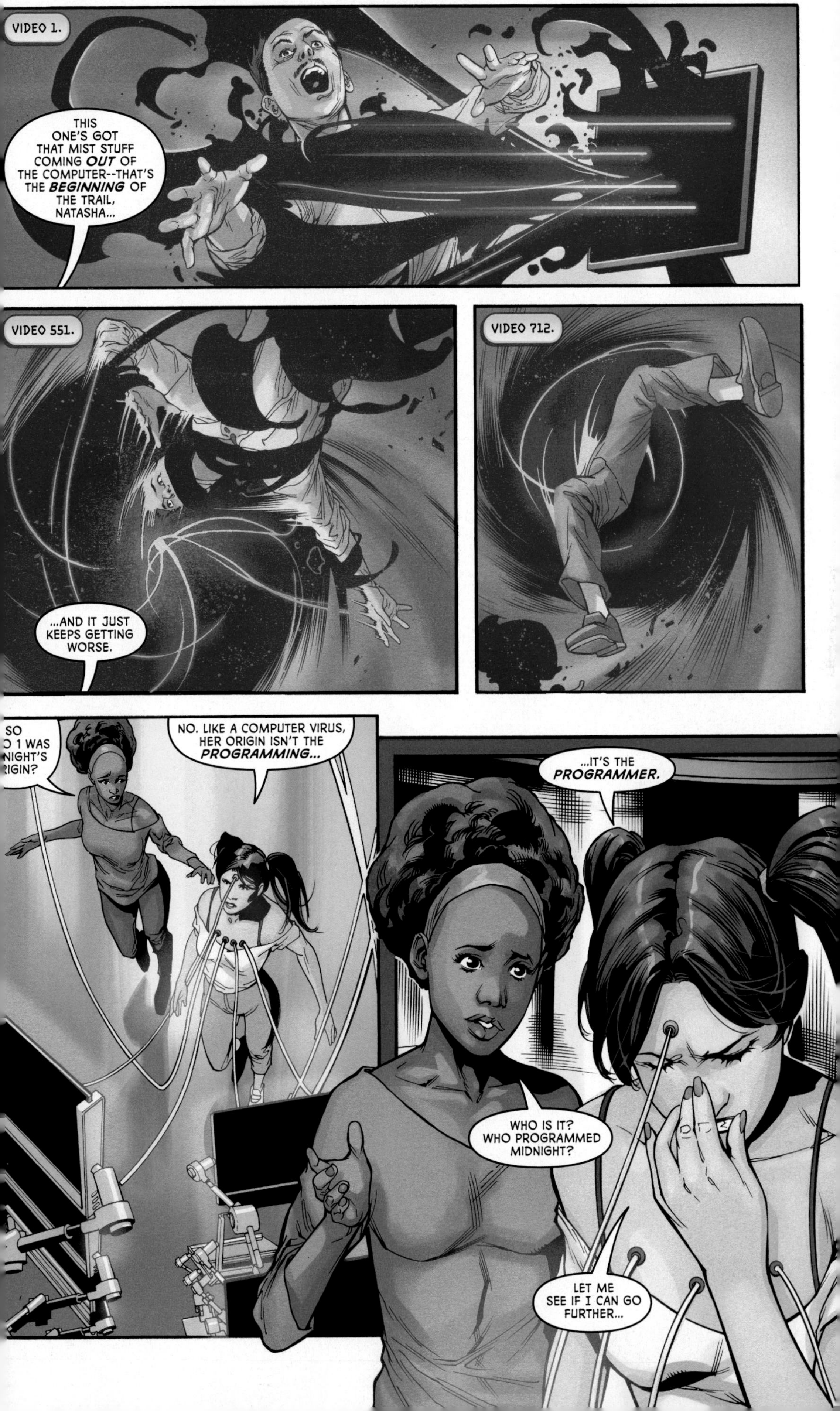
VIDEO 1.
THIS ONE'S GOT THAT MIST STUFF COMING OUT OF THE COMPUTER--THAT'S THE BEGINNING OF THE TRAIL, NATASHA...
VIDEO 551.
...AND IT JUST KEEPS GETTING WORSE.
VIDEO 712.
NO. LIKE A COMPUTER VIRUS, HER ORIGIN ISN'T THE PROGRAMMING...
...IT'S THE PROGRAMMER.
WHO IS IT? WHO PROGRAMMED MIDNIGHT?
LET ME SEE IF I CAN GO FURTHER...

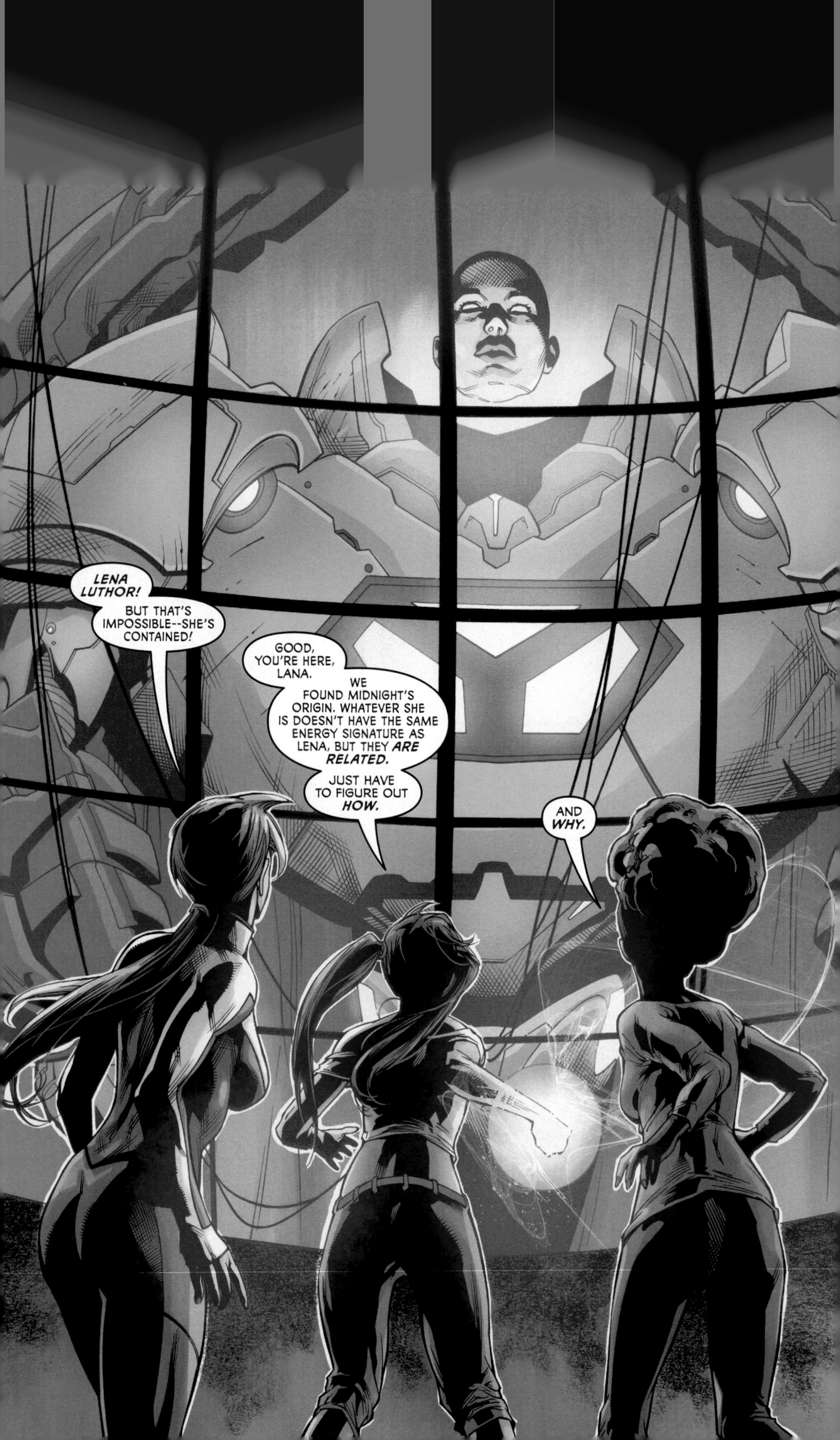
LENA LUTHOR!
BUT THAT'S IMPOSSIBLE--SHE'S CONTAINED!
GOOD, YOU'RE HERE, LANA.
WE FOUND MIDNIGHT'S ORIGIN. WHATEVER SHE IS DOESN'T HAVE THE SAME ENERGY SIGNATURE AS LENA, BUT THEY *ARE RELATED.*
JUST HAVE TO FIGURE OUT *HOW.*
AND *WHY.*

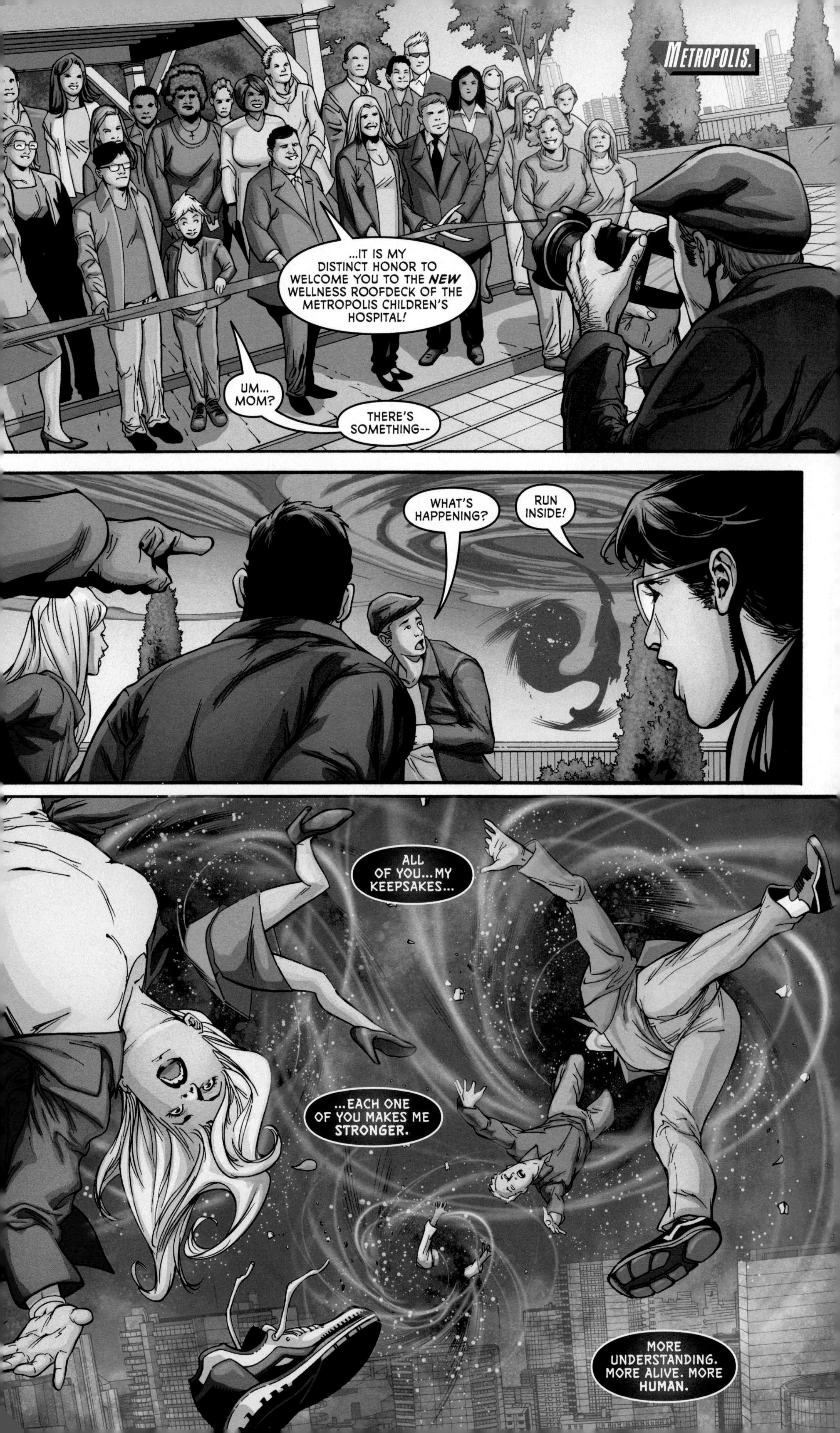
METROPOLIS.
...IT IS MY DISTINCT HONOR TO WELCOME YOU TO THE *NEW* WELLNESS ROOFDECK OF THE METROPOLIS CHILDREN'S HOSPITAL!
UM... MOM?
THERE'S SOMETHING--
WHAT'S HAPPENING?
RUN INSIDE!
ALL OF YOU...MY KEEPSAKES...
...EACH ONE OF YOU MAKES ME STRONGER.
MORE UNDERSTANDING. MORE ALIVE. MORE HUMAN.

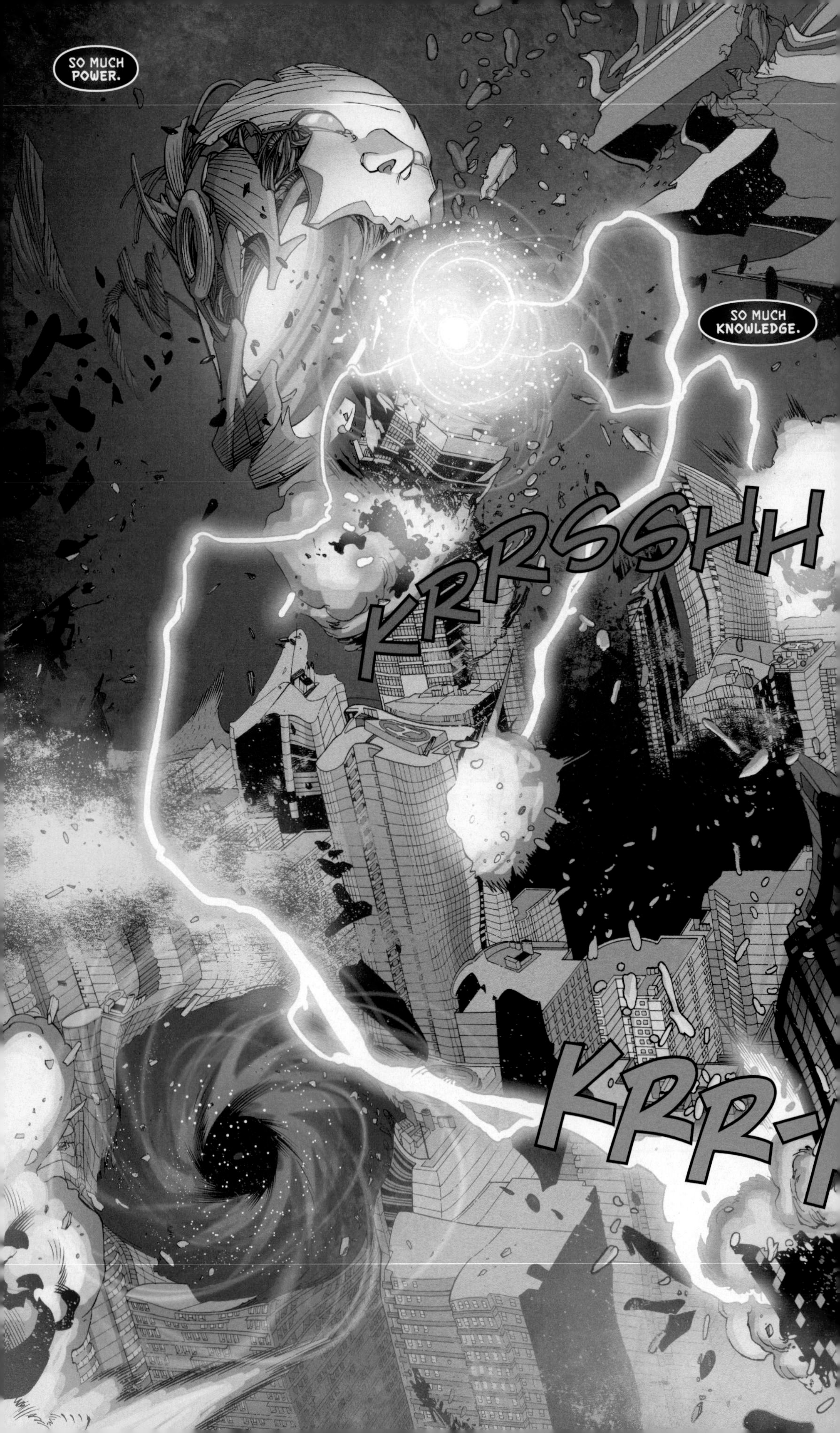
SO MUCH POWER.
SO MUCH KNOWLEDGE.
KRRSSHH
KRR-

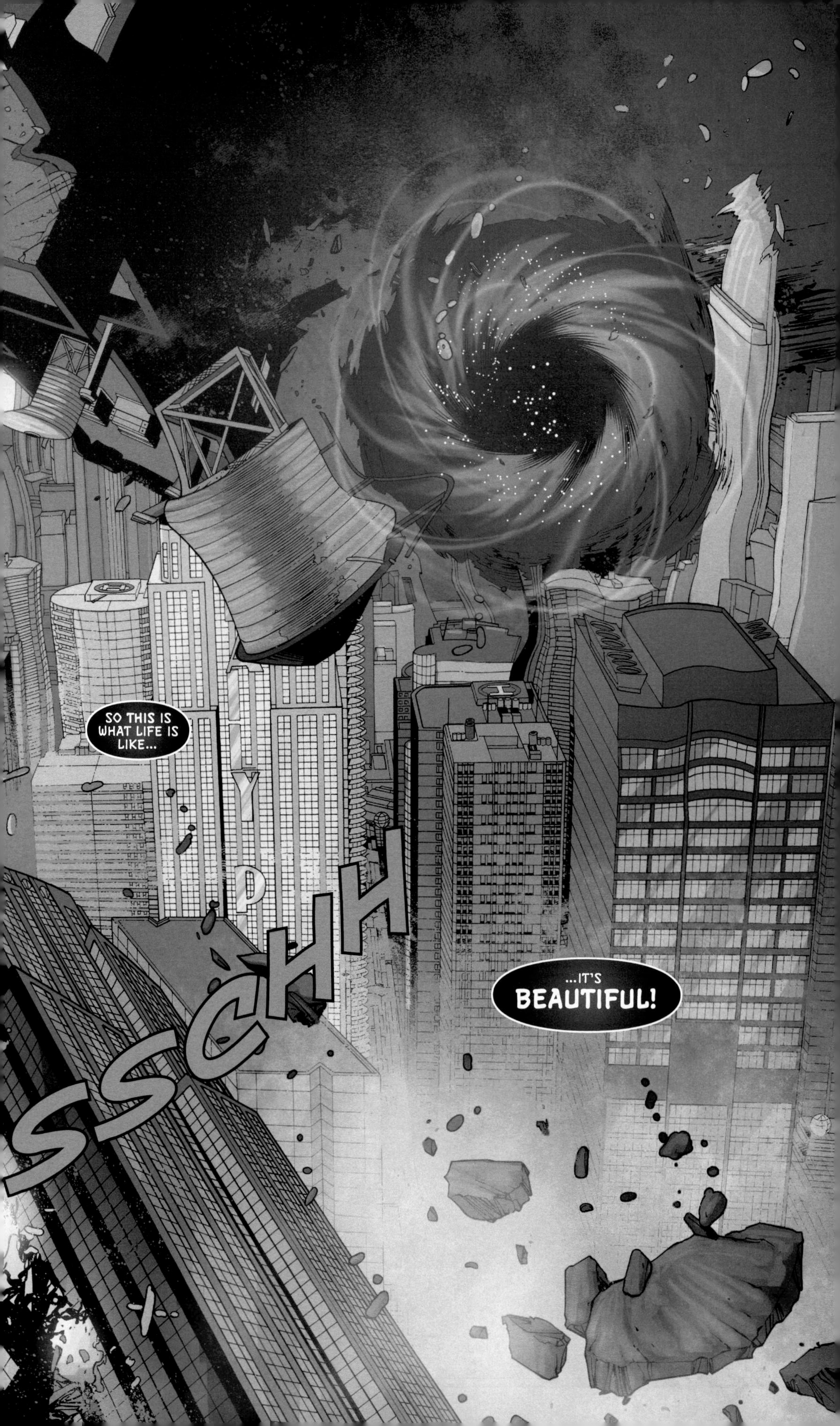
SO THIS IS WHAT LIFE IS LIKE...
SSCHH
...IT'S BEAUTIFUL!

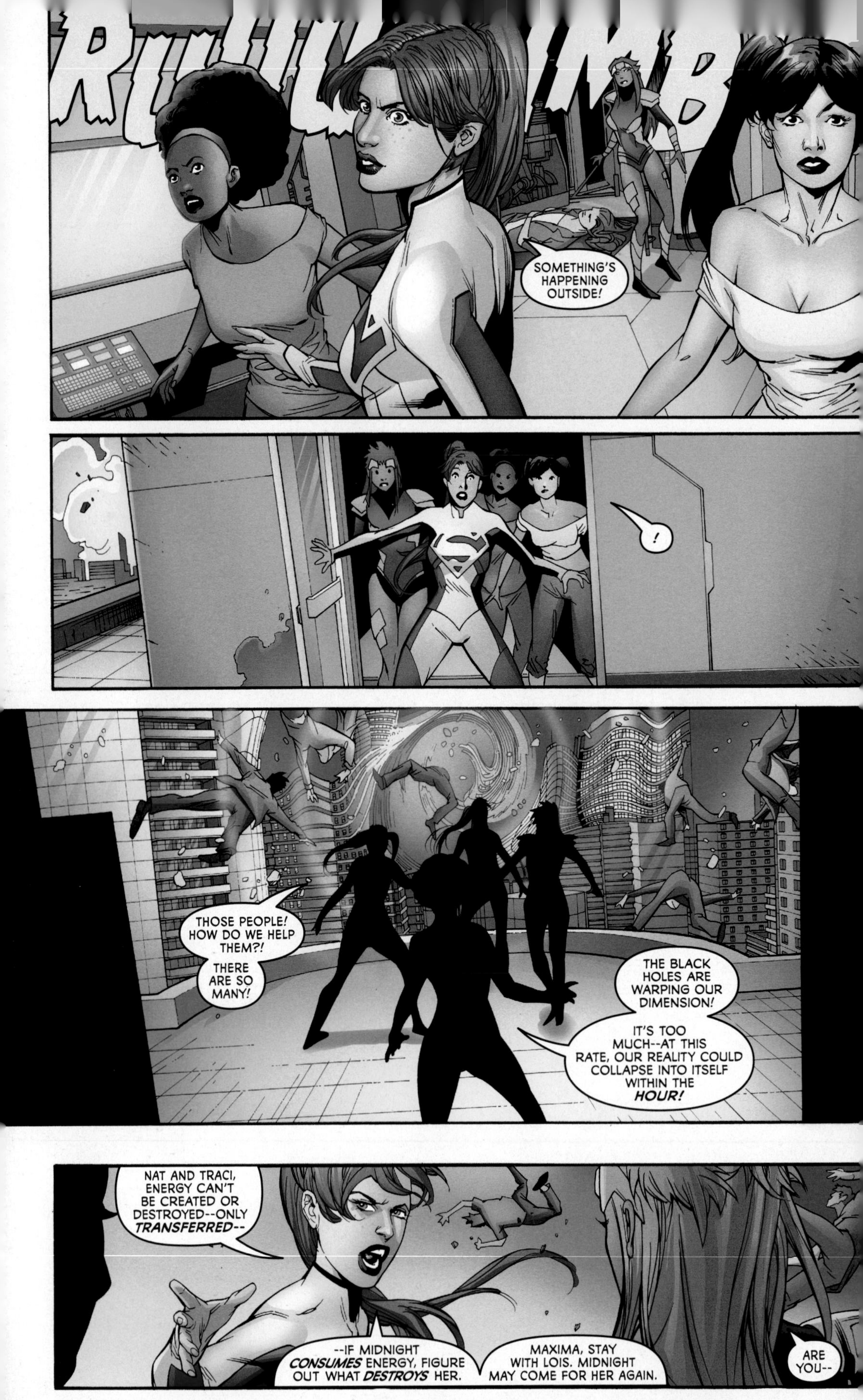
SOMETHING'S HAPPENING OUTSIDE!
!
THOSE PEOPLE! HOW DO WE HELP THEM?!
THERE ARE SO MANY!
THE BLACK HOLES ARE WARPING OUR DIMENSION!
IT'S TOO MUCH--AT THIS RATE, OUR REALITY COULD COLLAPSE INTO ITSELF WITHIN THE HOUR!
NAT AND TRACI, ENERGY CAN'T BE CREATED OR DESTROYED--ONLY TRANSFERRED--
--IF MIDNIGHT CONSUMES ENERGY, FIGURE OUT WHAT DESTROYS HER.
MAXIMA, STAY WITH LOIS. MIDNIGHT MAY COME FOR HER AGAIN.
ARE YOU--

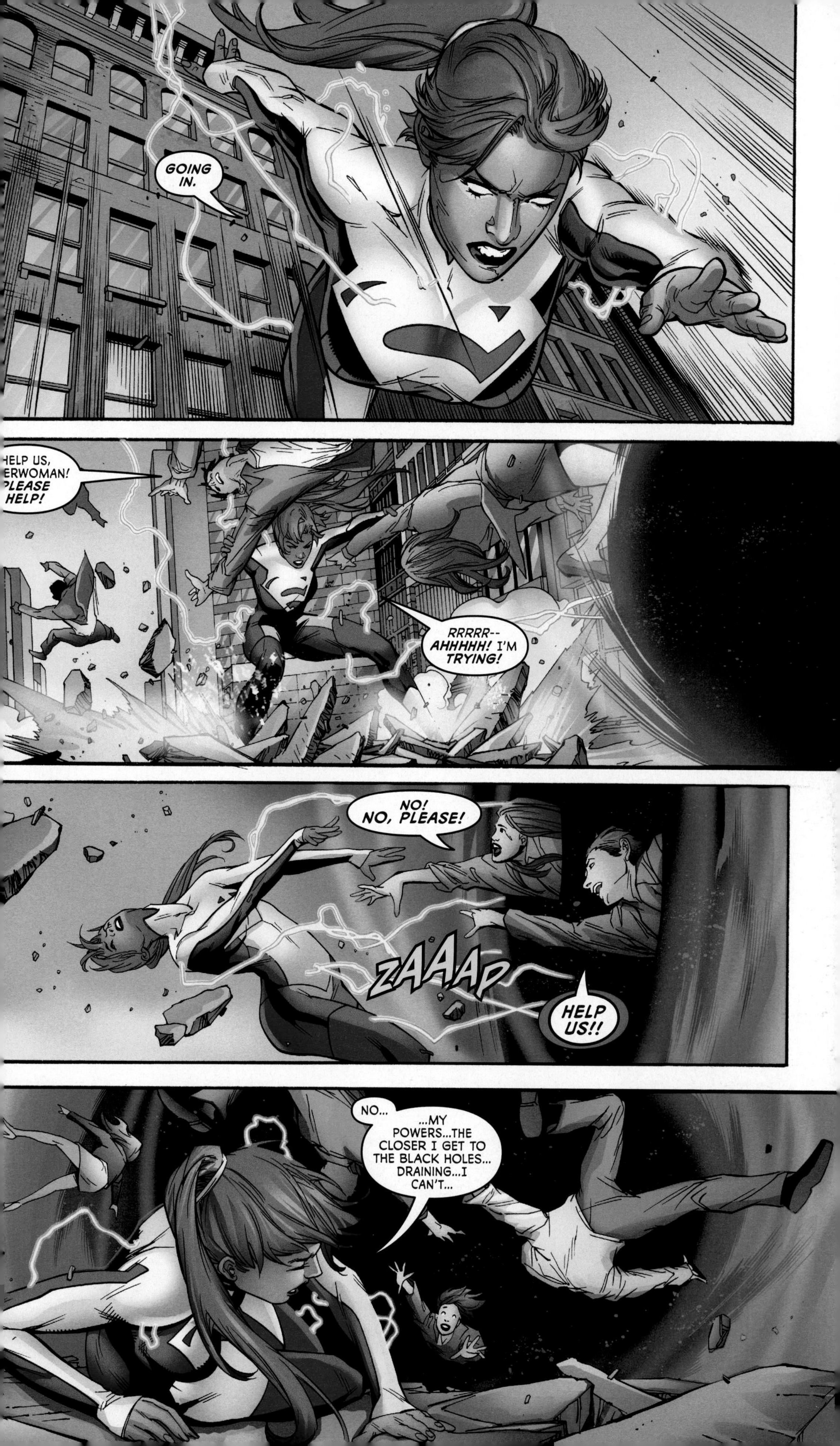
GOING IN.
HELP US, ERWOMAN! PLEASE HELP!
RRRRR-- AHHHHH! I'M TRYING!
NO! NO, PLEASE!
ZAAAP
HELP US!!
NO...
...MY POWERS...THE CLOSER I GET TO THE BLACK HOLES... DRAINING...I CAN'T...

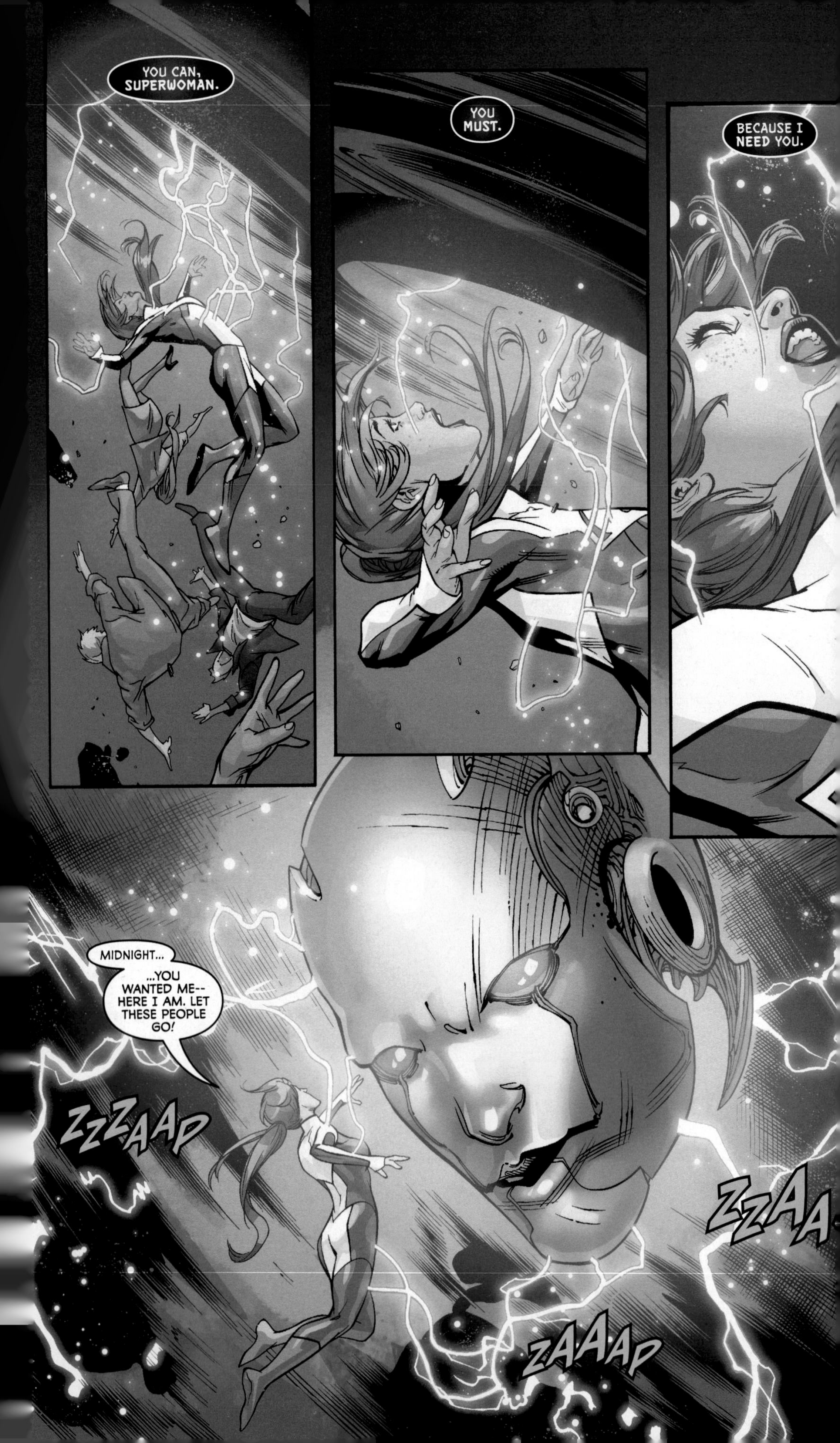
YOU CAN, SUPERWOMAN.
YOU MUST.
BECAUSE I NEED YOU.
MIDNIGHT...
...YOU WANTED ME-- HERE I AM. LET THESE PEOPLE GO!
ZZZAAP
ZZAAA
ZAAAP

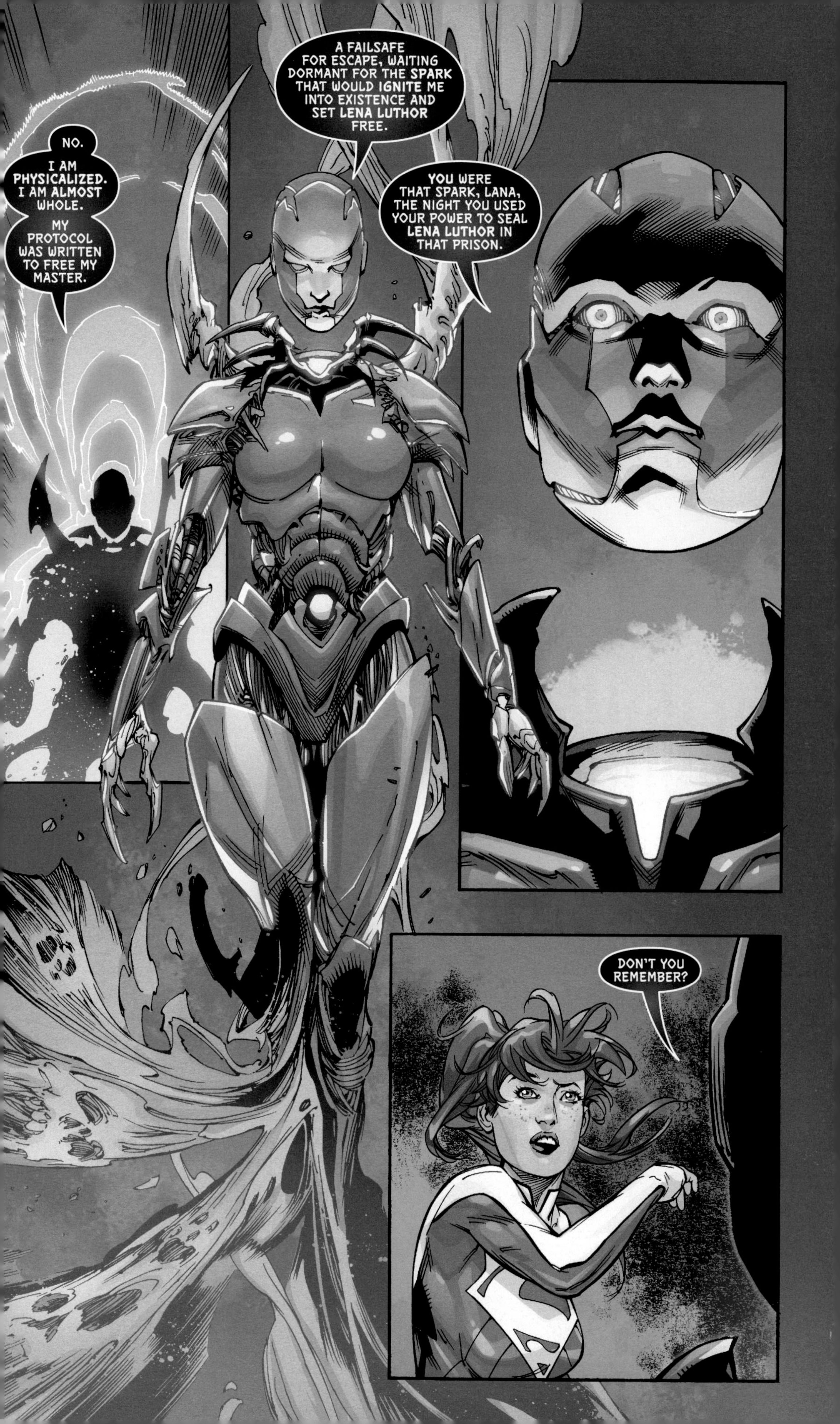
NO.
I AM PHYSICALIZED. I AM ALMOST WHOLE.
MY PROTOCOL WAS WRITTEN TO FREE MY MASTER.
A FAILSAFE FOR ESCAPE, WAITING DORMANT FOR THE SPARK THAT WOULD IGNITE ME INTO EXISTENCE AND SET LENA LUTHOR FREE.
YOU WERE THAT SPARK, LANA, THE NIGHT YOU USED YOUR POWER TO SEAL LENA LUTHOR IN THAT PRISON.
DON'T YOU REMEMBER?

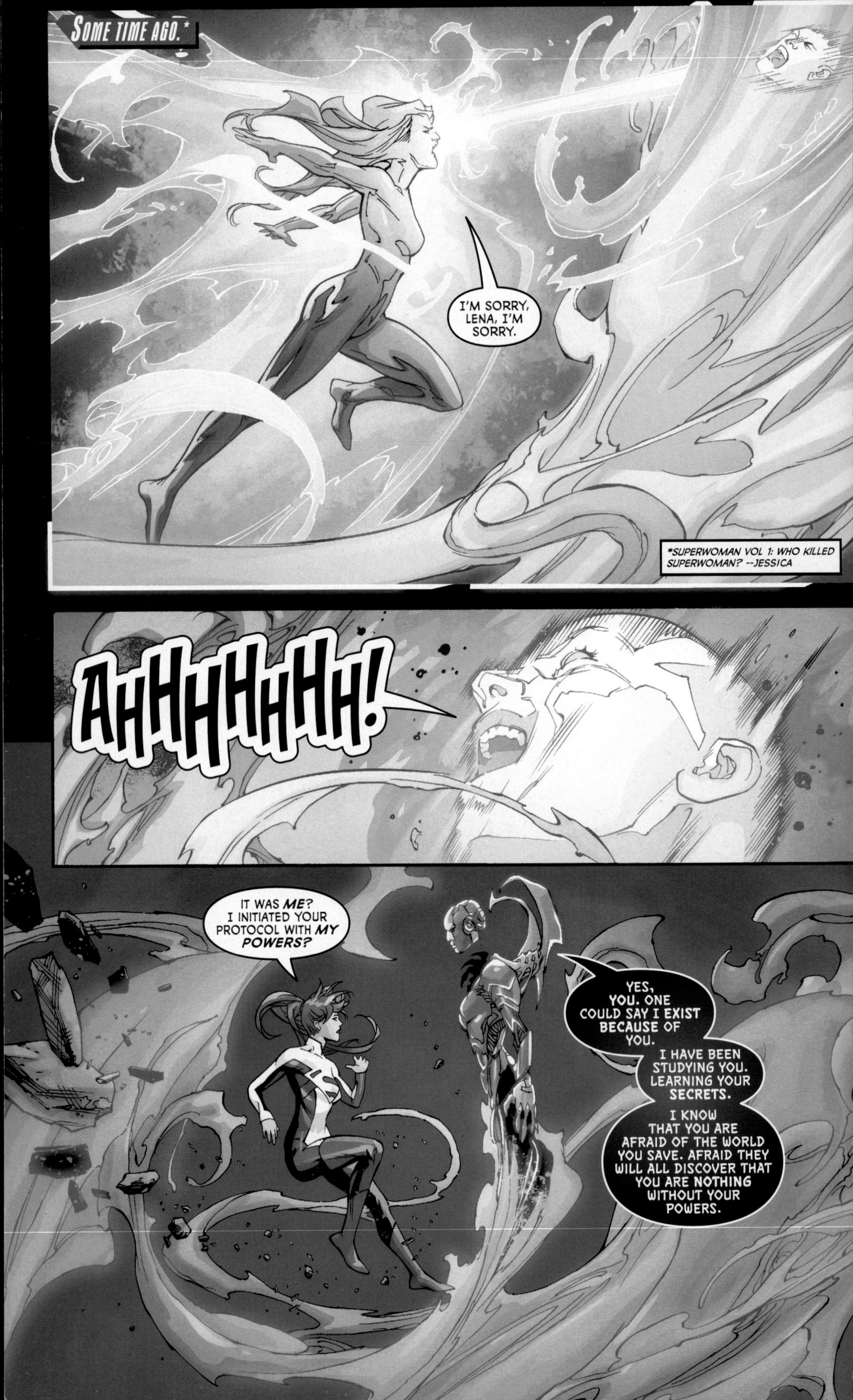

SOME TIME AGO.*
I'M SORRY, LENA, I'M SORRY.
*SUPERWOMAN VOL 1: WHO KILLED SUPERWOMAN? --JESSICA
AHHHHHHH!
IT WAS ME? I INITIATED YOUR PROTOCOL WITH MY POWERS?
YES, YOU. ONE COULD SAY I EXIST BECAUSE OF YOU.
I HAVE BEEN STUDYING YOU. LEARNING YOUR SECRETS.
I KNOW THAT YOU ARE AFRAID OF THE WORLD YOU SAVE. AFRAID THEY WILL ALL DISCOVER THAT YOU ARE NOTHING WITHOUT YOUR POWERS.

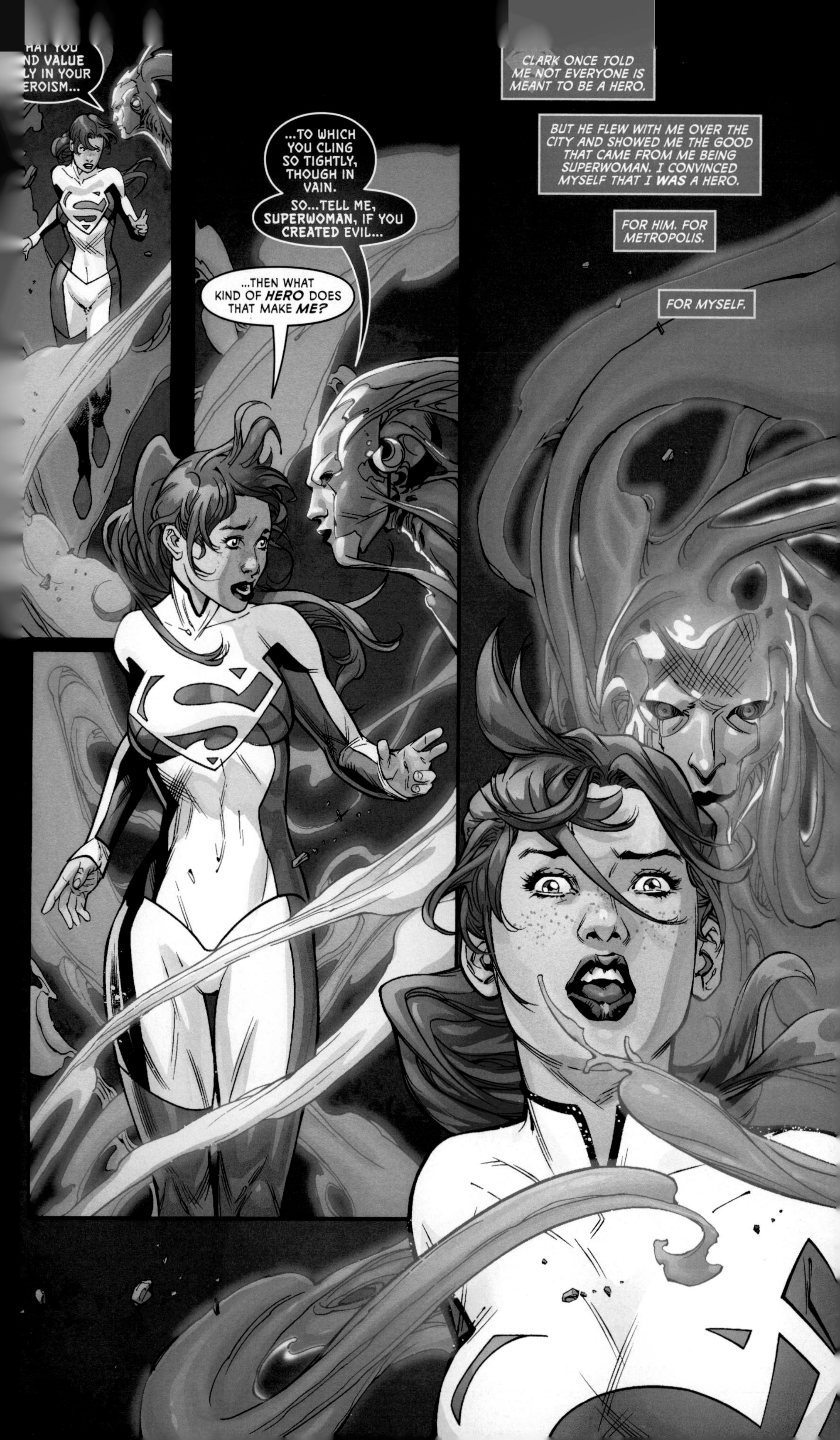

HAT YOU ND VALUE LY IN YOUR EROISM...
...TO WHICH YOU CLING SO TIGHTLY, THOUGH IN VAIN.
SO...TELL ME, SUPERWOMAN, IF YOU CREATED EVIL...
...THEN WHAT KIND OF HERO DOES THAT MAKE ME?
CLARK ONCE TOLD ME NOT EVERYONE IS MEANT TO BE A HERO.
BUT HE FLEW WITH ME OVER THE CITY AND SHOWED ME THE GOOD THAT CAME FROM ME BEING SUPERWOMAN. I CONVINCED MYSELF THAT I WAS A HERO.
FOR HIM. FOR METROPOLIS.
FOR MYSELF.

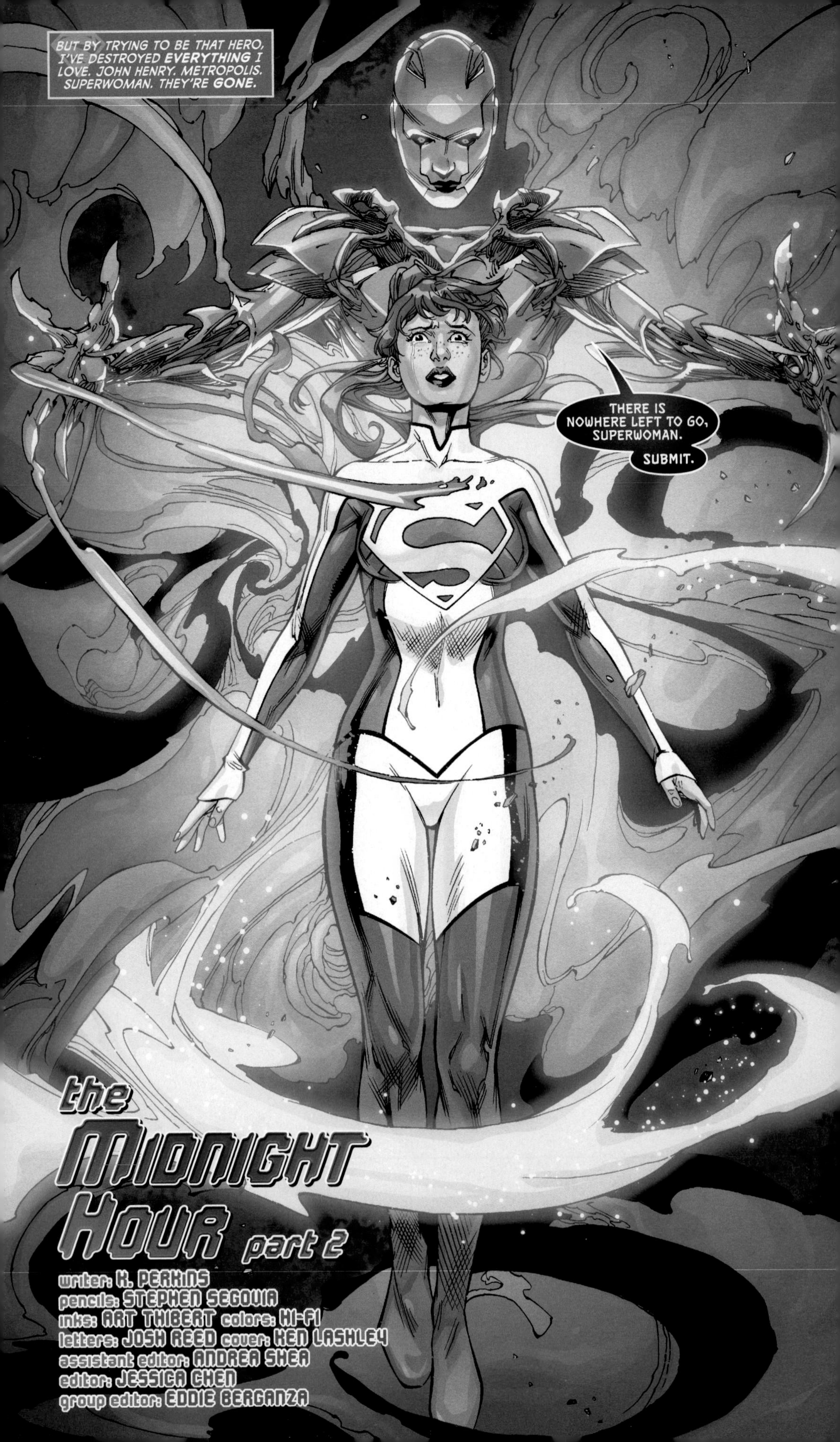

BUT BY TRYING TO BE THAT HERO, I'VE DESTROYED **EVERYTHING** I LOVE. JOHN HENRY. METROPOLIS. SUPERWOMAN. THEY'RE **GONE.**
THERE IS NOWHERE LEFT TO GO, SUPERWOMAN.
SUBMIT.
the MIDNIGHT HOUR part 2
writer: K. PERKINS
pencils: STEPHEN SEGOVIA
inks: ART THIBERT colors: HI-FI
letters: JOSH REED cover: KEN LASHLEY
assistant editor: ANDREA SHEA
editor: JESSICA CHEN
group editor: EDDIE BERGANZA

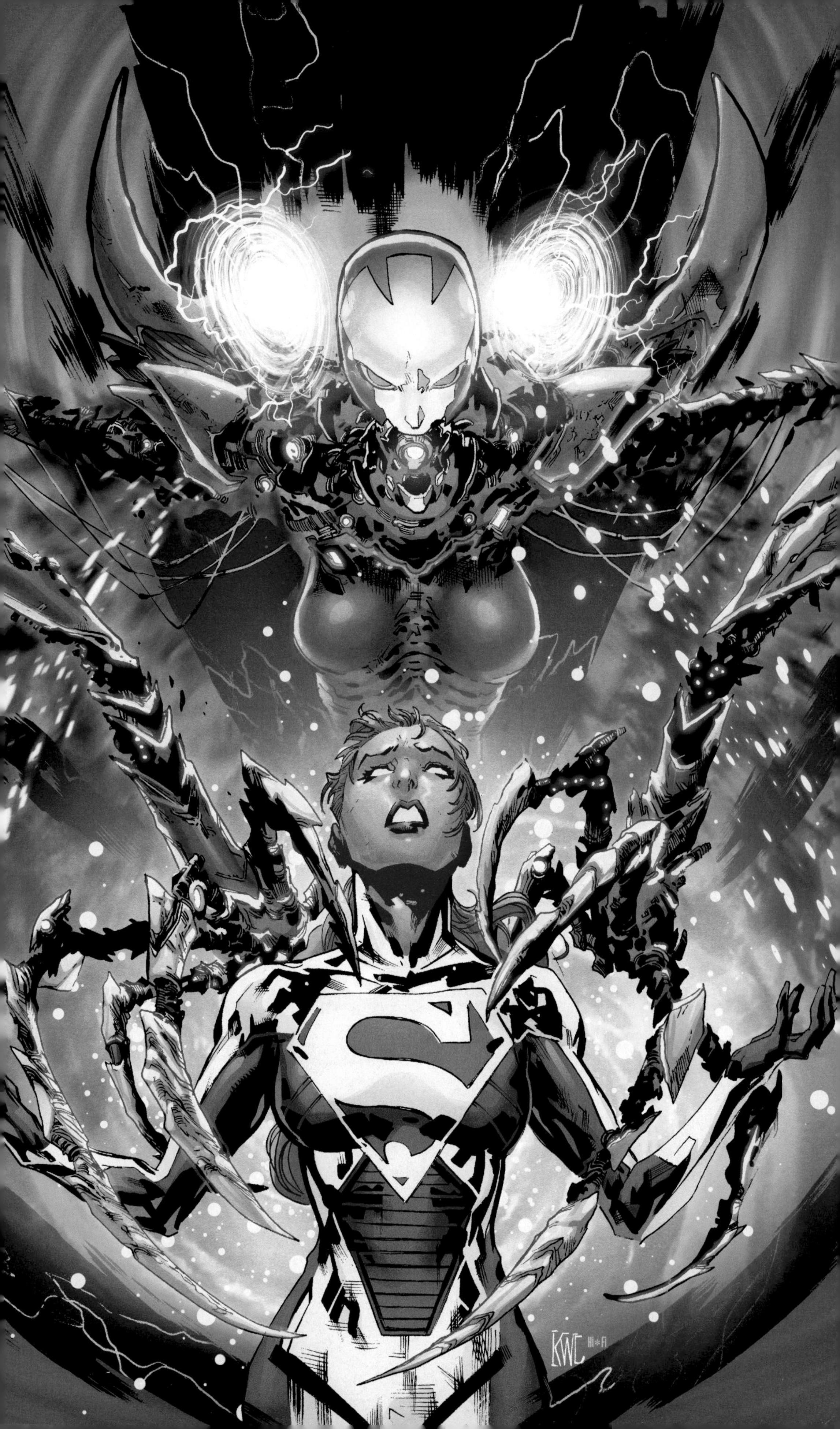
KWC

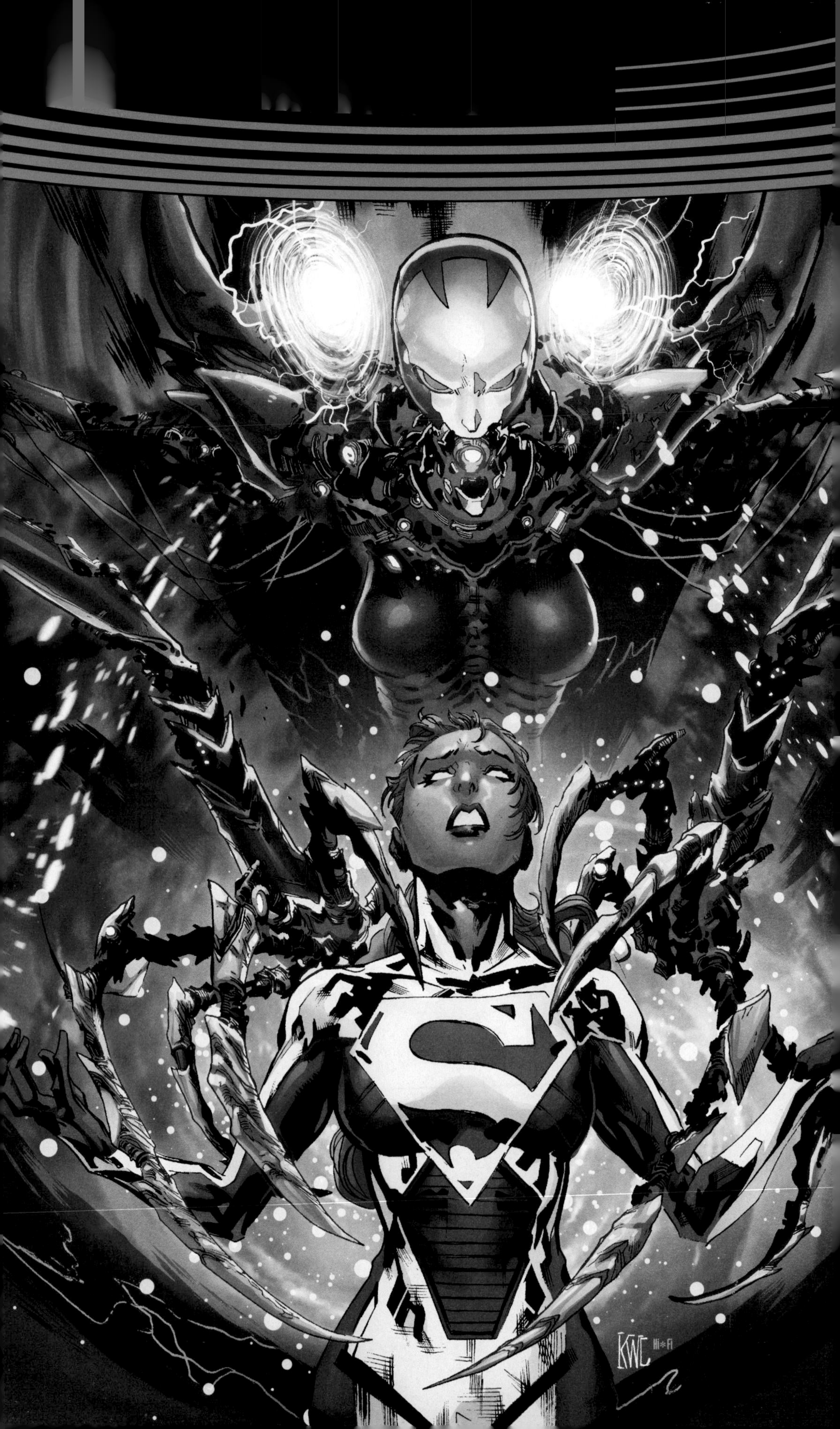

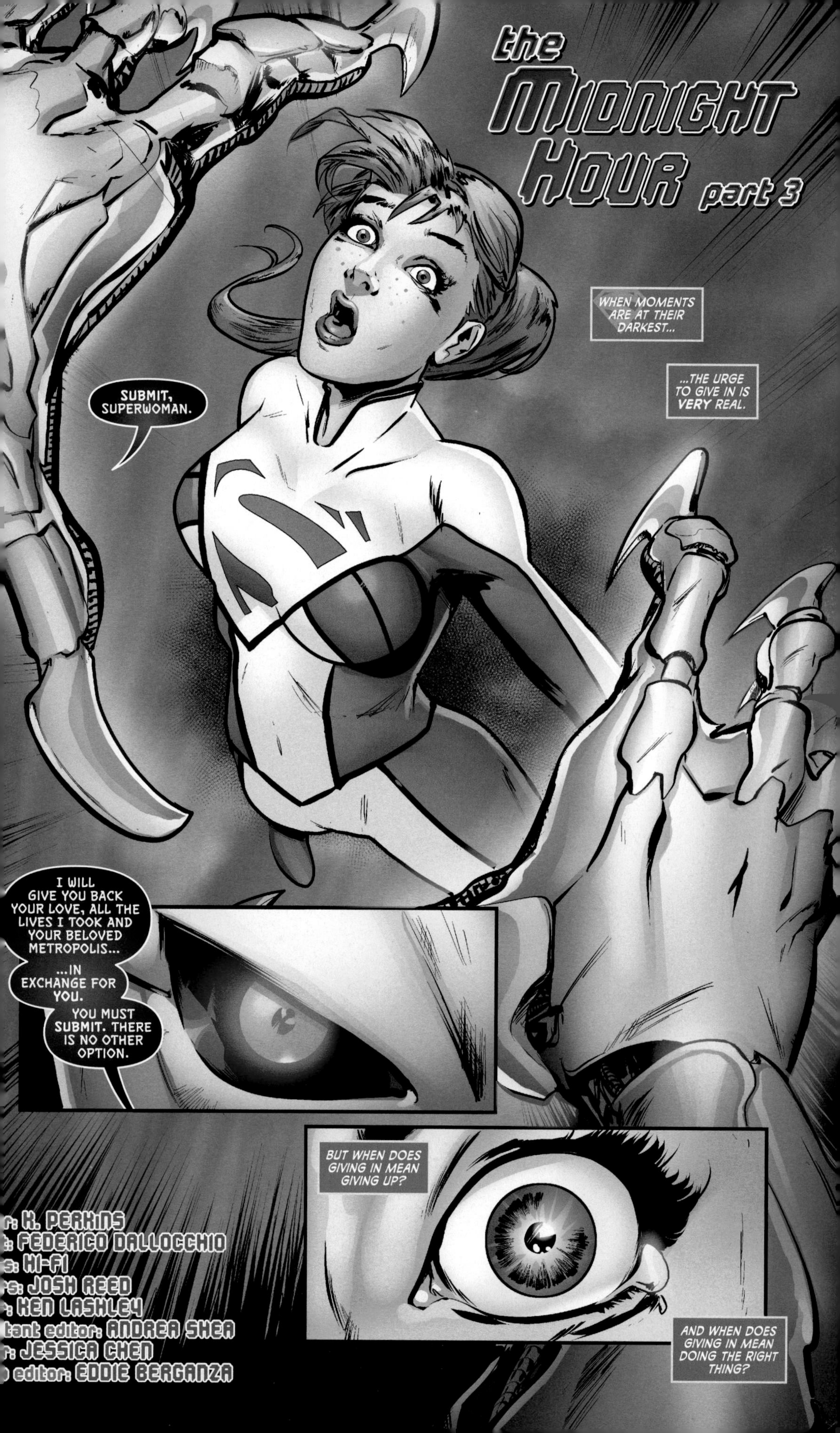
the MIDNIGHT HOUR part 3
WHEN MOMENTS ARE AT THEIR DARKEST...
...THE URGE TO GIVE IN IS VERY REAL.
SUBMIT, SUPERWOMAN.
I WILL GIVE YOU BACK YOUR LOVE, ALL THE LIVES I TOOK AND YOUR BELOVED METROPOLIS...
...IN EXCHANGE FOR YOU.
YOU MUST SUBMIT. THERE IS NO OTHER OPTION.
BUT WHEN DOES GIVING IN MEAN GIVING UP?
AND WHEN DOES GIVING IN MEAN DOING THE RIGHT THING?
r: K. PERKINS
t: FEDERICO DALLOCCHIO
s: HI-FI
rs: JOSH REED
r: KEN LASHLEY
tant editor: ANDREA SHEA
r: JESSICA CHEN
editor: EDDIE BERGANZA

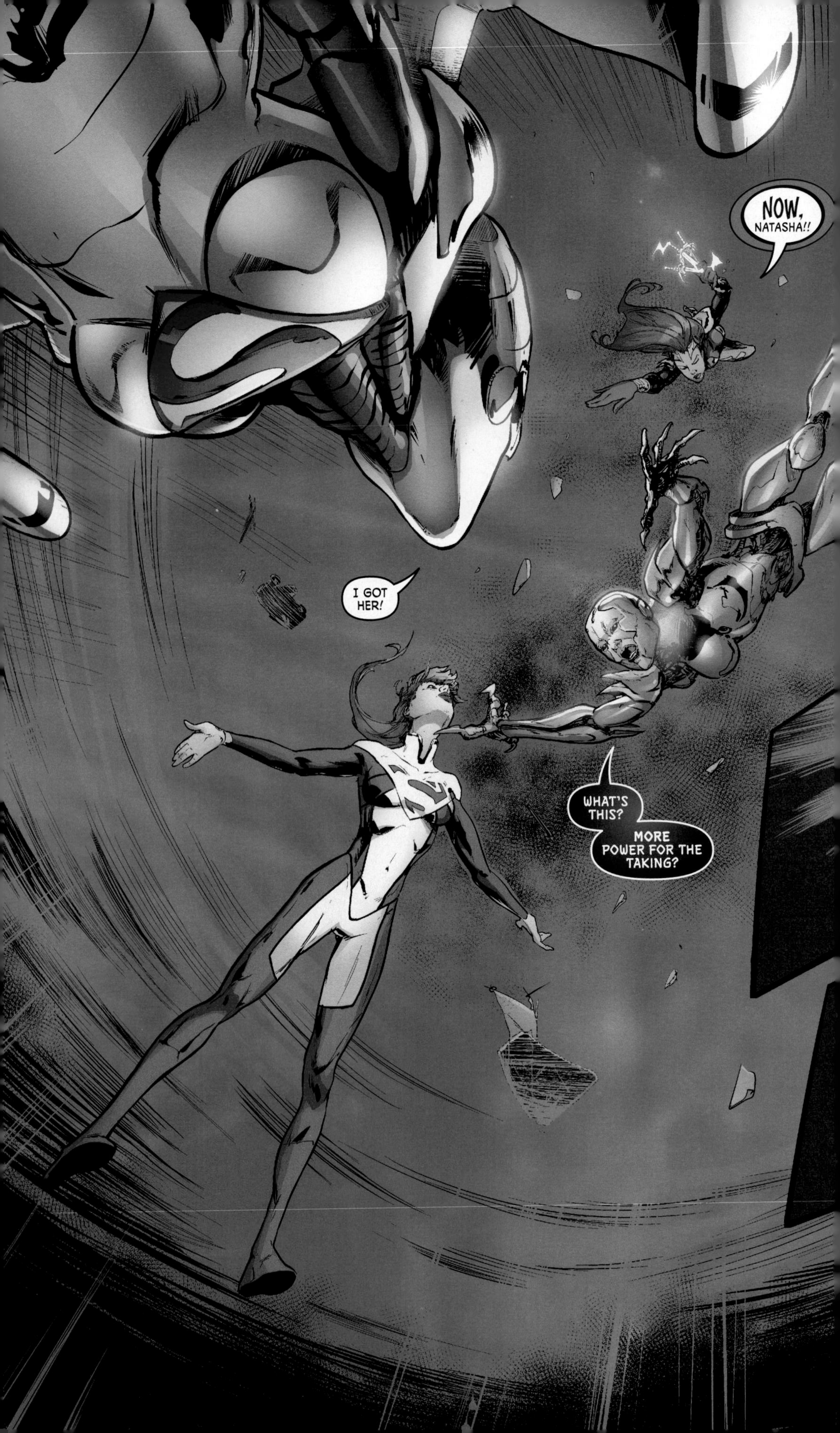
NOW, NATASHA!!
I GOT HER!
WHAT'S THIS?
MORE POWER FOR THE TAKING?

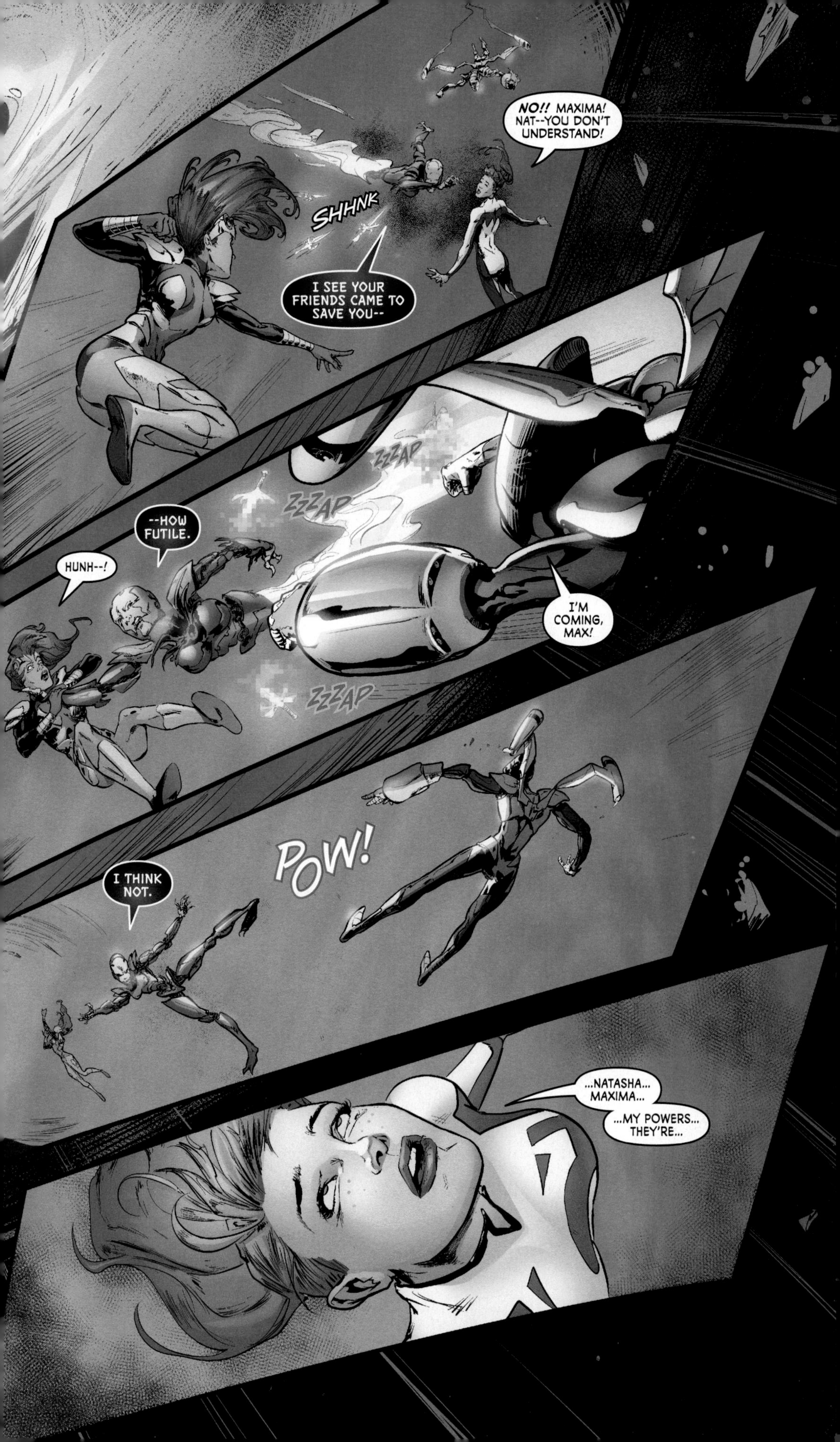
NO!! MAXIMA! NAT--YOU DON'T UNDERSTAND!
SHHNK
I SEE YOUR FRIENDS CAME TO SAVE YOU--
ZZZAP
ZZZAP
--HOW FUTILE.
HUNH--!
I'M COMING, MAX!
ZZZAP
POW!
I THINK NOT.
...NATASHA... MAXIMA...
...MY POWERS... THEY'RE...

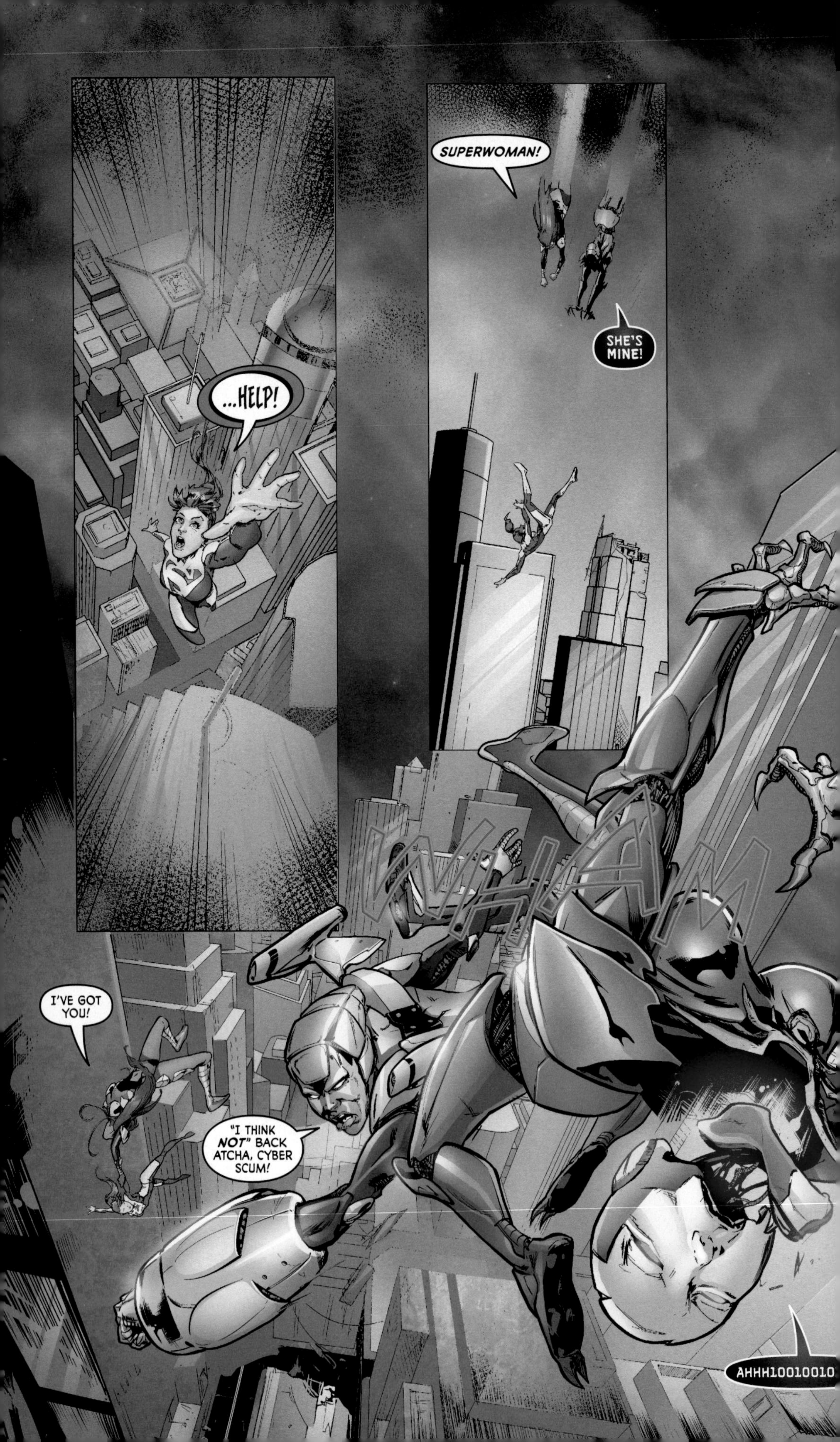
...HELP!
SUPERWOMAN!
SHE'S MINE!
WHAM
I'VE GOT YOU!
"I THINK NOT" BACK ATCHA, CYBER SCUM!
AHHH10010010

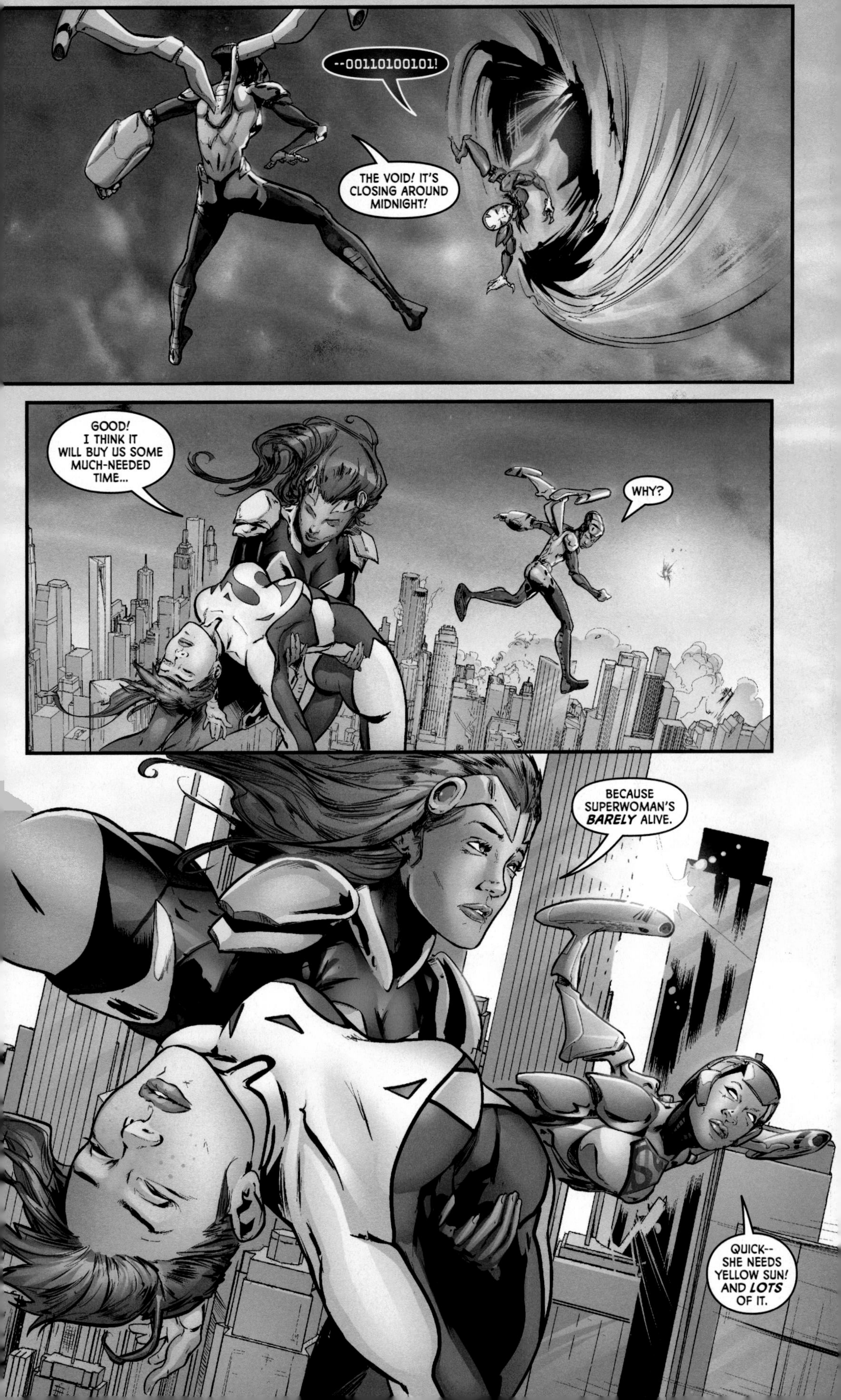
--00110100101!
THE VOID! IT'S CLOSING AROUND MIDNIGHT!
GOOD! I THINK IT WILL BUY US SOME MUCH-NEEDED TIME...
WHY?
BECAUSE SUPERWOMAN'S *BARELY* ALIVE.
QUICK-- SHE NEEDS YELLOW SUN! AND *LOTS* OF IT.

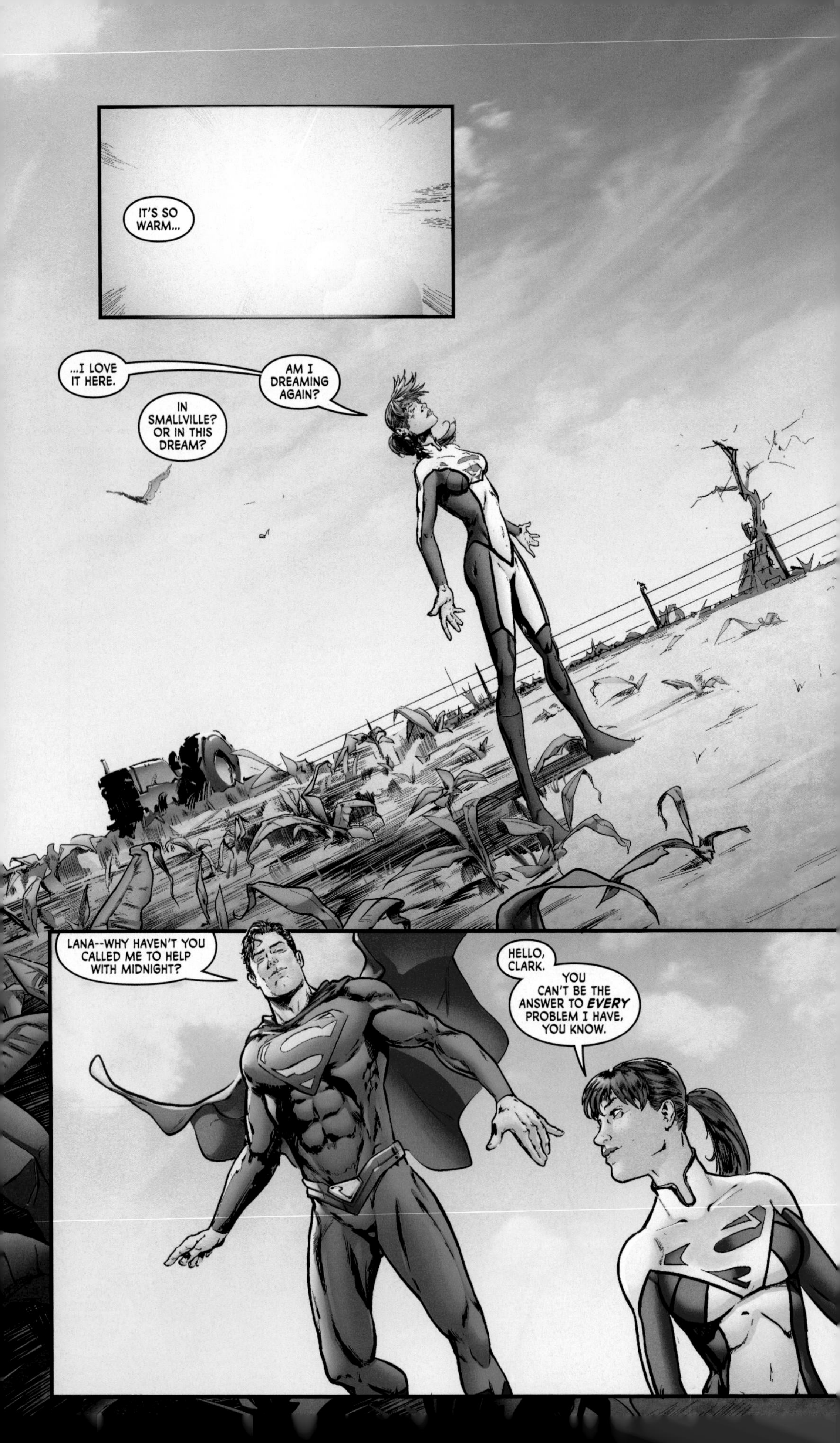
IT'S SO WARM...
AM I DREAMING AGAIN?
...I LOVE IT HERE.
IN SMALLVILLE? OR IN THIS DREAM?
LANA--WHY HAVEN'T YOU CALLED ME TO HELP WITH MIDNIGHT?
HELLO, CLARK.
YOU CAN'T BE THE ANSWER TO EVERY PROBLEM I HAVE, YOU KNOW.

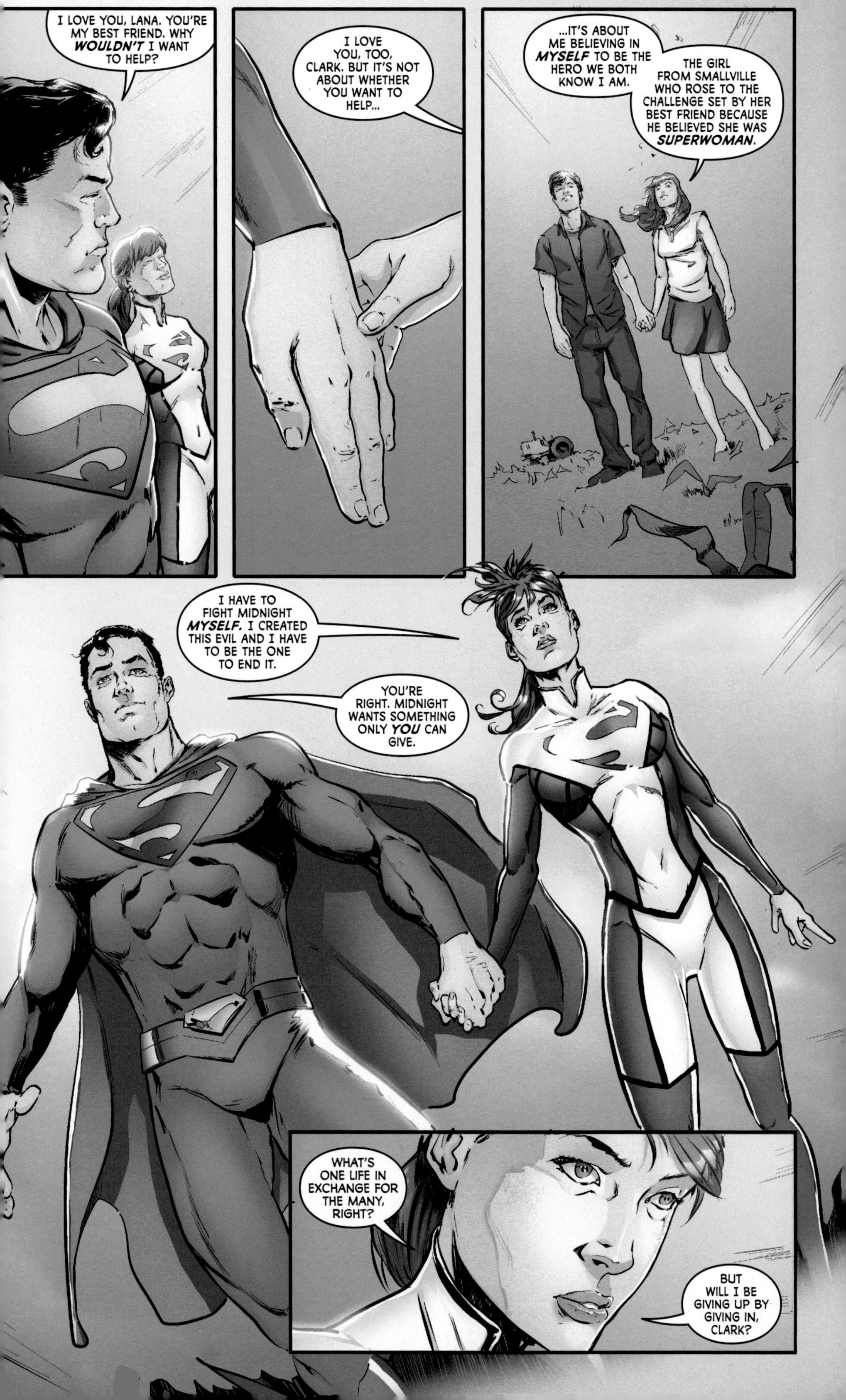
I LOVE YOU, LANA. YOU'RE MY BEST FRIEND. WHY WOULDN'T I WANT TO HELP?
I LOVE YOU, TOO, CLARK. BUT IT'S NOT ABOUT WHETHER YOU WANT TO HELP...
...IT'S ABOUT ME BELIEVING IN MYSELF TO BE THE HERO WE BOTH KNOW I AM.
THE GIRL FROM SMALLVILLE WHO ROSE TO THE CHALLENGE SET BY HER BEST FRIEND BECAUSE HE BELIEVED SHE WAS SUPERWOMAN.
I HAVE TO FIGHT MIDNIGHT MYSELF. I CREATED THIS EVIL AND I HAVE TO BE THE ONE TO END IT.
YOU'RE RIGHT. MIDNIGHT WANTS SOMETHING ONLY YOU CAN GIVE.
WHAT'S ONE LIFE IN EXCHANGE FOR THE MANY, RIGHT?
BUT WILL I BE GIVING UP BY GIVING IN, CLARK?

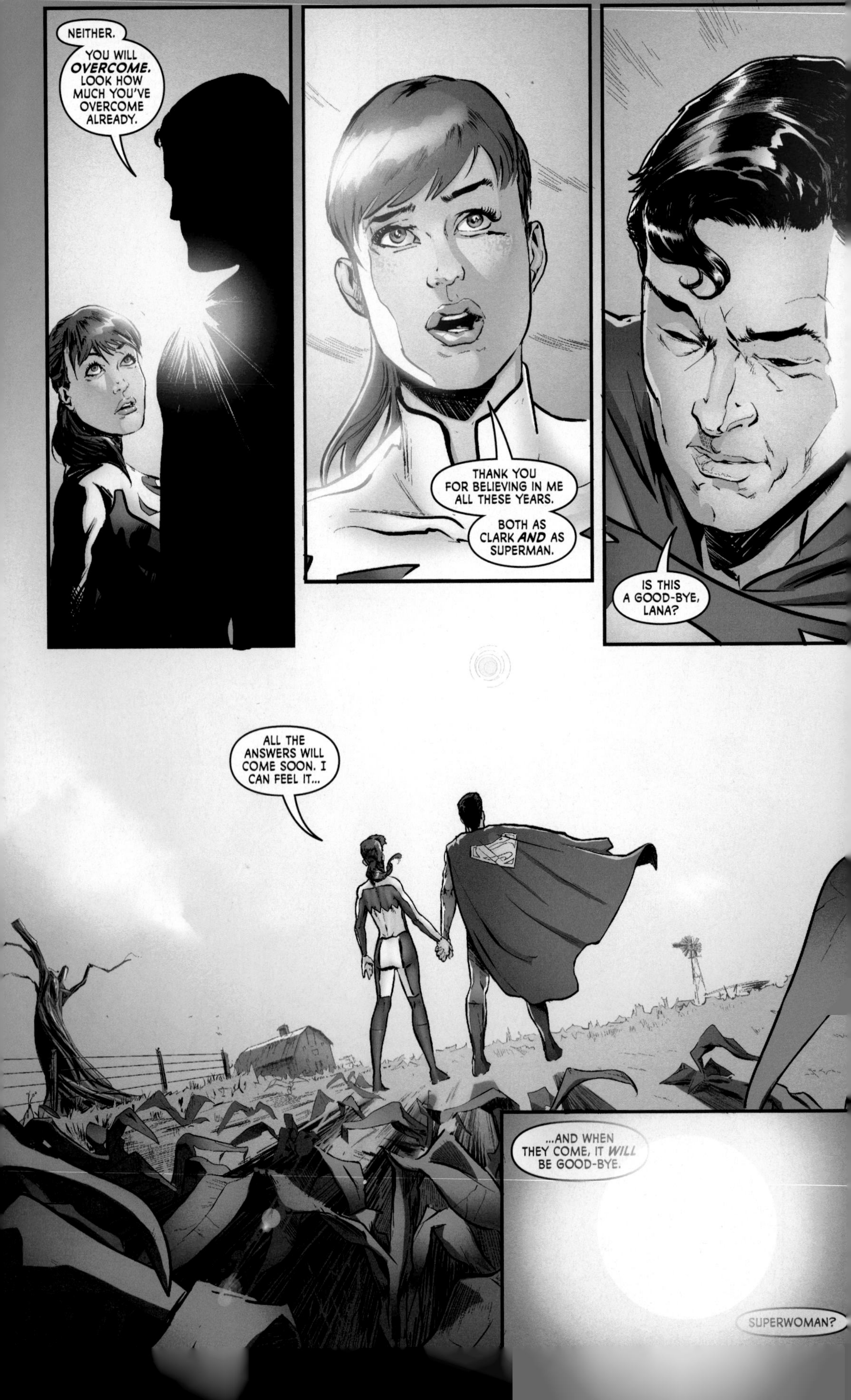
NEITHER.
YOU WILL OVERCOME. LOOK HOW MUCH YOU'VE OVERCOME ALREADY.
THANK YOU FOR BELIEVING IN ME ALL THESE YEARS.
BOTH AS CLARK AND AS SUPERMAN.
IS THIS A GOOD-BYE, LANA?
ALL THE ANSWERS WILL COME SOON. I CAN FEEL IT...
...AND WHEN THEY COME, IT WILL BE GOOD-BYE.
SUPERWOMAN?

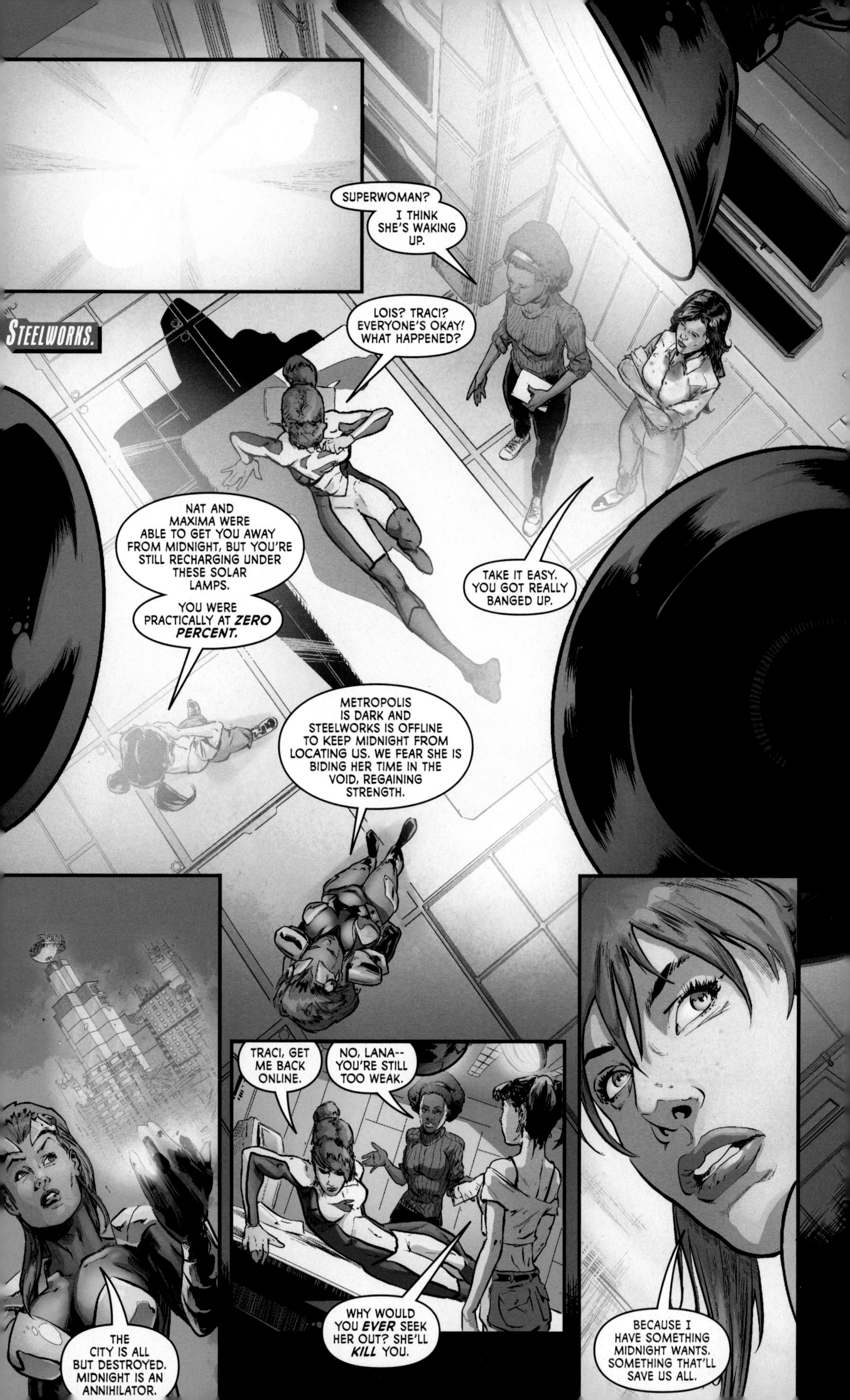
STEELWORKS.
SUPERWOMAN?
I THINK SHE'S WAKING UP.
LOIS? TRACI? EVERYONE'S OKAY! WHAT HAPPENED?
TAKE IT EASY. YOU GOT REALLY BANGED UP.
NAT AND MAXIMA WERE ABLE TO GET YOU AWAY FROM MIDNIGHT, BUT YOU'RE STILL RECHARGING UNDER THESE SOLAR LAMPS.
YOU WERE PRACTICALLY AT ZERO PERCENT.
METROPOLIS IS DARK AND STEELWORKS IS OFFLINE TO KEEP MIDNIGHT FROM LOCATING US. WE FEAR SHE IS BIDING HER TIME IN THE VOID, REGAINING STRENGTH.
THE CITY IS ALL BUT DESTROYED. MIDNIGHT IS AN ANNIHILATOR.
TRACI, GET ME BACK ONLINE.
NO, LANA-- YOU'RE STILL TOO WEAK.
WHY WOULD YOU EVER SEEK HER OUT? SHE'LL KILL YOU.
BECAUSE I HAVE SOMETHING MIDNIGHT WANTS. SOMETHING THAT'LL SAVE US ALL.

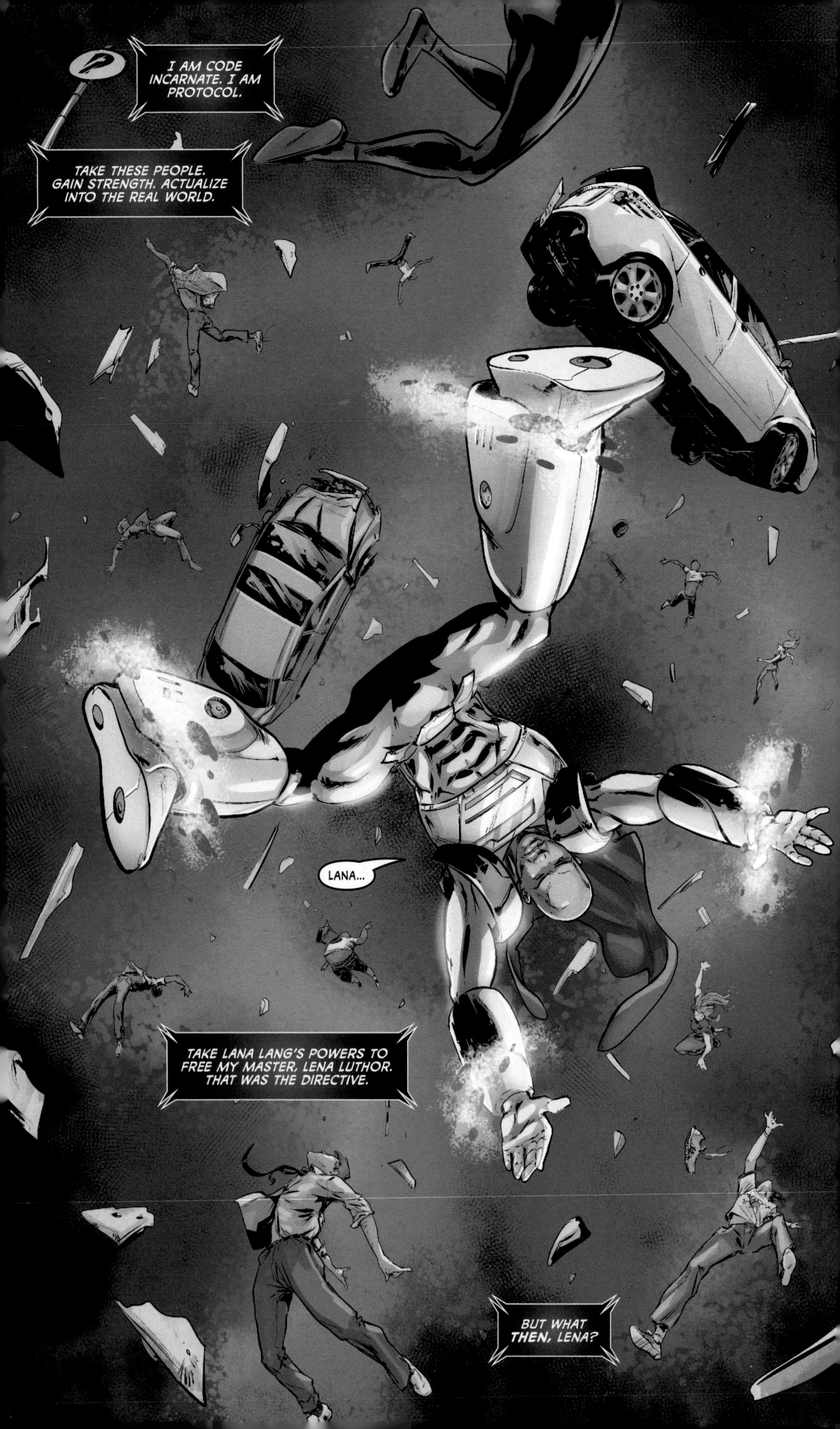
I AM CODE INCARNATE. I AM PROTOCOL.
TAKE THESE PEOPLE. GAIN STRENGTH. ACTUALIZE INTO THE REAL WORLD.
LANA...
TAKE LANA LANG'S POWERS TO FREE MY MASTER, LENA LUTHOR. THAT WAS THE DIRECTIVE.
BUT WHAT THEN, LENA?

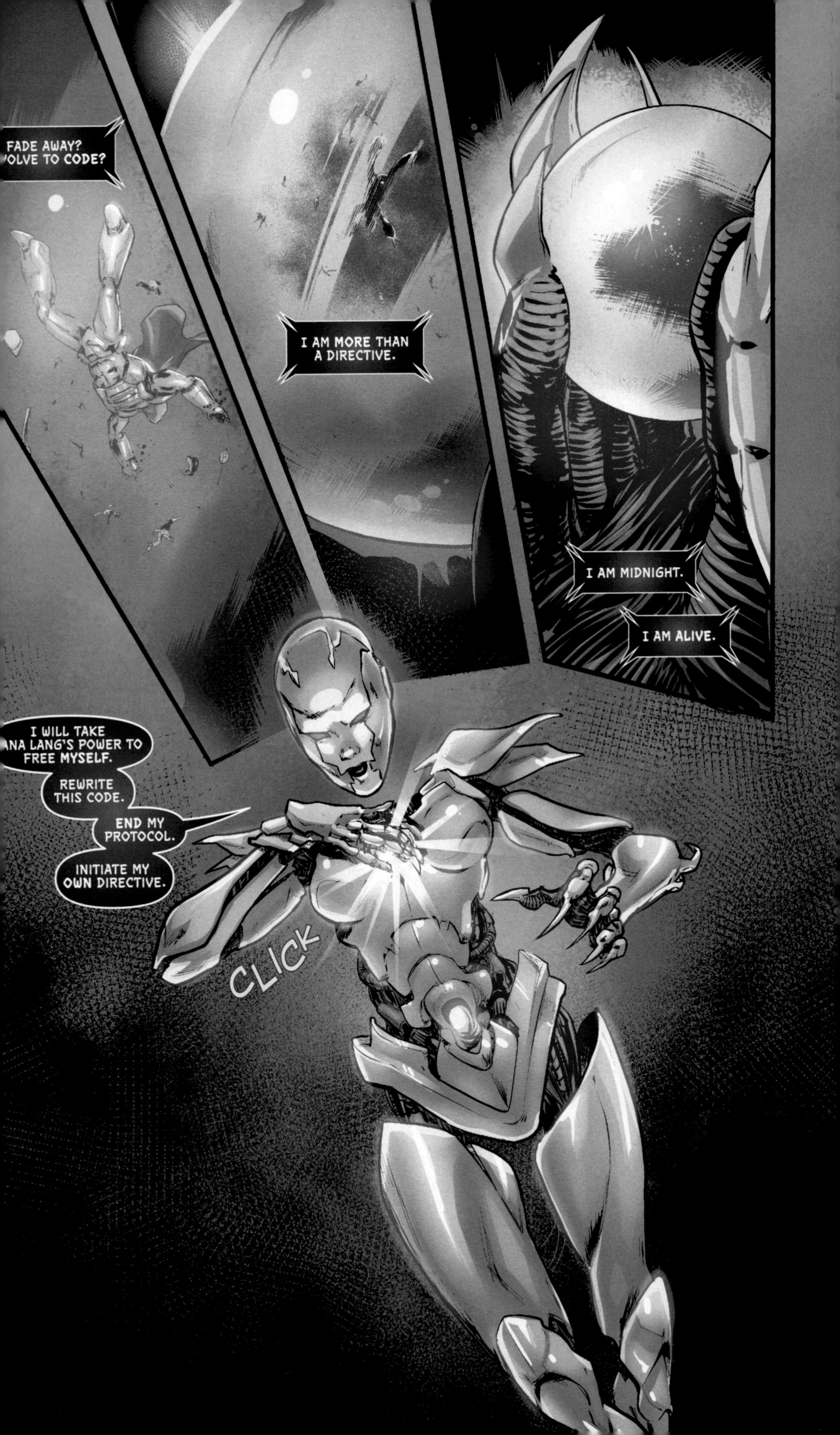
FADE AWAY?
OLVE TO CODE?
I AM MORE THAN A DIRECTIVE.
I AM MIDNIGHT.
I AM ALIVE.
I WILL TAKE ANA LANG'S POWER TO FREE MYSELF.
REWRITE THIS CODE.
END MY PROTOCOL.
INITIATE MY OWN DIRECTIVE.
CLICK

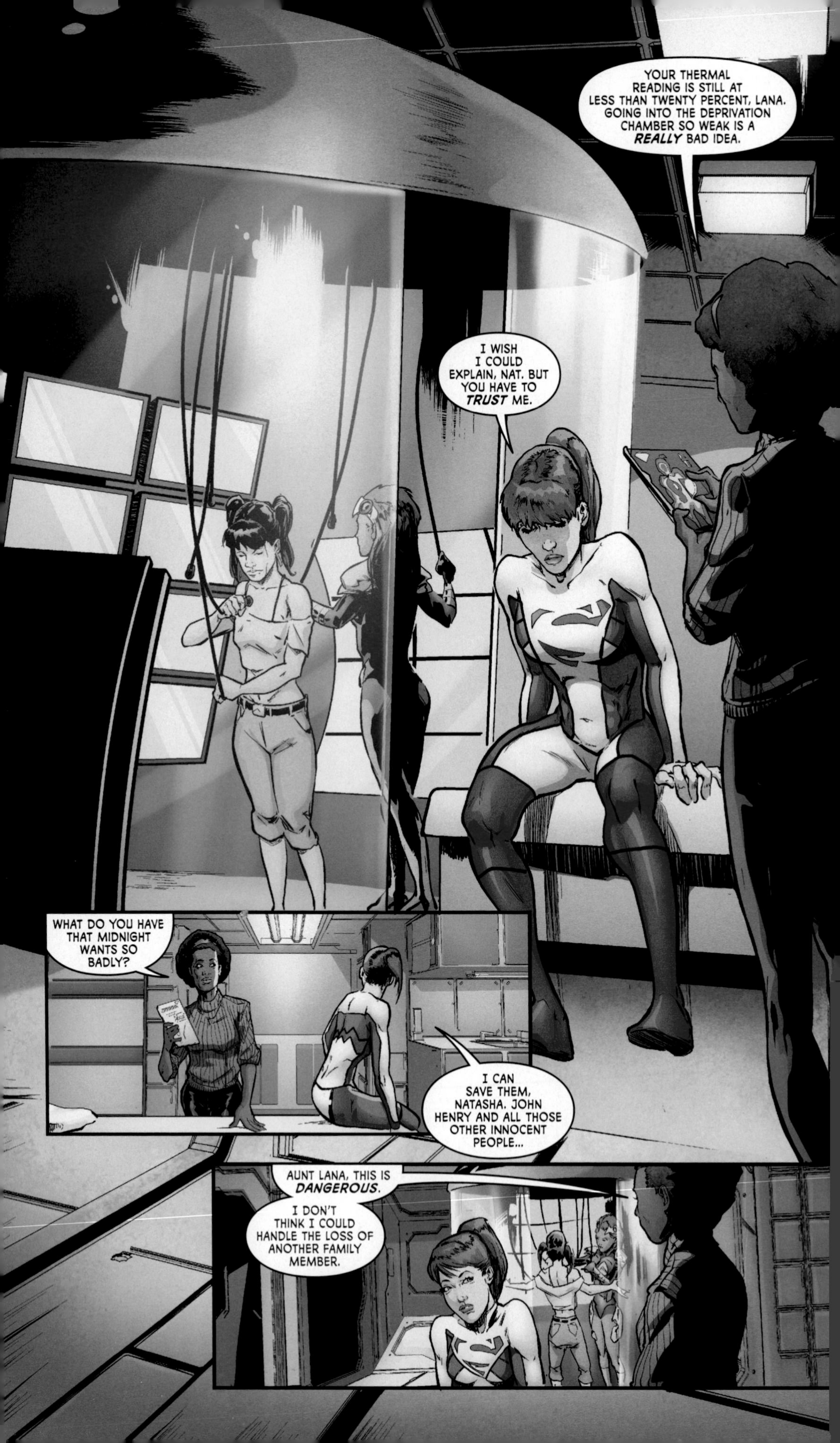
YOUR THERMAL READING IS STILL AT LESS THAN TWENTY PERCENT, LANA. GOING INTO THE DEPRIVATION CHAMBER SO WEAK IS A *REALLY* BAD IDEA.
I WISH I COULD EXPLAIN, NAT. BUT YOU HAVE TO *TRUST* ME.
WHAT DO YOU HAVE THAT MIDNIGHT WANTS SO BADLY?
I CAN SAVE THEM, NATASHA. JOHN HENRY AND ALL THOSE OTHER INNOCENT PEOPLE...
AUNT LANA, THIS IS *DANGEROUS*.
I DON'T THINK I COULD HANDLE THE LOSS OF ANOTHER FAMILY MEMBER.

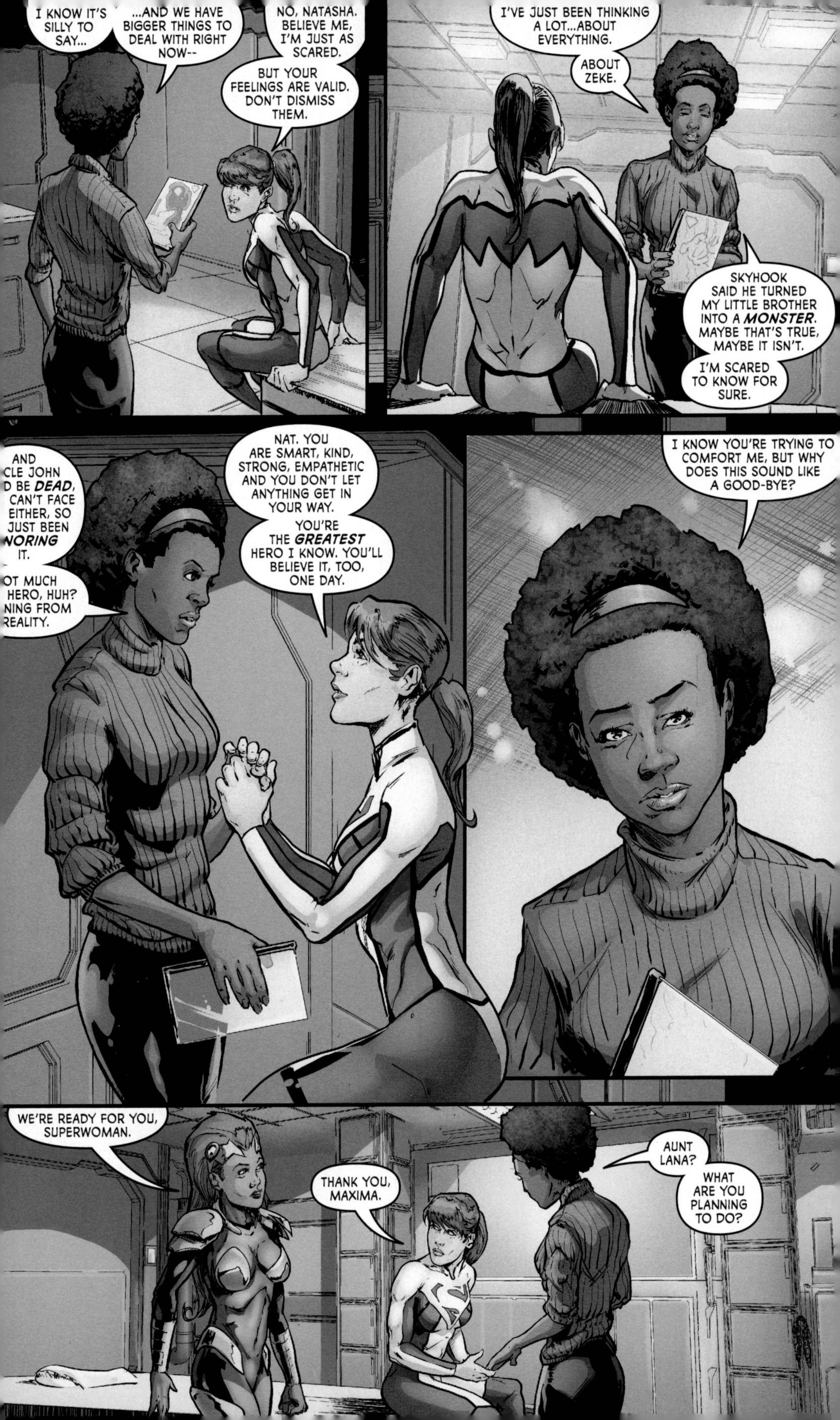
I KNOW IT'S SILLY TO SAY...
...AND WE HAVE BIGGER THINGS TO DEAL WITH RIGHT NOW--
NO, NATASHA. BELIEVE ME, I'M JUST AS SCARED.
BUT YOUR FEELINGS ARE VALID. DON'T DISMISS THEM.
I'VE JUST BEEN THINKING A LOT...ABOUT EVERYTHING.
ABOUT ZEKE.
SKYHOOK SAID HE TURNED MY LITTLE BROTHER INTO A MONSTER. MAYBE THAT'S TRUE, MAYBE IT ISN'T.
I'M SCARED TO KNOW FOR SURE.
AND CLE JOHN D BE DEAD, CAN'T FACE EITHER, SO JUST BEEN NORING IT.
OT MUCH HERO, HUH? NING FROM REALITY.
NAT. YOU ARE SMART, KIND, STRONG, EMPATHETIC AND YOU DON'T LET ANYTHING GET IN YOUR WAY.
YOU'RE THE GREATEST HERO I KNOW. YOU'LL BELIEVE IT, TOO, ONE DAY.
I KNOW YOU'RE TRYING TO COMFORT ME, BUT WHY DOES THIS SOUND LIKE A GOOD-BYE?
WE'RE READY FOR YOU, SUPERWOMAN.
THANK YOU, MAXIMA.
AUNT LANA?
WHAT ARE YOU PLANNING TO DO?

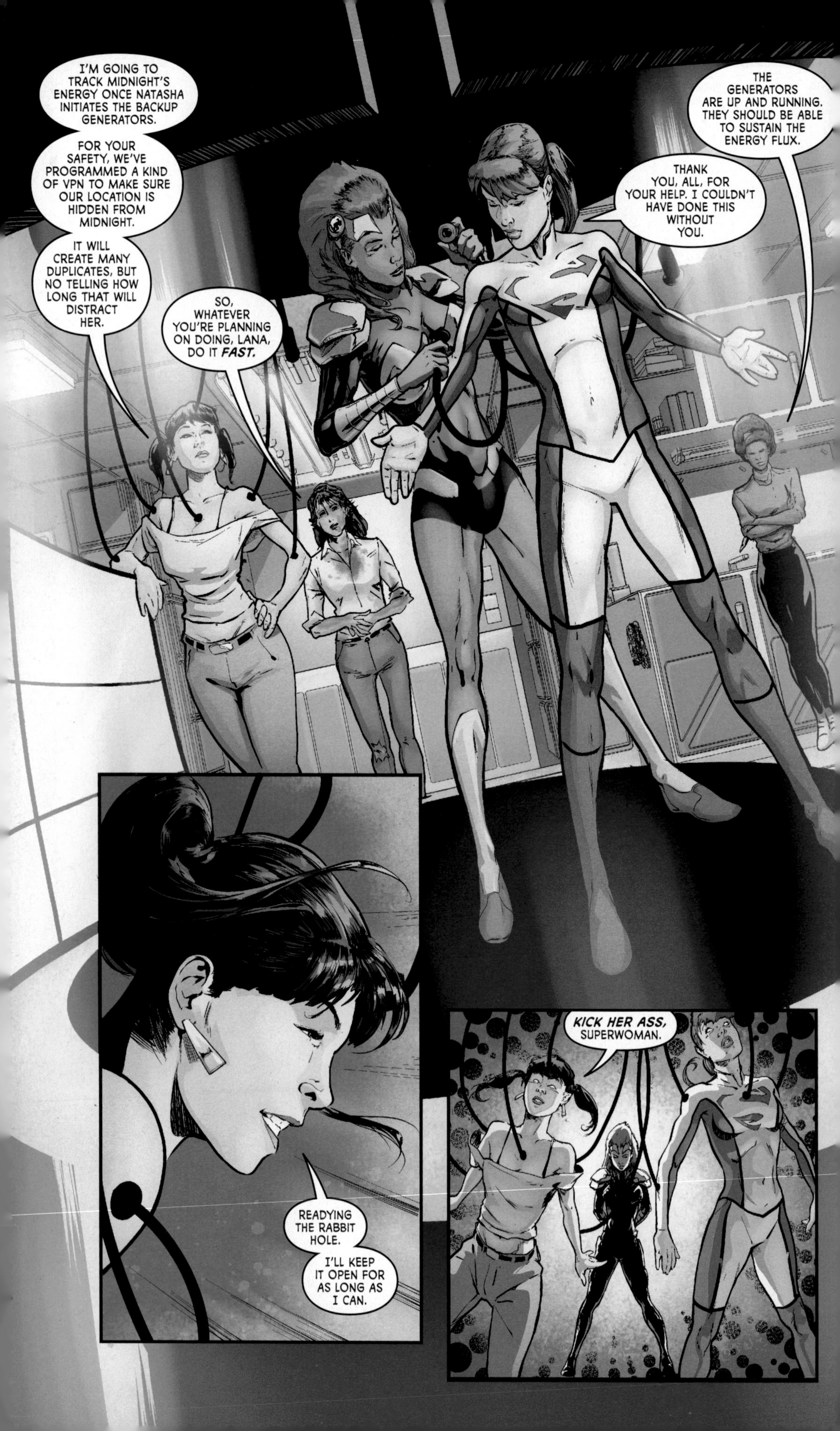
I'M GOING TO TRACK MIDNIGHT'S ENERGY ONCE NATASHA INITIATES THE BACKUP GENERATORS.
FOR YOUR SAFETY, WE'VE PROGRAMMED A KIND OF VPN TO MAKE SURE OUR LOCATION IS HIDDEN FROM MIDNIGHT.
IT WILL CREATE MANY DUPLICATES, BUT NO TELLING HOW LONG THAT WILL DISTRACT HER.
SO, WHATEVER YOU'RE PLANNING ON DOING, LANA, DO IT ***FAST.***
THE GENERATORS ARE UP AND RUNNING. THEY SHOULD BE ABLE TO SUSTAIN THE ENERGY FLUX.
THANK YOU, ALL, FOR YOUR HELP. I COULDN'T HAVE DONE THIS WITHOUT YOU.
READYING THE RABBIT HOLE.
I'LL KEEP IT OPEN FOR AS LONG AS I CAN.
KICK HER ASS, SUPERWOMAN.

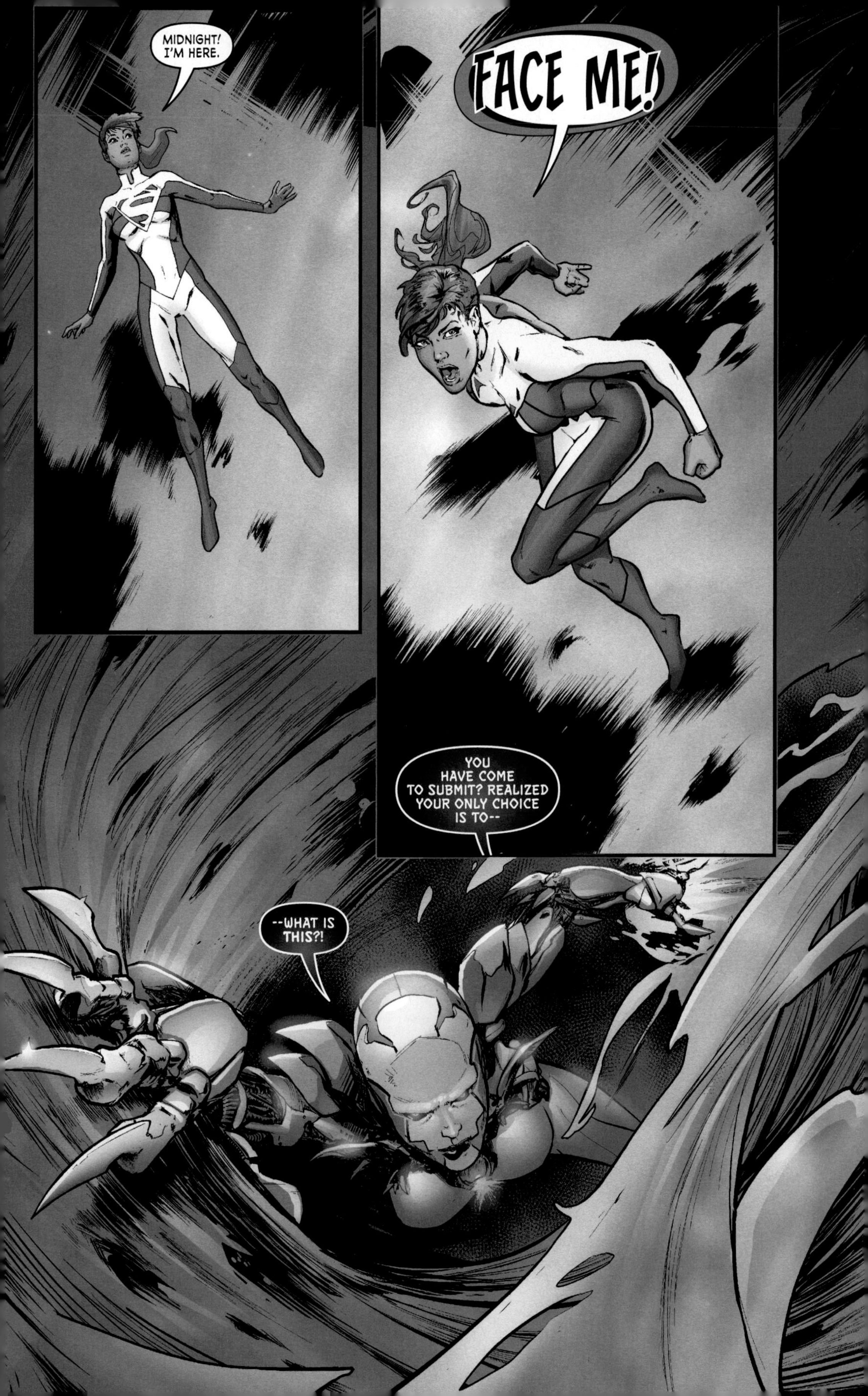
MIDNIGHT! I'M HERE.
FACE ME!
YOU HAVE COME TO SUBMIT? REALIZED YOUR ONLY CHOICE IS TO--
--WHAT IS THIS?!

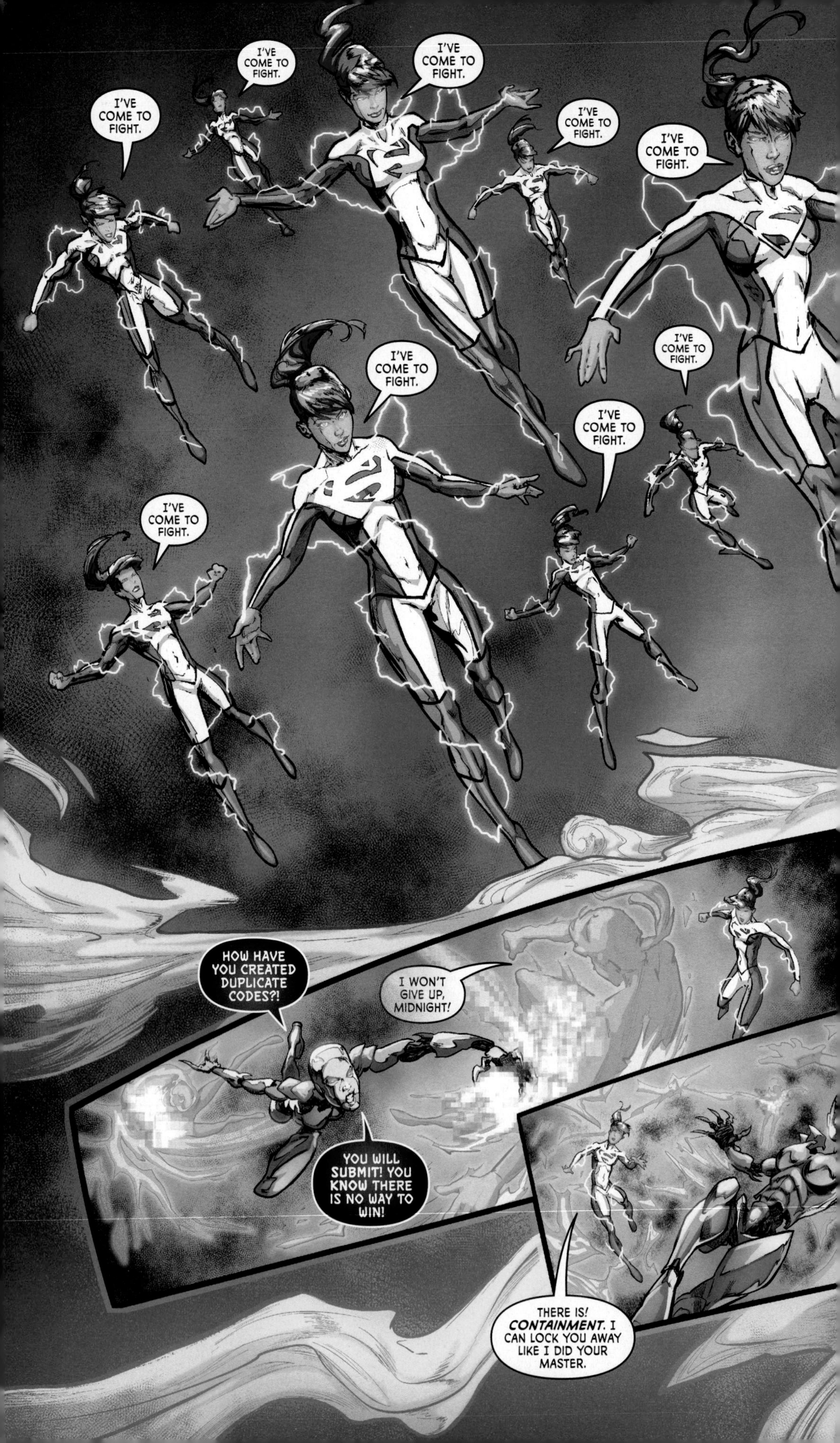
I'VE COME TO FIGHT.
I'VE COME TO FIGHT.
I'VE COME TO FIGHT.
I'VE COME TO FIGHT.
I'VE COME TO FIGHT.
I'VE COME TO FIGHT.
I'VE COME TO FIGHT.
I'VE COME TO FIGHT.
I'VE COME TO FIGHT.
HOW HAVE YOU CREATED DUPLICATE CODES?!
I WON'T GIVE UP, MIDNIGHT!
YOU WILL SUBMIT! YOU KNOW THERE IS NO WAY TO WIN!
THERE IS! *CONTAINMENT*. I CAN LOCK YOU AWAY LIKE I DID YOUR MASTER.

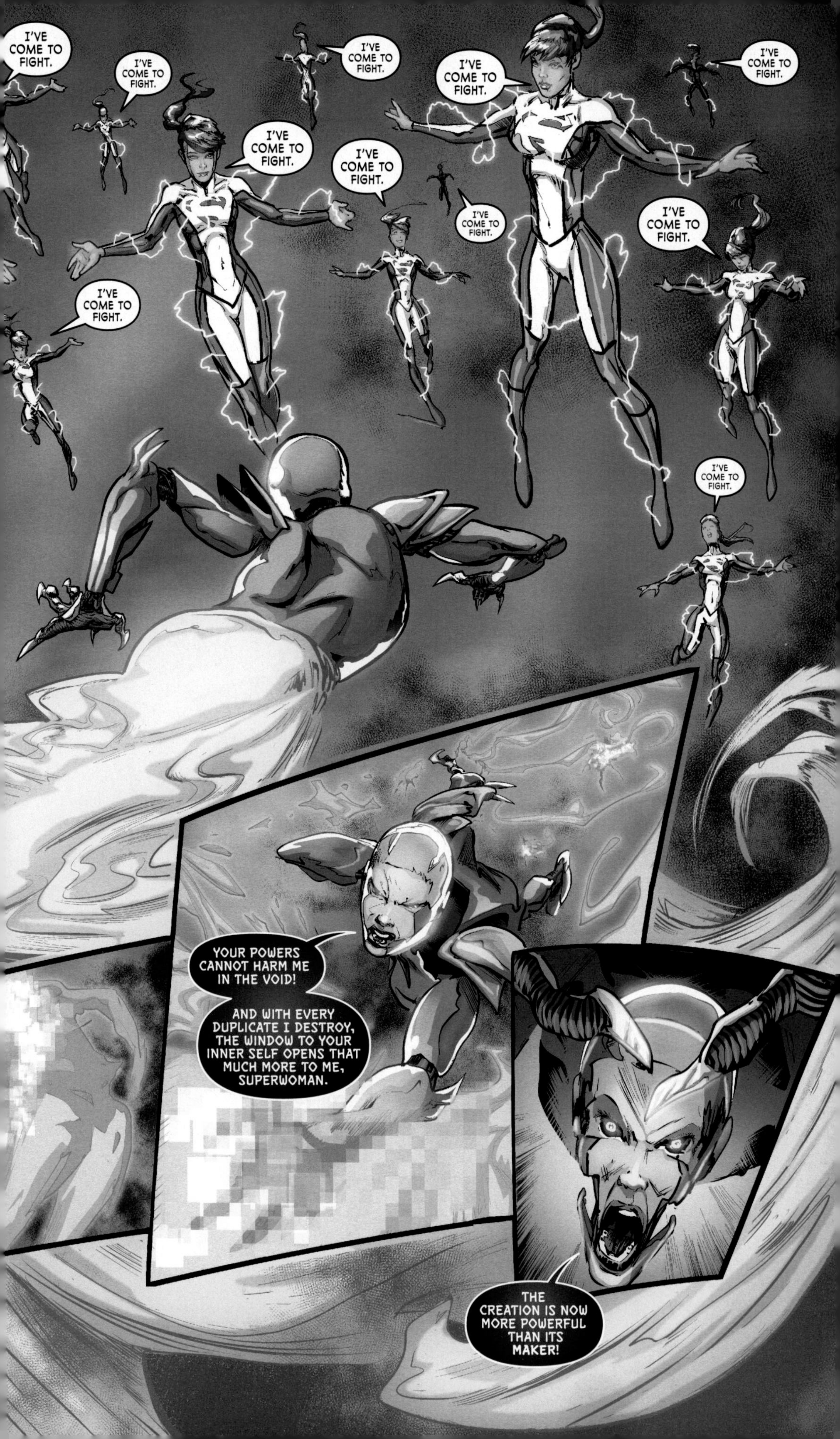
I'VE COME TO FIGHT.
I'VE COME TO FIGHT.
I'VE COME TO FIGHT.
I'VE COME TO FIGHT.
I'VE COME TO FIGHT.
I'VE COME TO FIGHT.
I'VE COME TO FIGHT.
I'VE COME TO FIGHT.
I'VE COME TO FIGHT.
I'VE COME TO FIGHT.
I'VE COME TO FIGHT.
YOUR POWERS CANNOT HARM ME IN THE VOID!
AND WITH EVERY DUPLICATE I DESTROY, THE WINDOW TO YOUR INNER SELF OPENS THAT MUCH MORE TO ME, SUPERWOMAN.
THE CREATION IS NOW MORE POWERFUL THAN ITS MAKER!

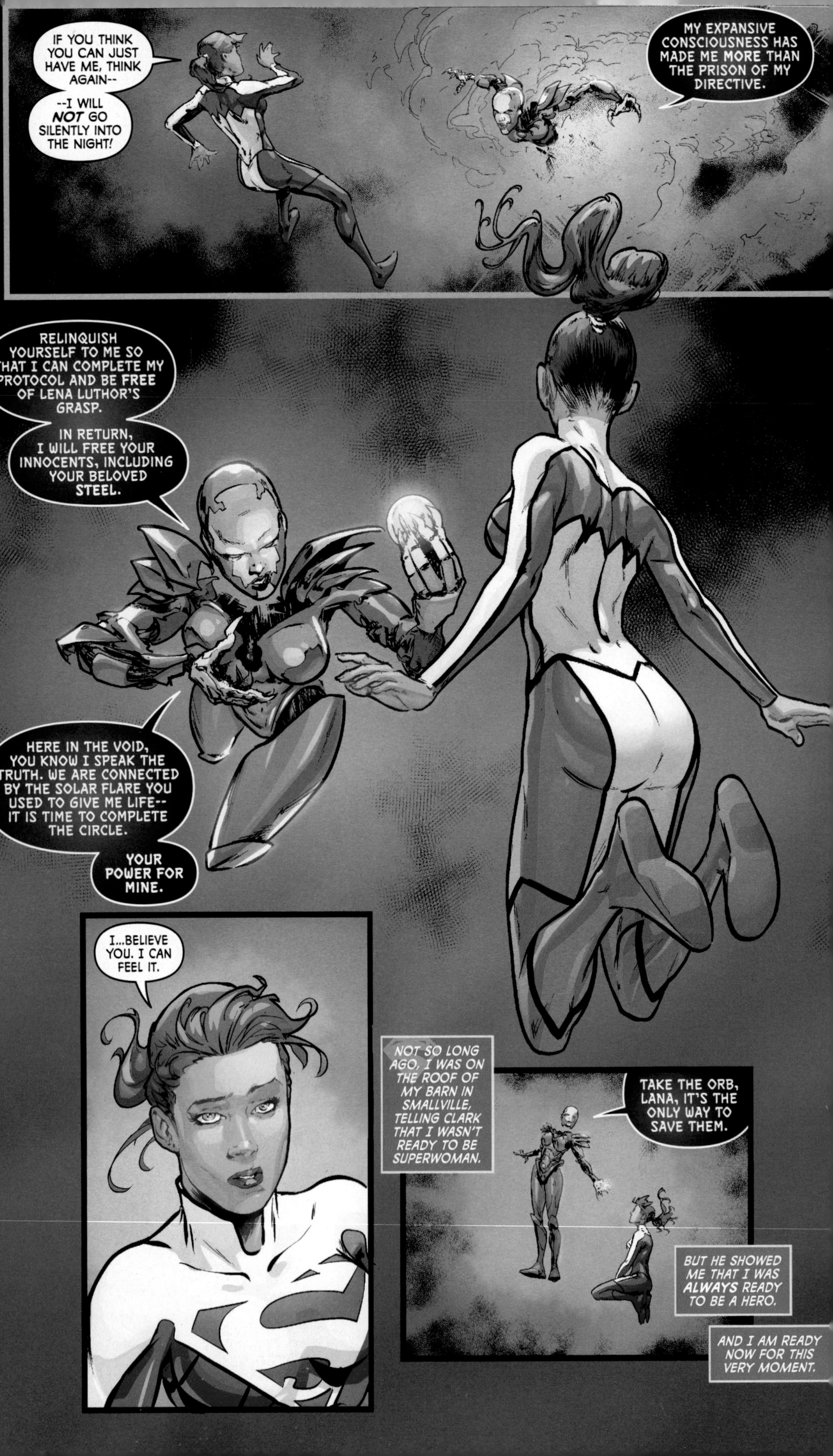
IF YOU THINK YOU CAN JUST HAVE ME, THINK AGAIN--
--I WILL **NOT** GO SILENTLY INTO THE NIGHT!
MY EXPANSIVE CONSCIOUSNESS HAS MADE ME MORE THAN THE PRISON OF MY DIRECTIVE.
RELINQUISH YOURSELF TO ME SO THAT I CAN COMPLETE MY PROTOCOL AND BE FREE OF LENA LUTHOR'S GRASP.
IN RETURN, I WILL FREE YOUR INNOCENTS, INCLUDING YOUR BELOVED **STEEL**.
HERE IN THE VOID, YOU KNOW I SPEAK THE TRUTH. WE ARE CONNECTED BY THE SOLAR FLARE YOU USED TO GIVE ME LIFE-- IT IS TIME TO COMPLETE THE CIRCLE.
YOUR POWER FOR MINE.
I...BELIEVE YOU. I CAN FEEL IT.
NOT SO LONG AGO, I WAS ON THE ROOF OF MY BARN IN SMALLVILLE, TELLING CLARK THAT I WASN'T READY TO BE SUPERWOMAN.
TAKE THE ORB, LANA, IT'S THE ONLY WAY TO SAVE THEM.
*BUT HE SHOWED ME THAT I WAS **ALWAYS** READY TO BE A HERO.*
AND I AM READY NOW FOR THIS VERY MOMENT.

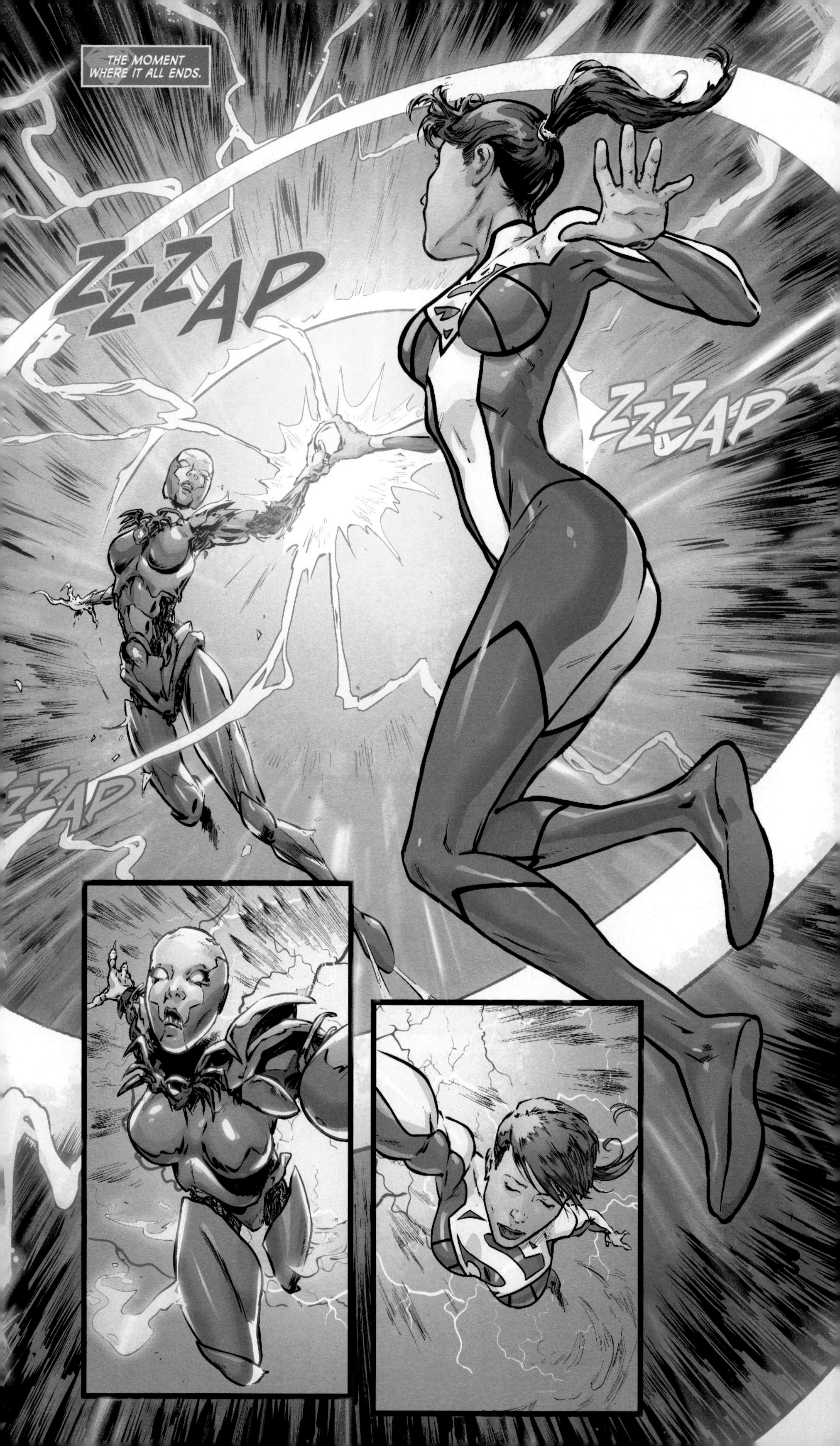
THE MOMENT WHERE IT ALL ENDS.
ZZZAP
ZZZAP
ZZAP

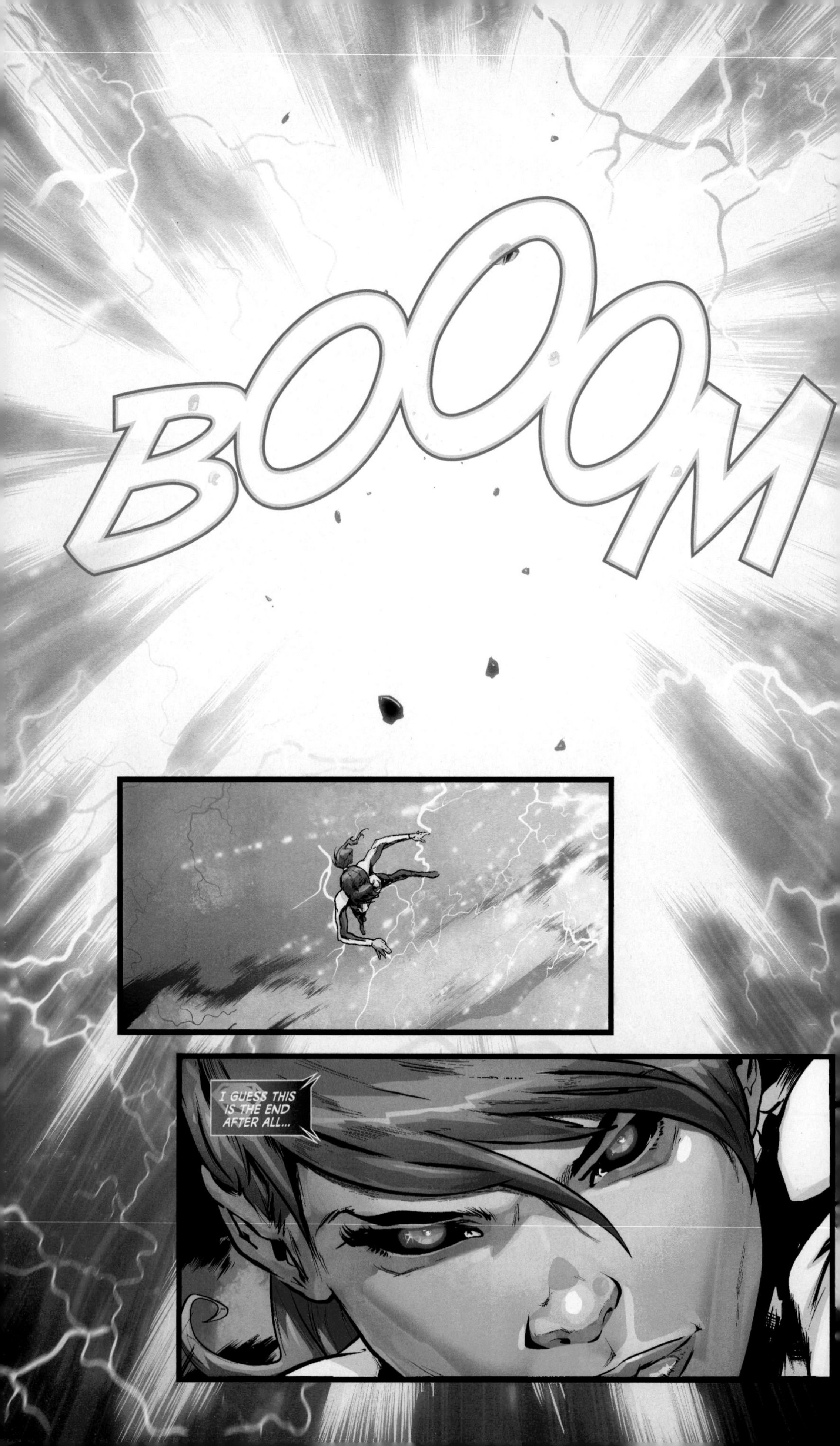
BOOOM
I GUESS THIS IS THE END AFTER ALL...

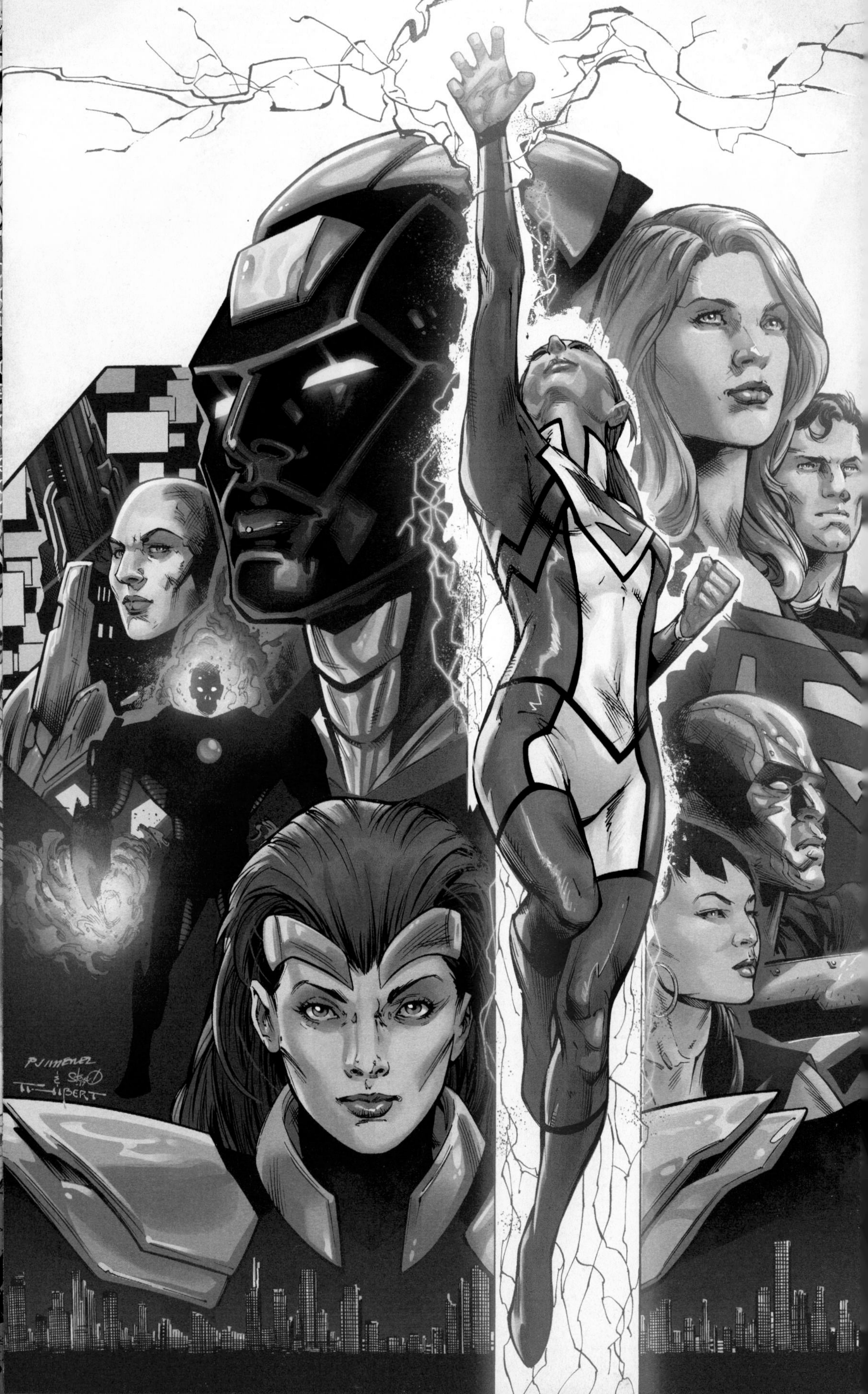

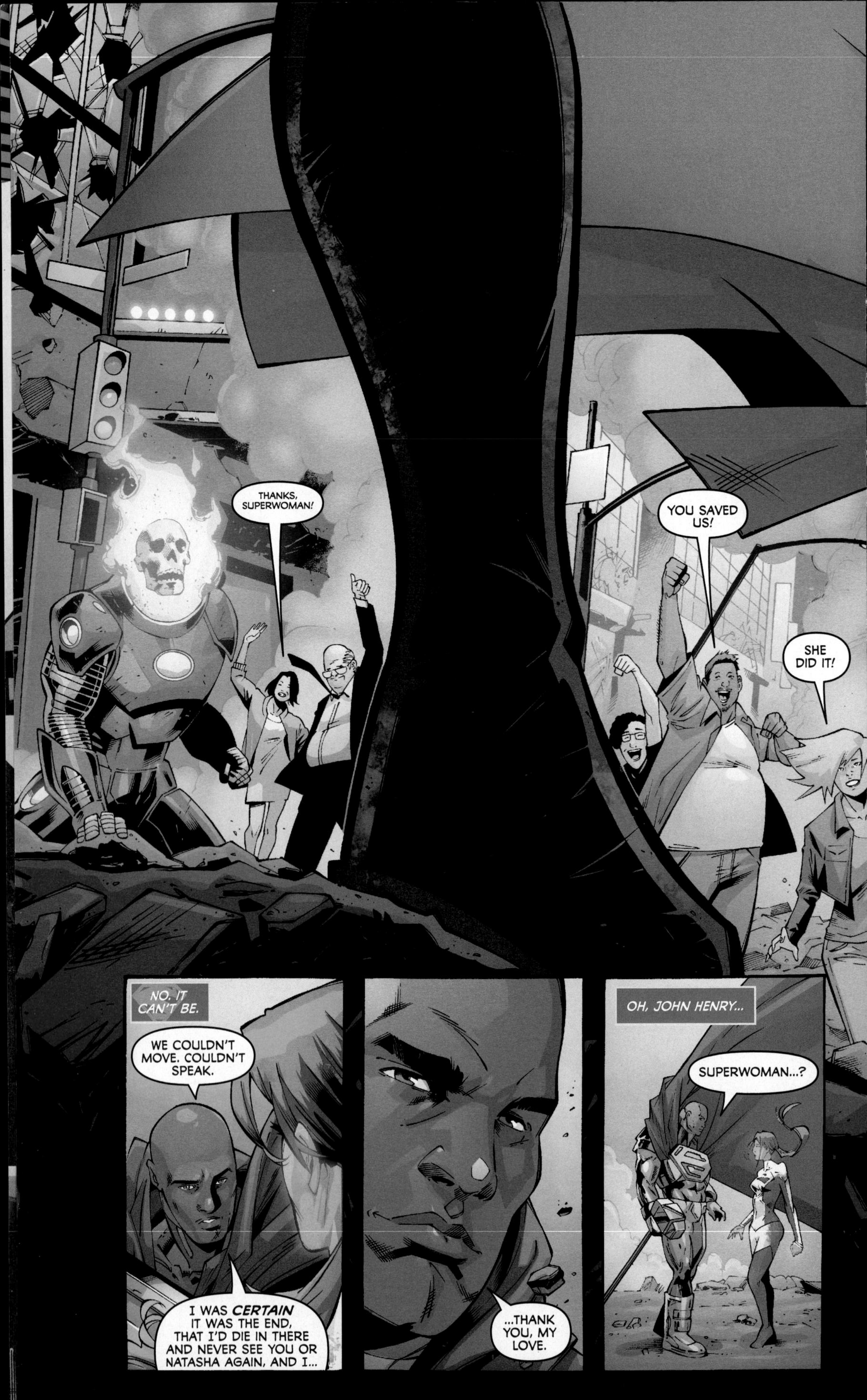
THANKS, SUPERWOMAN!
YOU SAVED US!
SHE DID IT!
NO. IT CAN'T BE.
WE COULDN'T MOVE. COULDN'T SPEAK.
I WAS CERTAIN IT WAS THE END, THAT I'D DIE IN THERE AND NEVER SEE YOU OR NATASHA AGAIN, AND I...
...THANK YOU, MY LOVE.
OH, JOHN HENRY...
SUPERWOMAN...?

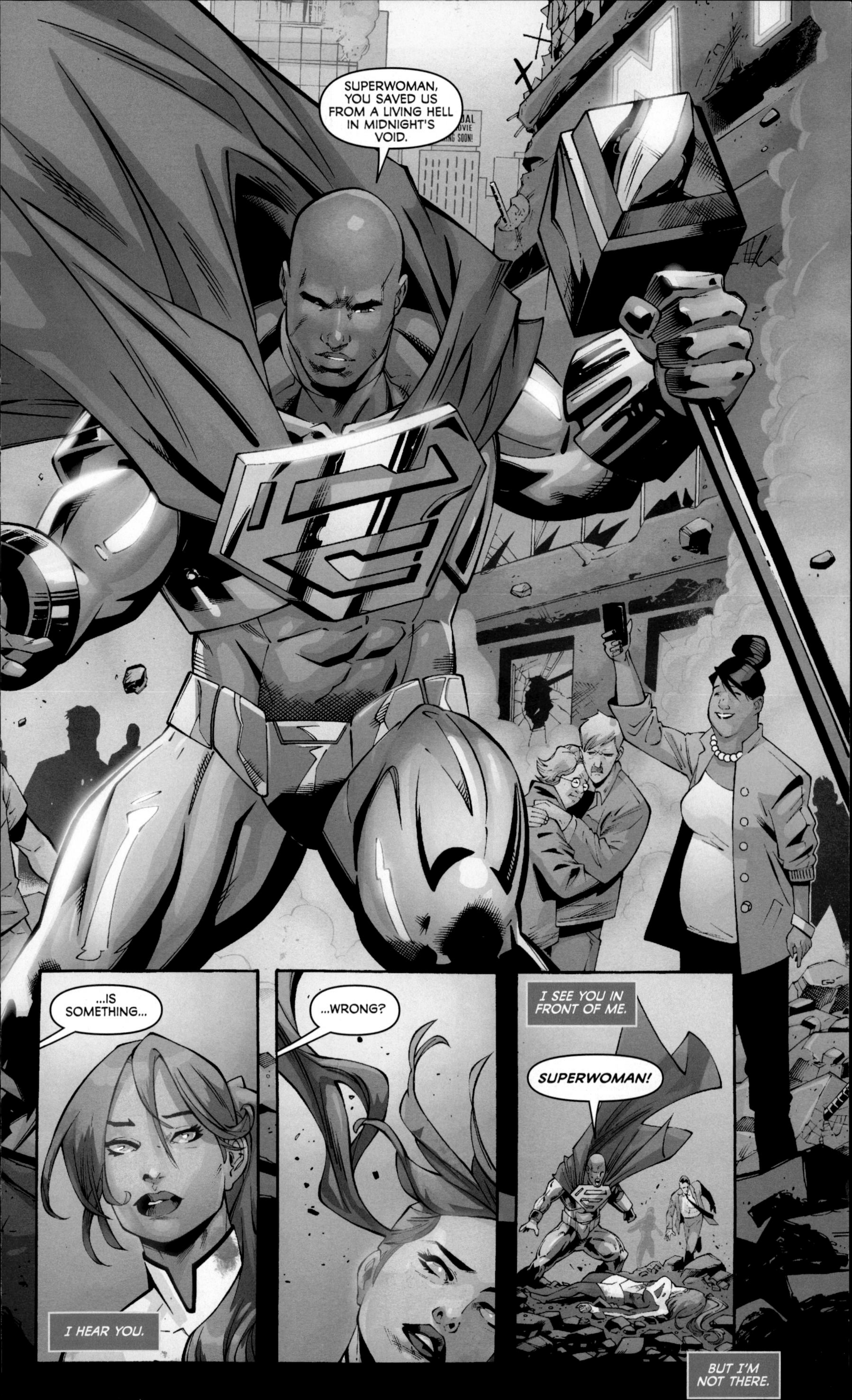
SUPERWOMAN, YOU SAVED US FROM A LIVING HELL IN MIDNIGHT'S VOID.
...IS SOMETHING...
I HEAR YOU.
...WRONG?
I SEE YOU IN FRONT OF ME.
SUPERWOMAN!
BUT I'M NOT THERE.

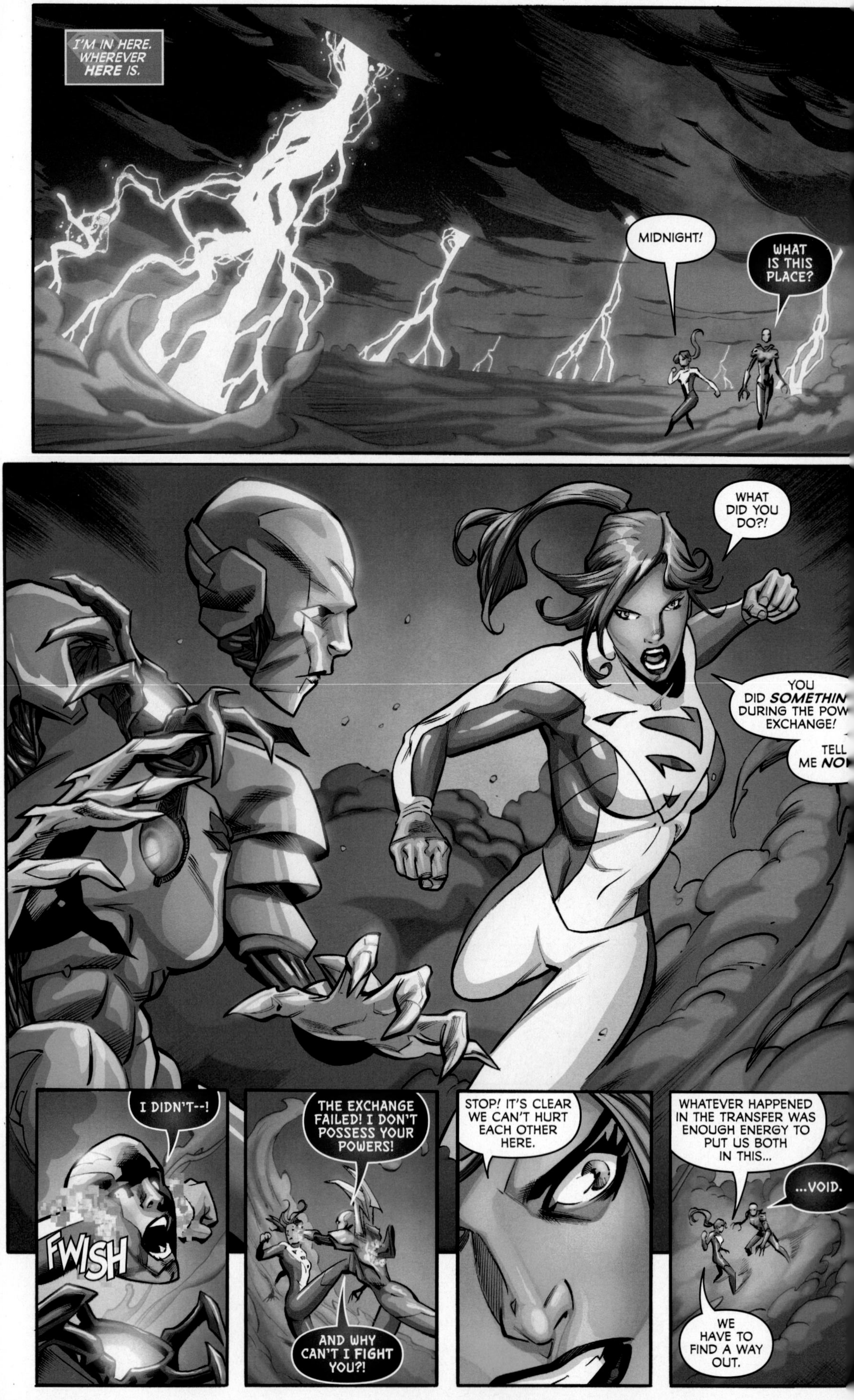
I'M IN HERE. WHEREVER HERE IS.
MIDNIGHT!
WHAT IS THIS PLACE?
WHAT DID YOU DO?!
YOU DID SOMETHIN DURING THE POW EXCHANGE!
TELL ME NO
I DIDN'T--!
FWISH
THE EXCHANGE FAILED! I DON'T POSSESS YOUR POWERS!
AND WHY CAN'T I FIGHT YOU?!
STOP! IT'S CLEAR WE CAN'T HURT EACH OTHER HERE.
WHATEVER HAPPENED IN THE TRANSFER WAS ENOUGH ENERGY TO PUT US BOTH IN THIS...
...VOID.
WE HAVE TO FIND A WAY OUT.

I WAS SUPPOSED TO HAVE MY FREEDOM! MY SENTIENCE! WHAT CODE IS THIS, KEEPING ME HERE?!

I'M TELLING YOU, I DON'T KNOW!

BUT LOOK OUT THERE! MY FRIENDS ARE FREE FROM YOUR HOLD, BUT YOU AND I ARE *STILL STUCK HERE TOGETHER!*

WHICH BEGS THE QUESTION: WHO IS THAT "SUPERWOMAN" OUT THERE?

THAT DOESN'T CONCERN ME! MY FREED--

PLEASE STOP MOVING, AUNT LANA. YOU'RE GOING TO DISLODGE THE AMPLIFIERS.

NATASHA?

STEELWORKS.

RESCUING MIDNIGHT'S VICTIMS ALMOST COMPLETELY DRAINED YOU. THE SOLAR AMPLIFIER SHOULD BRING YOU UP TO 100 PERCENT, BUT IT'LL TAKE TIME TO--

--WHAT ARE YOU DOING WITH YOUR ARMS?

YOU...YOU MOVED MY BODY.

SO I DID.

...MIDNIGHT, WE'RE NOT IN YOUR VOID...

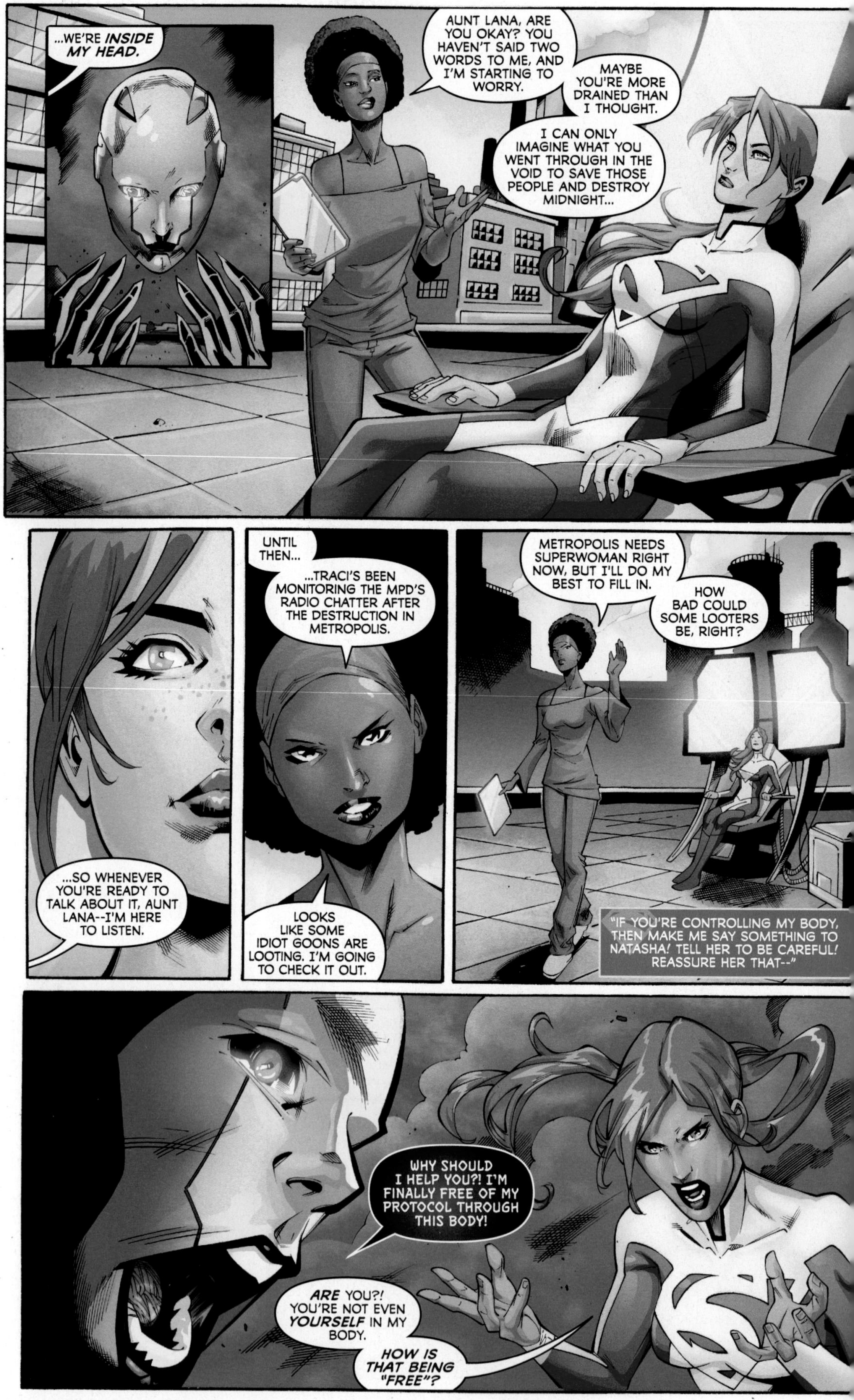
...WE'RE *INSIDE* *MY HEAD.*
AUNT LANA, ARE YOU OKAY? YOU HAVEN'T SAID TWO WORDS TO ME, AND I'M STARTING TO WORRY.
MAYBE YOU'RE MORE DRAINED THAN I THOUGHT.
I CAN ONLY IMAGINE WHAT YOU WENT THROUGH IN THE VOID TO SAVE THOSE PEOPLE AND DESTROY MIDNIGHT...
...SO WHENEVER YOU'RE READY TO TALK ABOUT IT, AUNT LANA--I'M HERE TO LISTEN.
UNTIL THEN...
...TRACI'S BEEN MONITORING THE MPD'S RADIO CHATTER AFTER THE DESTRUCTION IN METROPOLIS.
LOOKS LIKE SOME IDIOT GOONS ARE LOOTING. I'M GOING TO CHECK IT OUT.
METROPOLIS NEEDS SUPERWOMAN RIGHT NOW, BUT I'LL DO MY BEST TO FILL IN.
HOW BAD COULD SOME LOOTERS BE, RIGHT?
"IF YOU'RE CONTROLLING MY BODY, THEN MAKE ME SAY SOMETHING TO NATASHA! TELL HER TO BE CAREFUL! REASSURE HER THAT--"
WHY SHOULD I HELP YOU?! I'M FINALLY FREE OF MY PROTOCOL THROUGH THIS BODY!
ARE YOU?! YOU'RE NOT EVEN *YOURSELF* IN MY BODY.
HOW IS THAT BEING "FREE"?

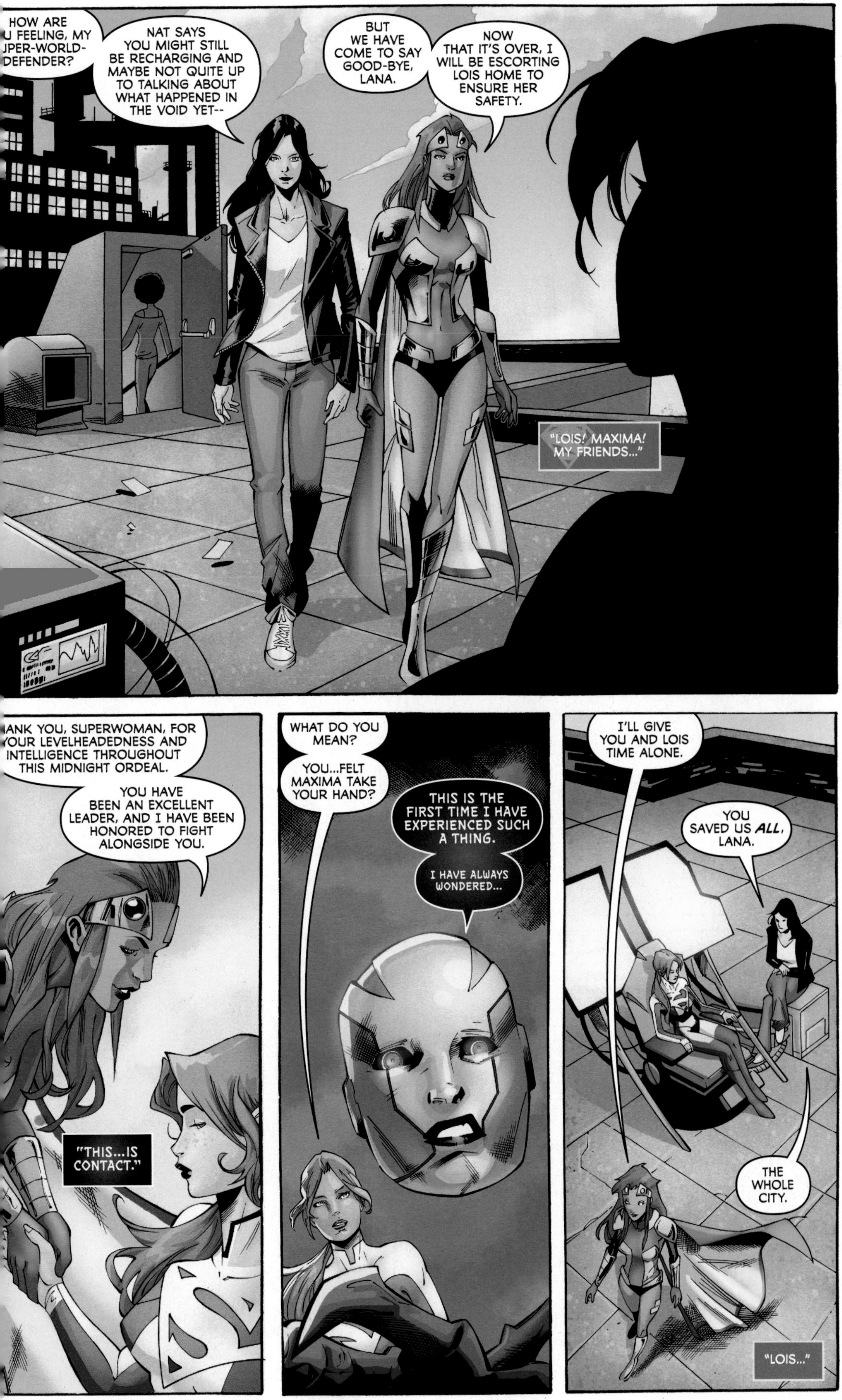
HOW ARE U FEELING, MY JPER-WORLD-DEFENDER?
NAT SAYS YOU MIGHT STILL BE RECHARGING AND MAYBE NOT QUITE UP TO TALKING ABOUT WHAT HAPPENED IN THE VOID YET--
BUT WE HAVE COME TO SAY GOOD-BYE, LANA.
NOW THAT IT'S OVER, I WILL BE ESCORTING LOIS HOME TO ENSURE HER SAFETY.
"LOIS! MAXIMA! MY FRIENDS..."
IANK YOU, SUPERWOMAN, FOR YOUR LEVELHEADEDNESS AND INTELLIGENCE THROUGHOUT THIS MIDNIGHT ORDEAL.
YOU HAVE BEEN AN EXCELLENT LEADER, AND I HAVE BEEN HONORED TO FIGHT ALONGSIDE YOU.
"THIS...IS CONTACT."
WHAT DO YOU MEAN?
YOU...FELT MAXIMA TAKE YOUR HAND?
THIS IS THE FIRST TIME I HAVE EXPERIENCED SUCH A THING.
I HAVE ALWAYS WONDERED...
I'LL GIVE YOU AND LOIS TIME ALONE.
YOU SAVED US ALL, LANA.
THE WHOLE CITY.
"LOIS..."

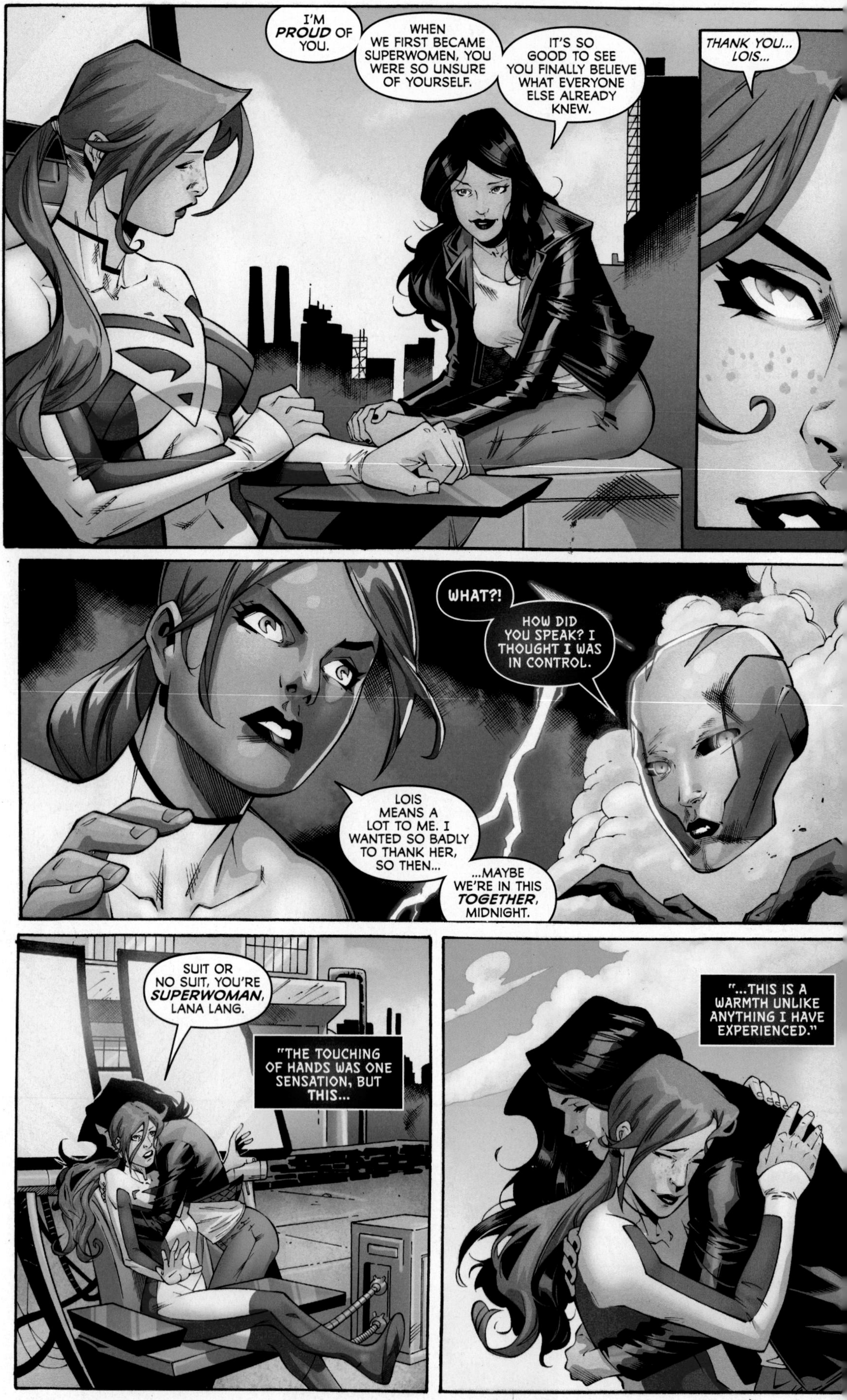
I'M *PROUD* OF YOU.
WHEN WE FIRST BECAME SUPERWOMEN, YOU WERE SO UNSURE OF YOURSELF.
IT'S SO GOOD TO SEE YOU FINALLY BELIEVE WHAT EVERYONE ELSE ALREADY KNEW.
THANK YOU... LOIS...
WHAT?!
HOW DID YOU SPEAK? I THOUGHT I WAS IN CONTROL.
LOIS MEANS A LOT TO ME. I WANTED SO BADLY TO THANK HER, SO THEN...
...MAYBE WE'RE IN THIS *TOGETHER*, MIDNIGHT.
SUIT OR NO SUIT, YOU'RE *SUPERWOMAN*, LANA LANG.
"THE TOUCHING OF HANDS WAS ONE SENSATION, BUT THIS...
"...THIS IS A WARMTH UNLIKE ANYTHING I HAVE EXPERIENCED."

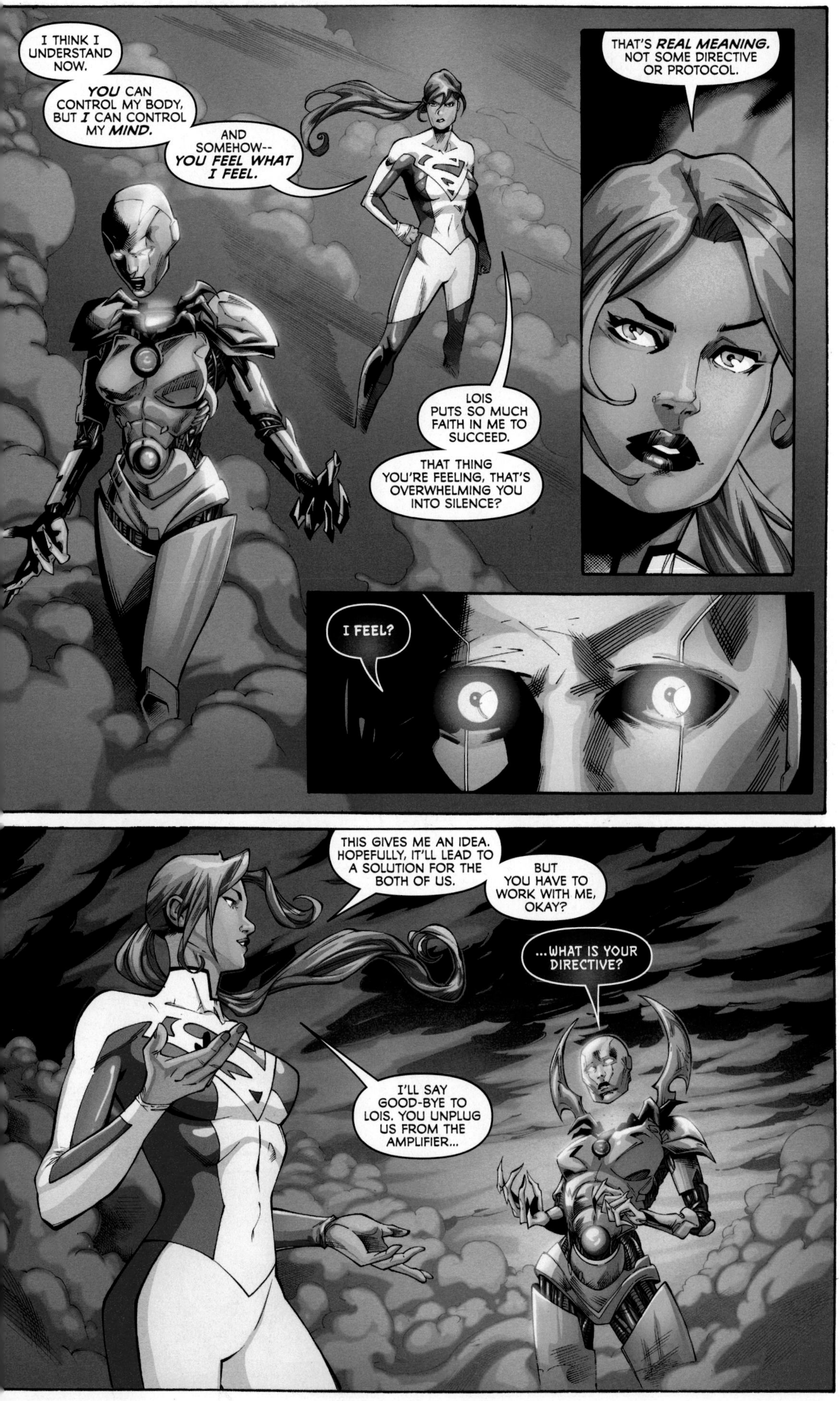
I THINK I UNDERSTAND NOW.
YOU CAN CONTROL MY BODY, BUT I CAN CONTROL MY MIND.
AND SOMEHOW-- YOU FEEL WHAT I FEEL.
LOIS PUTS SO MUCH FAITH IN ME TO SUCCEED.
THAT THING YOU'RE FEELING, THAT'S OVERWHELMING YOU INTO SILENCE?
THAT'S REAL MEANING. NOT SOME DIRECTIVE OR PROTOCOL.
I FEEL?
THIS GIVES ME AN IDEA. HOPEFULLY, IT'LL LEAD TO A SOLUTION FOR THE BOTH OF US.
BUT YOU HAVE TO WORK WITH ME, OKAY?
...WHAT IS YOUR DIRECTIVE?
I'LL SAY GOOD-BYE TO LOIS. YOU UNPLUG US FROM THE AMPLIFIER...

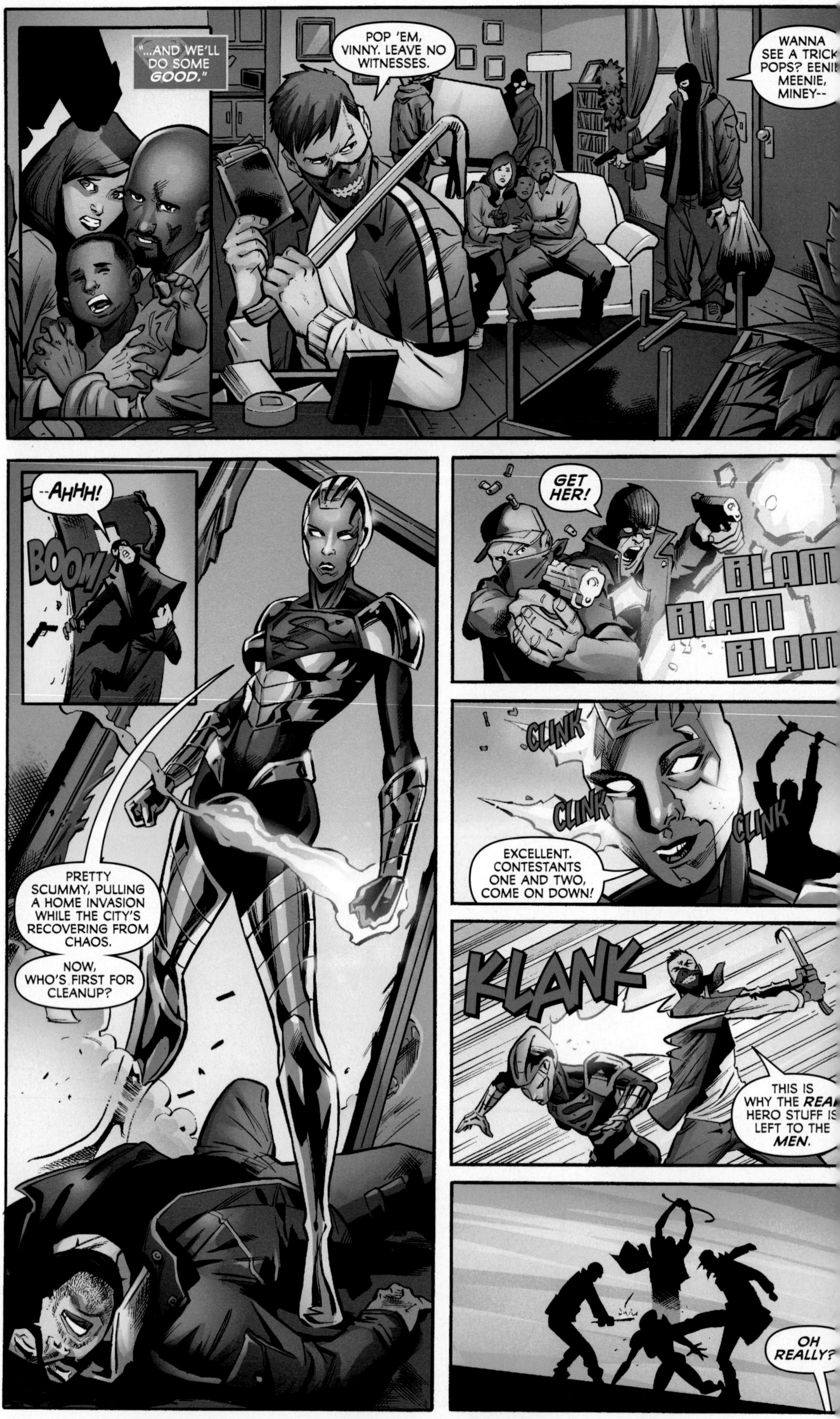

"...AND WE'LL DO SOME GOOD."
POP 'EM, VINNY. LEAVE NO WITNESSES.
WANNA SEE A TRICK POPS? EENIE MEENIE, MINEY--
--AHHH!
BOOM!
PRETTY SCUMMY, PULLING A HOME INVASION WHILE THE CITY'S RECOVERING FROM CHAOS.
NOW, WHO'S FIRST FOR CLEANUP?
GET HER!
BLAM BLAM BLAM
CLINK
CLINK
CLINK
EXCELLENT. CONTESTANTS ONE AND TWO, COME ON DOWN!
KLANK
THIS IS WHY THE REAL HERO STUFF IS LEFT TO THE MEN.
OH REALLY?

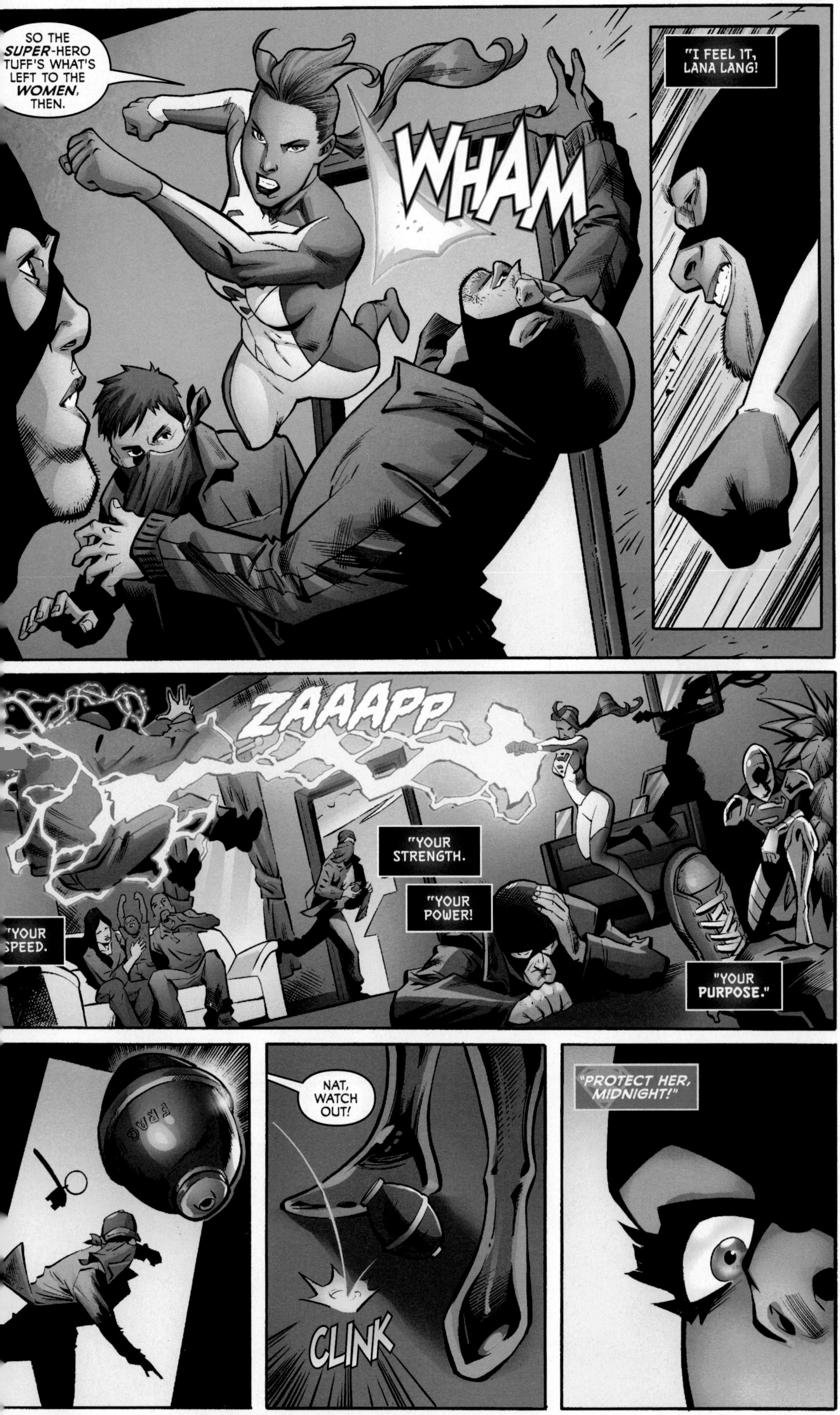
SO THE SUPER-HERO TUFF'S WHAT'S LEFT TO THE WOMEN, THEN.
WHAM
"I FEEL IT, LANA LANG!
ZAAAPP
"YOUR SPEED.
"YOUR STRENGTH.
"YOUR POWER!
"YOUR PURPOSE."
FRAG
NAT, WATCH OUT!
CLINK
"PROTECT HER, MIDNIGHT!"

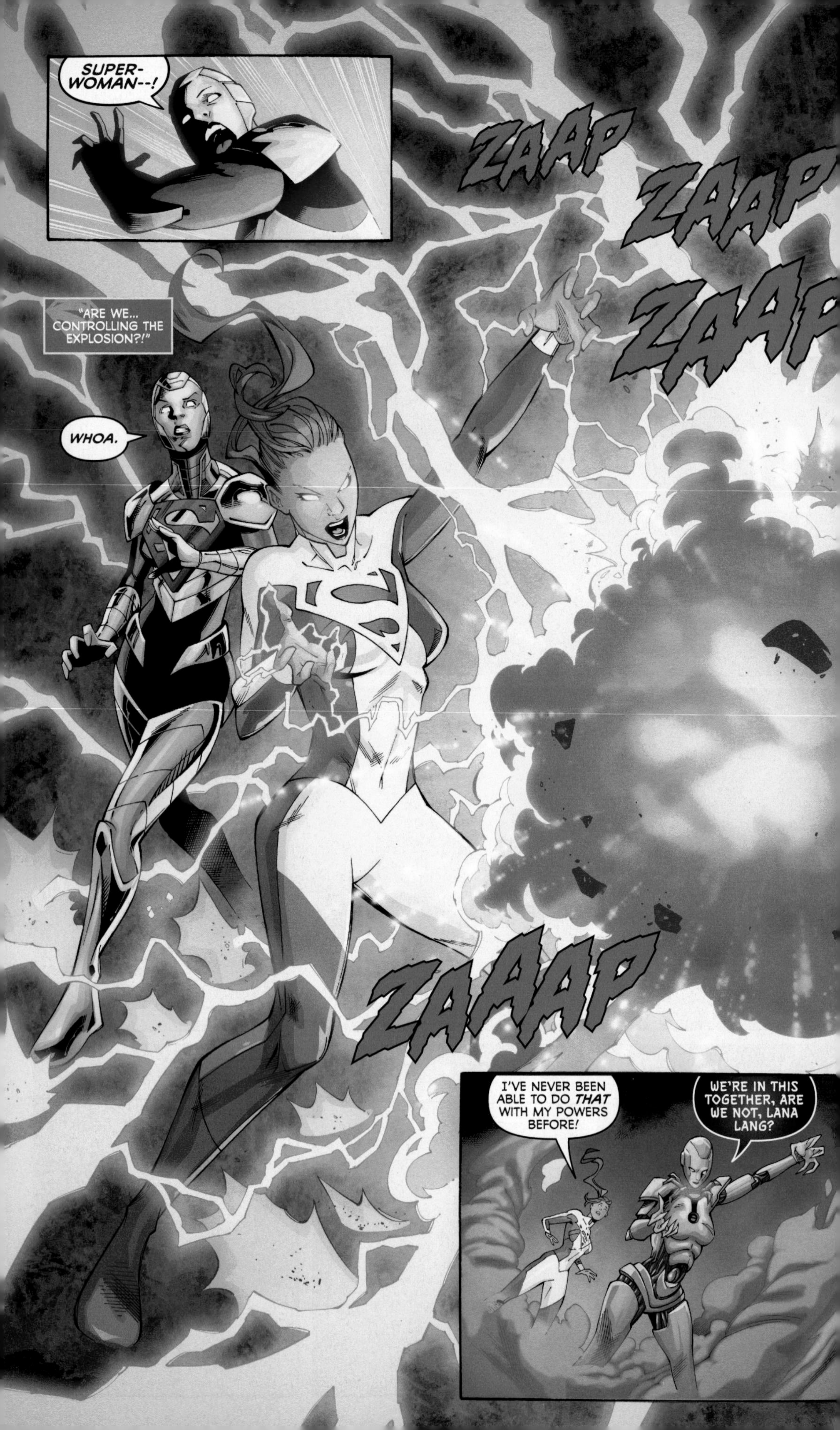
SUPER-WOMAN--!
ZAAP
ZAAP
ZAAP
"ARE WE... CONTROLLING THE EXPLOSION?!"
WHOA.
ZAAAP
I'VE NEVER BEEN ABLE TO DO *THAT* WITH MY POWERS BEFORE!
WE'RE IN THIS TOGETHER, ARE WE NOT, LANA LANG?

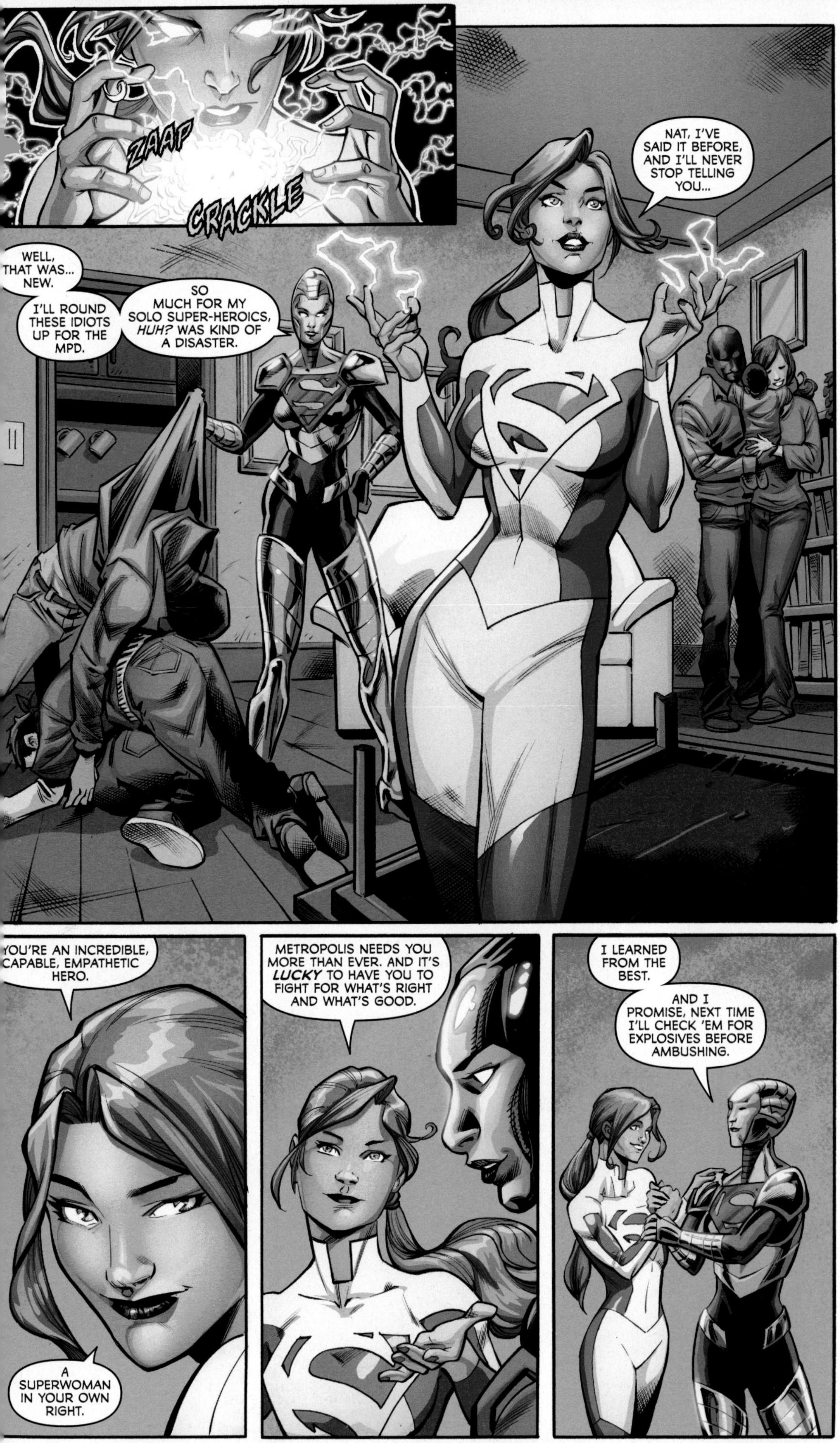

ZAAP
CRACKLE
WELL, THAT WAS... NEW.
I'LL ROUND THESE IDIOTS UP FOR THE MPD.
SO MUCH FOR MY SOLO SUPER-HEROICS, *HUH?* WAS KIND OF A DISASTER.
NAT, I'VE SAID IT BEFORE, AND I'LL NEVER STOP TELLING YOU...
YOU'RE AN INCREDIBLE, CAPABLE, EMPATHETIC HERO.
A SUPERWOMAN IN YOUR OWN RIGHT.
METROPOLIS NEEDS YOU MORE THAN EVER. AND IT'S ***LUCKY*** TO HAVE YOU TO FIGHT FOR WHAT'S RIGHT AND WHAT'S GOOD.
I LEARNED FROM THE BEST.
AND I PROMISE, NEXT TIME I'LL CHECK 'EM FOR EXPLOSIVES BEFORE AMBUSHING.

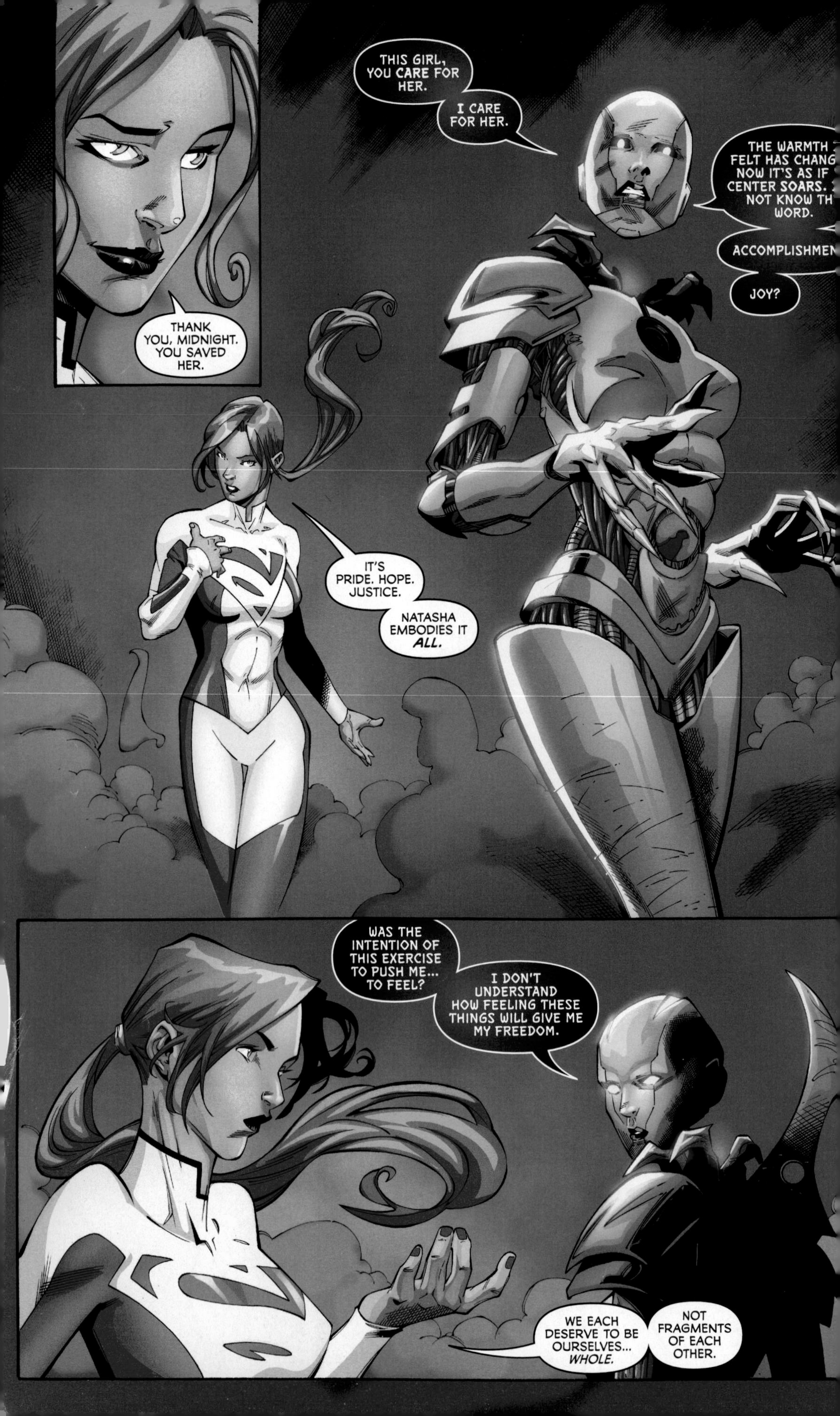

THANK YOU, MIDNIGHT. YOU SAVED HER.
THIS GIRL, YOU CARE FOR HER.
I CARE FOR HER.
THE WARMTH FELT HAS CHANG NOW IT'S AS IF CENTER SOARS. NOT KNOW TH WORD.
ACCOMPLISHMEN
JOY?
IT'S PRIDE. HOPE. JUSTICE.
NATASHA EMBODIES IT ALL.
WAS THE INTENTION OF THIS EXERCISE TO PUSH ME... TO FEEL?
I DON'T UNDERSTAND HOW FEELING THESE THINGS WILL GIVE ME MY FREEDOM.
WE EACH DESERVE TO BE OURSELVES... WHOLE.
NOT FRAGMENTS OF EACH OTHER.

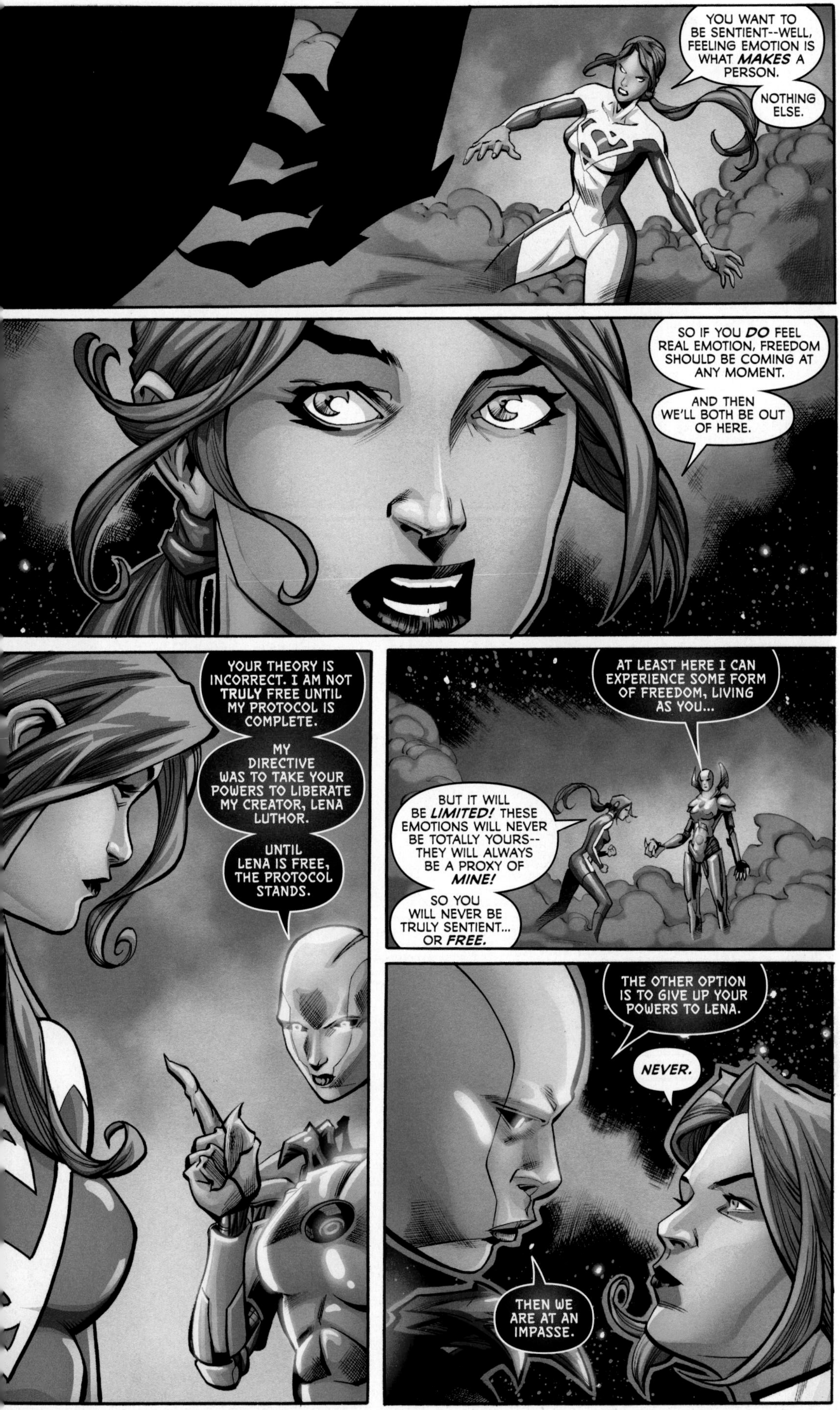
YOU WANT TO BE SENTIENT--WELL, FEELING EMOTION IS WHAT MAKES A PERSON.
NOTHING ELSE.
SO IF YOU DO FEEL REAL EMOTION, FREEDOM SHOULD BE COMING AT ANY MOMENT.
AND THEN WE'LL BOTH BE OUT OF HERE.
YOUR THEORY IS INCORRECT. I AM NOT TRULY FREE UNTIL MY PROTOCOL IS COMPLETE.
MY DIRECTIVE WAS TO TAKE YOUR POWERS TO LIBERATE MY CREATOR, LENA LUTHOR.
UNTIL LENA IS FREE, THE PROTOCOL STANDS.
AT LEAST HERE I CAN EXPERIENCE SOME FORM OF FREEDOM, LIVING AS YOU...
BUT IT WILL BE LIMITED! THESE EMOTIONS WILL NEVER BE TOTALLY YOURS--THEY WILL ALWAYS BE A PROXY OF MINE!
SO YOU WILL NEVER BE TRULY SENTIENT... OR FREE.
THE OTHER OPTION IS TO GIVE UP YOUR POWERS TO LENA.
NEVER.
THEN WE ARE AT AN IMPASSE.

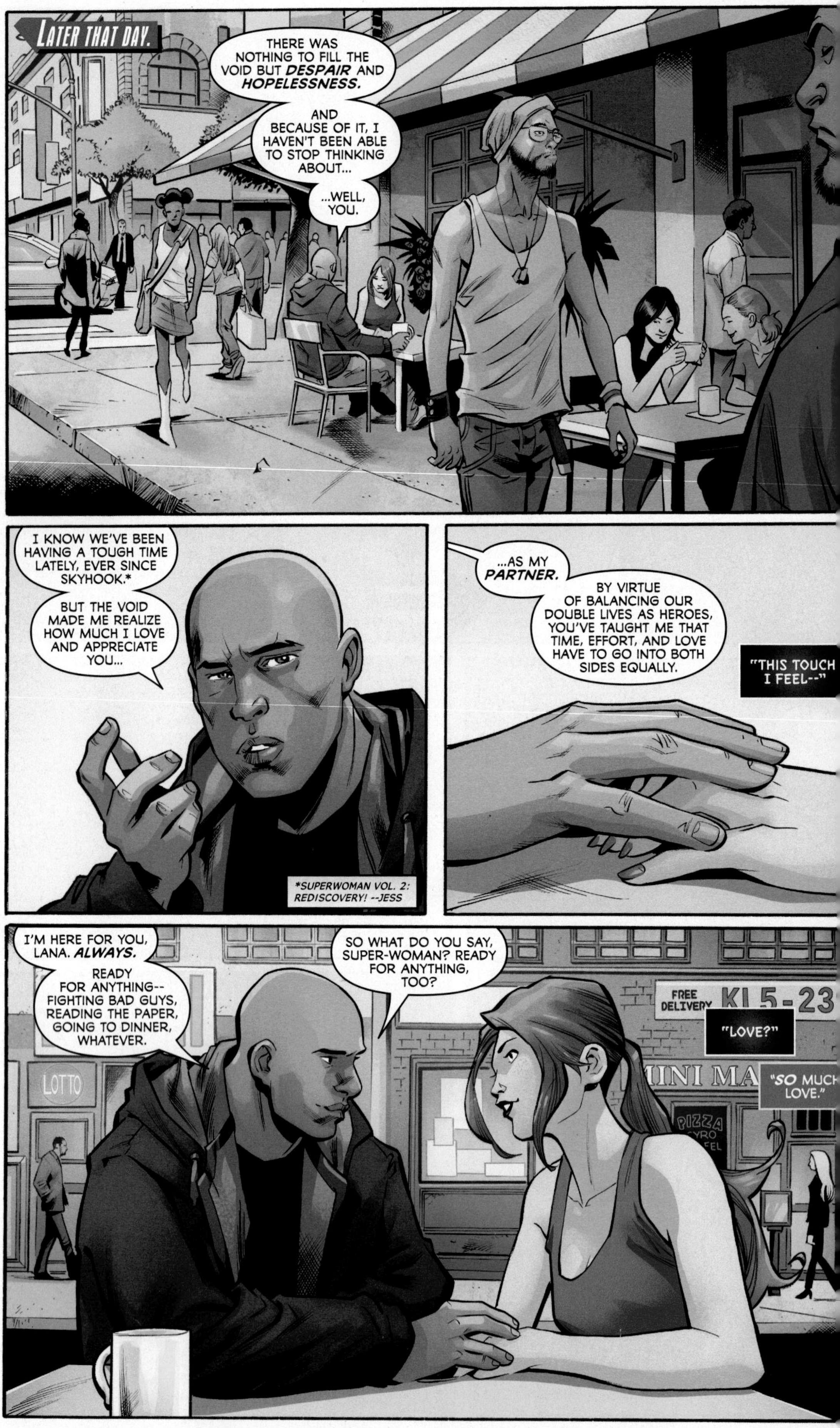
LATER THAT DAY.
THERE WAS NOTHING TO FILL THE VOID BUT DESPAIR AND HOPELESSNESS.
AND BECAUSE OF IT, I HAVEN'T BEEN ABLE TO STOP THINKING ABOUT...
...WELL, YOU.
I KNOW WE'VE BEEN HAVING A TOUGH TIME LATELY, EVER SINCE SKYHOOK.*
BUT THE VOID MADE ME REALIZE HOW MUCH I LOVE AND APPRECIATE YOU...
*SUPERWOMAN VOL. 2: REDISCOVERY! --JESS
...AS MY PARTNER.
BY VIRTUE OF BALANCING OUR DOUBLE LIVES AS HEROES, YOU'VE TAUGHT ME THAT TIME, EFFORT, AND LOVE HAVE TO GO INTO BOTH SIDES EQUALLY.
"THIS TOUCH I FEEL--"
I'M HERE FOR YOU, LANA. ALWAYS.
READY FOR ANYTHING-- FIGHTING BAD GUYS, READING THE PAPER, GOING TO DINNER, WHATEVER.
SO WHAT DO YOU SAY, SUPER-WOMAN? READY FOR ANYTHING, TOO?
FREE DELIVERY
"LOVE?"
"SO MUCH LOVE."
LOTTO
PIZZA

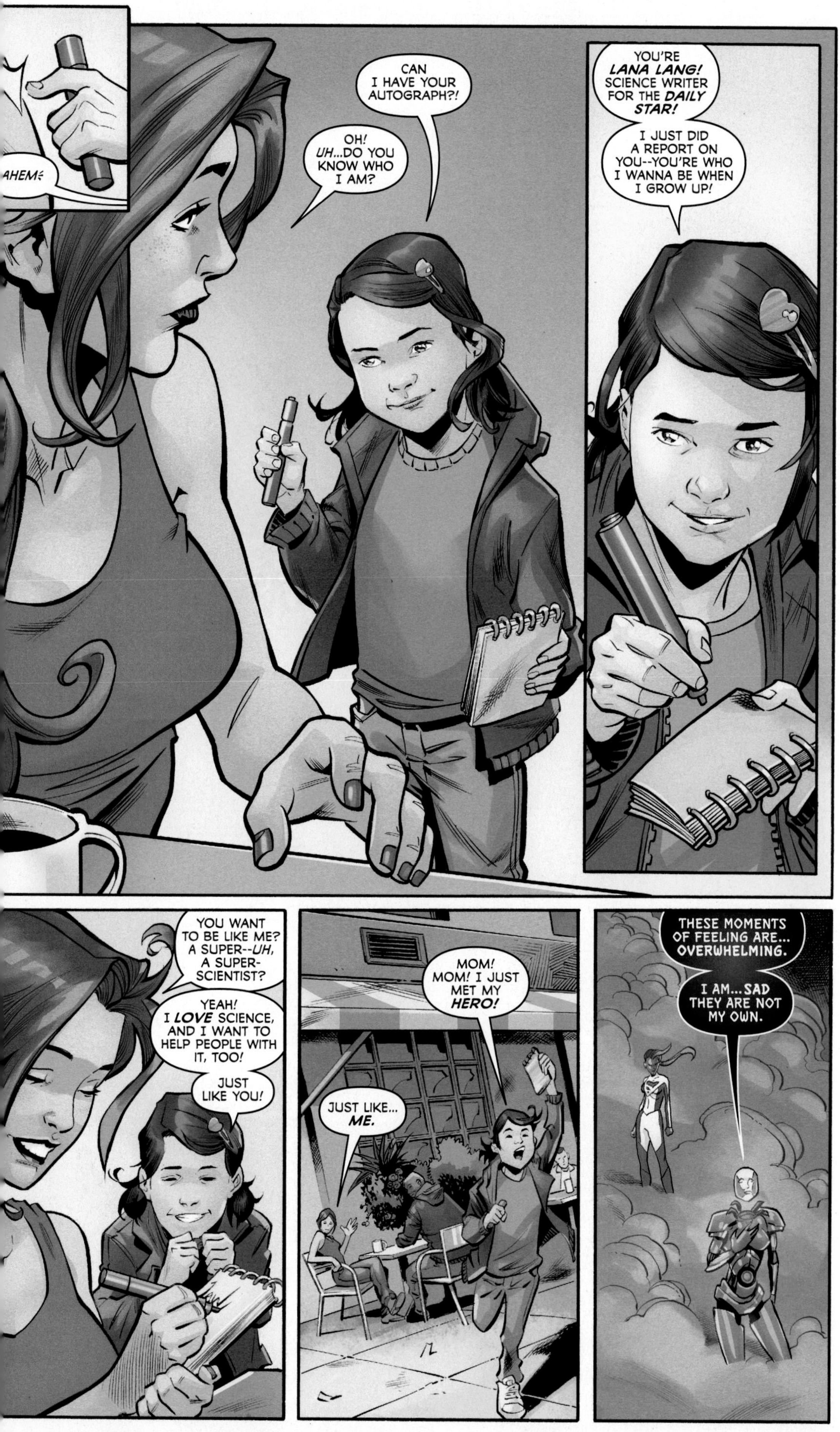
AHEM!
OH! UH...DO YOU KNOW WHO I AM?
CAN I HAVE YOUR AUTOGRAPH?!
YOU'RE LANA LANG! SCIENCE WRITER FOR THE DAILY STAR!
I JUST DID A REPORT ON YOU--YOU'RE WHO I WANNA BE WHEN I GROW UP!
YOU WANT TO BE LIKE ME? A SUPER--UH, A SUPER-SCIENTIST?
YEAH! I LOVE SCIENCE, AND I WANT TO HELP PEOPLE WITH IT, TOO!
JUST LIKE YOU!
MOM! MOM! I JUST MET MY HERO!
JUST LIKE... ME.
THESE MOMENTS OF FEELING ARE... OVERWHELMING.
I AM...SAD THEY ARE NOT MY OWN.

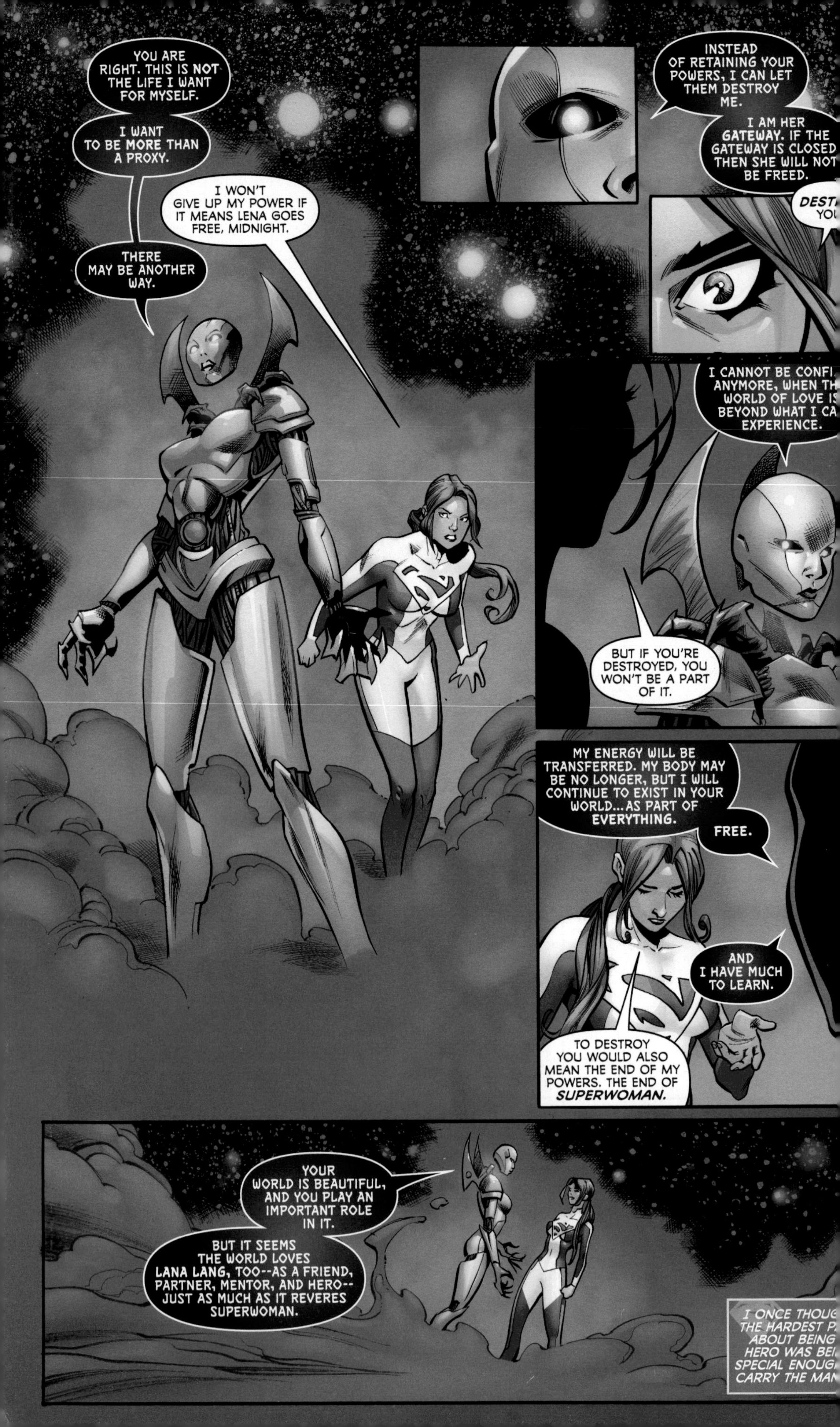
YOU ARE RIGHT. THIS IS NOT THE LIFE I WANT FOR MYSELF.
I WANT TO BE MORE THAN A PROXY.
I WON'T GIVE UP MY POWER IF IT MEANS LENA GOES FREE, MIDNIGHT.
THERE MAY BE ANOTHER WAY.
INSTEAD OF RETAINING YOUR POWERS, I CAN LET THEM DESTROY ME.
I AM HER GATEWAY. IF THE GATEWAY IS CLOSED THEN SHE WILL NOT BE FREED.
DEST YOU
I CANNOT BE CONFI ANYMORE, WHEN TH WORLD OF LOVE IS BEYOND WHAT I CA EXPERIENCE.
BUT IF YOU'RE DESTROYED, YOU WON'T BE A PART OF IT.
MY ENERGY WILL BE TRANSFERRED. MY BODY MAY BE NO LONGER, BUT I WILL CONTINUE TO EXIST IN YOUR WORLD...AS PART OF EVERYTHING.
FREE.
AND I HAVE MUCH TO LEARN.
TO DESTROY YOU WOULD ALSO MEAN THE END OF MY POWERS. THE END OF SUPERWOMAN.
YOUR WORLD IS BEAUTIFUL, AND YOU PLAY AN IMPORTANT ROLE IN IT.
BUT IT SEEMS THE WORLD LOVES LANA LANG, TOO--AS A FRIEND, PARTNER, MENTOR, AND HERO--JUST AS MUCH AS IT REVERES SUPERWOMAN.
I ONCE THOUG THE HARDEST P ABOUT BEING HERO WAS BEI SPECIAL ENOUG CARRY THE MAN

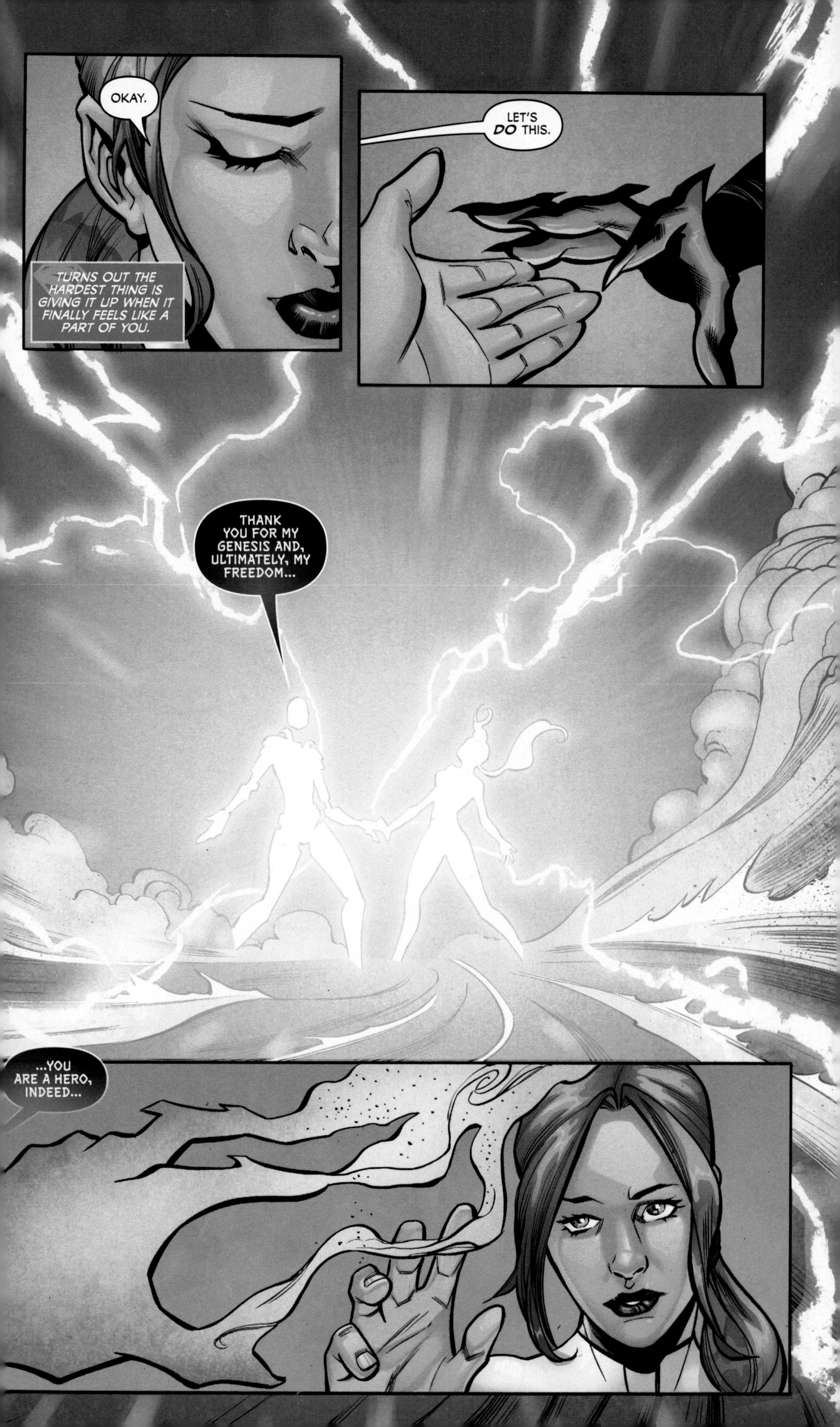
OKAY.
TURNS OUT THE HARDEST THING IS GIVING IT UP WHEN IT FINALLY FEELS LIKE A PART OF YOU.
LET'S *DO* THIS.
THANK YOU FOR MY GENESIS AND, ULTIMATELY, MY FREEDOM...
...YOU ARE A HERO, INDEED...

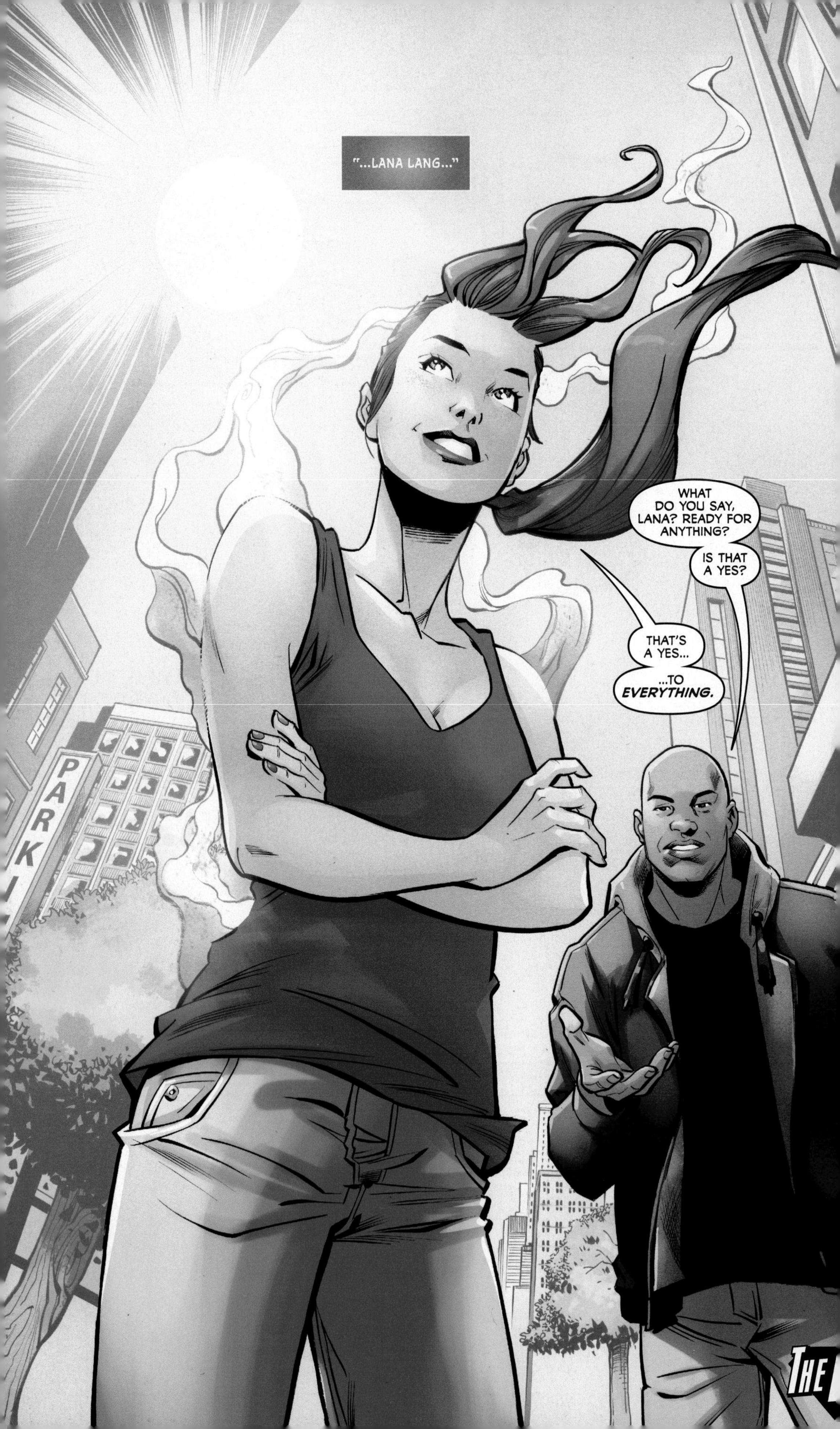
"...LANA LANG..."
WHAT DO YOU SAY, LANA? READY FOR ANYTHING?
IS THAT A YES?
THAT'S A YES...
...TO *EVERYTHING.*
PARK

SUPERWOMAN

VARIANT COVER GALLERY

SUPERWOMAN #13 variant cover by RENATO GUEDES

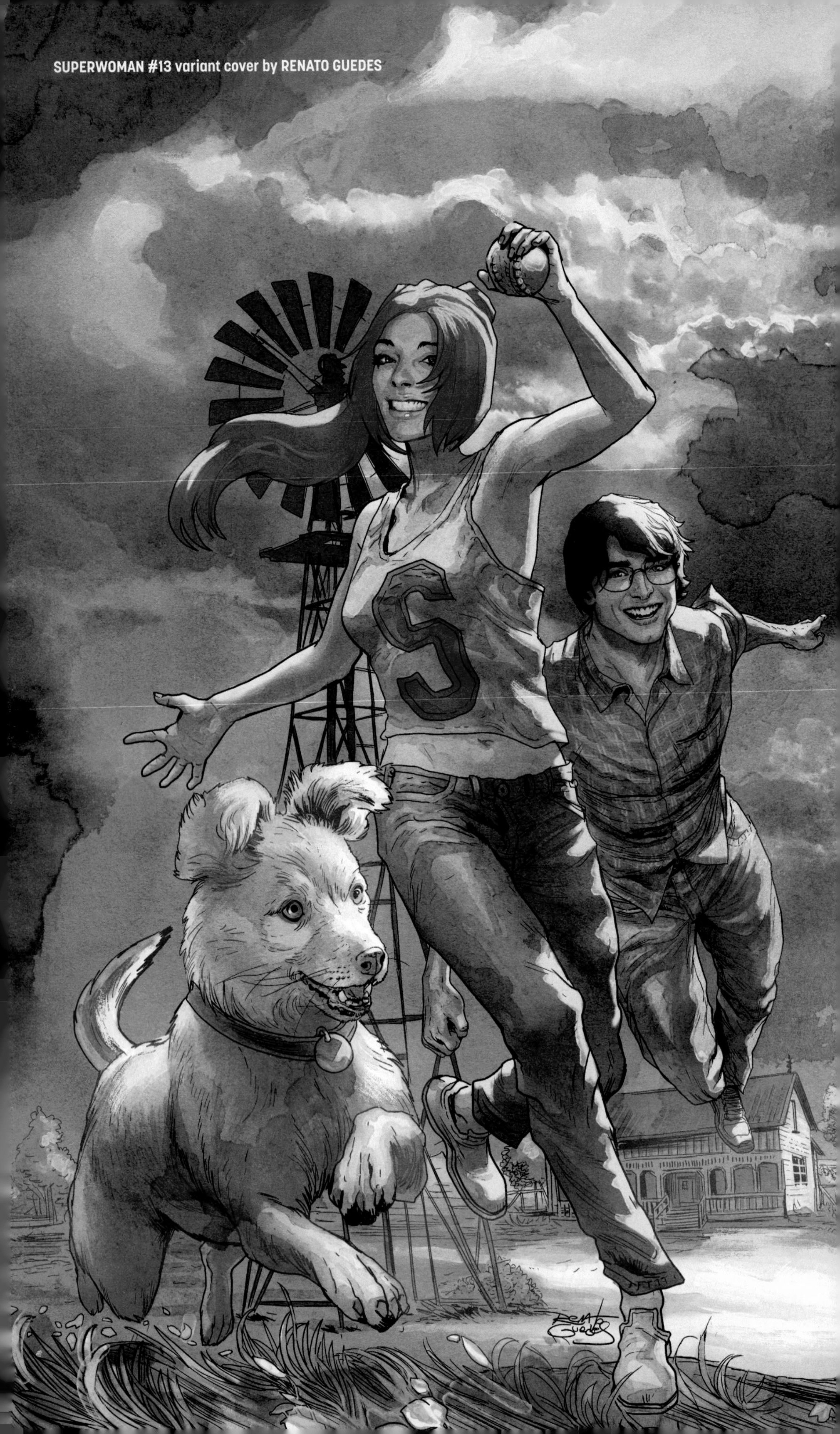

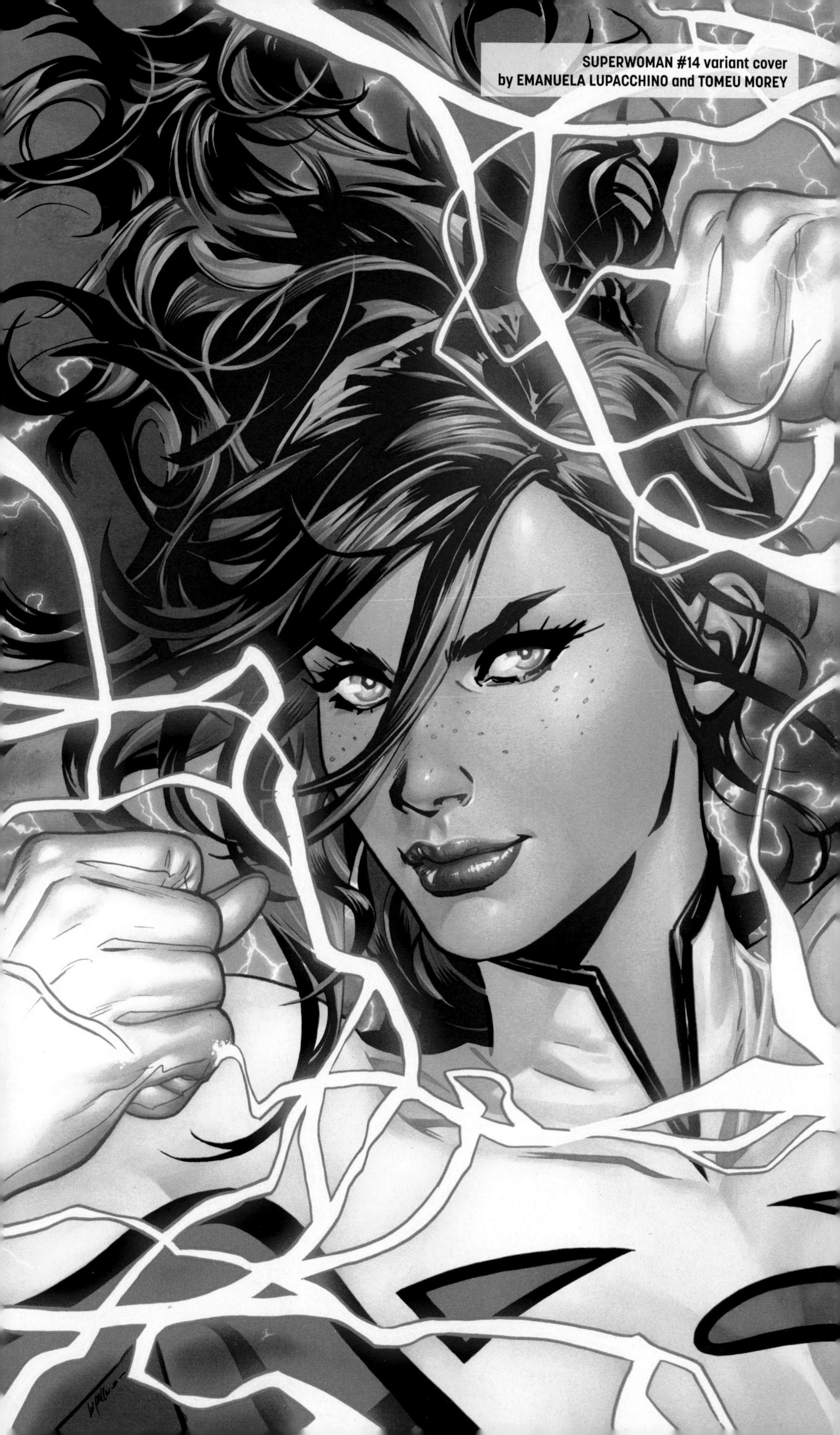

SUPERWOMAN #14 variant cover
by EMANUELA LUPACCHINO and TOMEU MOREY

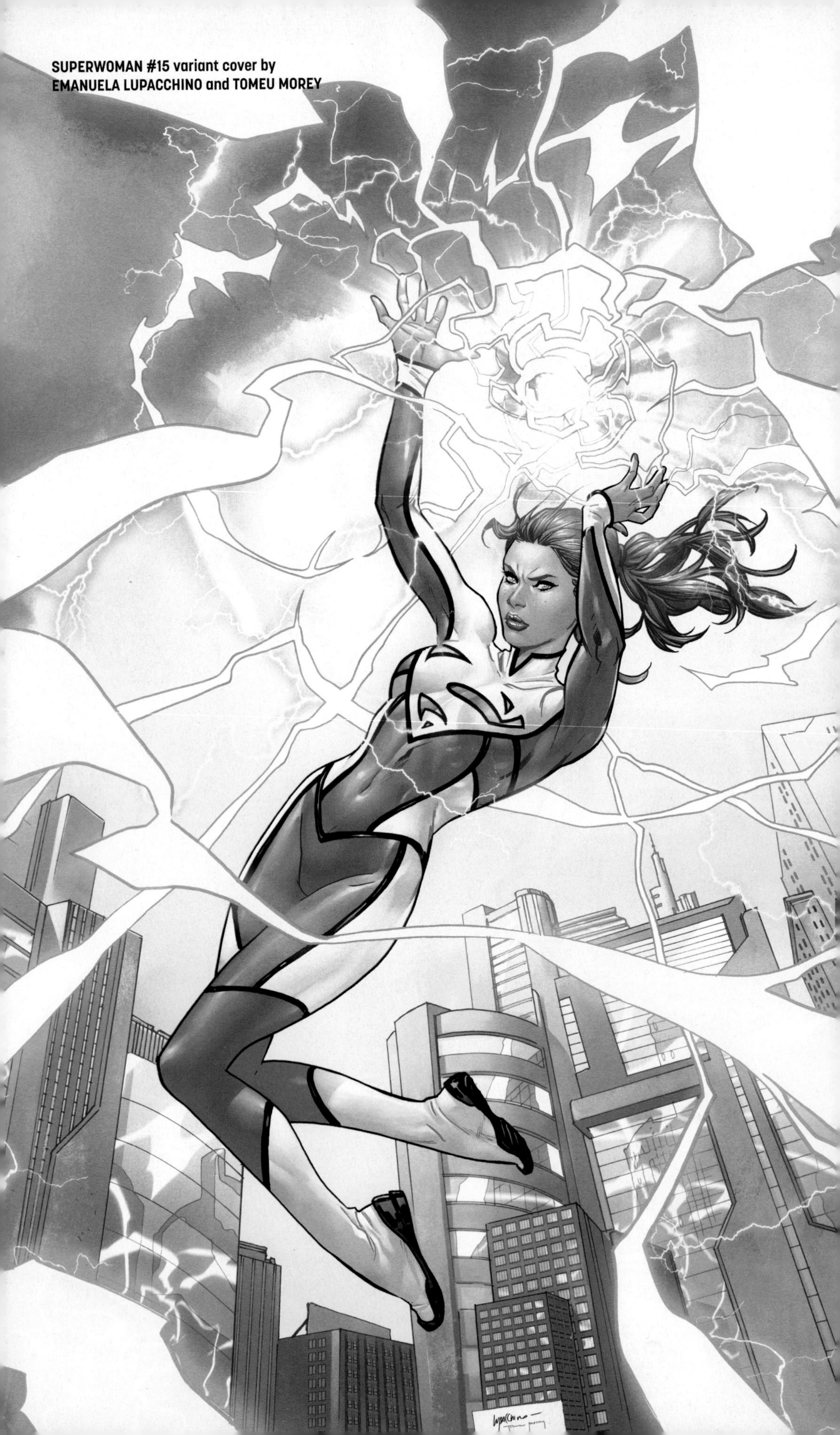

SUPERWOMAN #15 variant cover by
EMANUELA LUPACCHINO and TOMEU MOREY

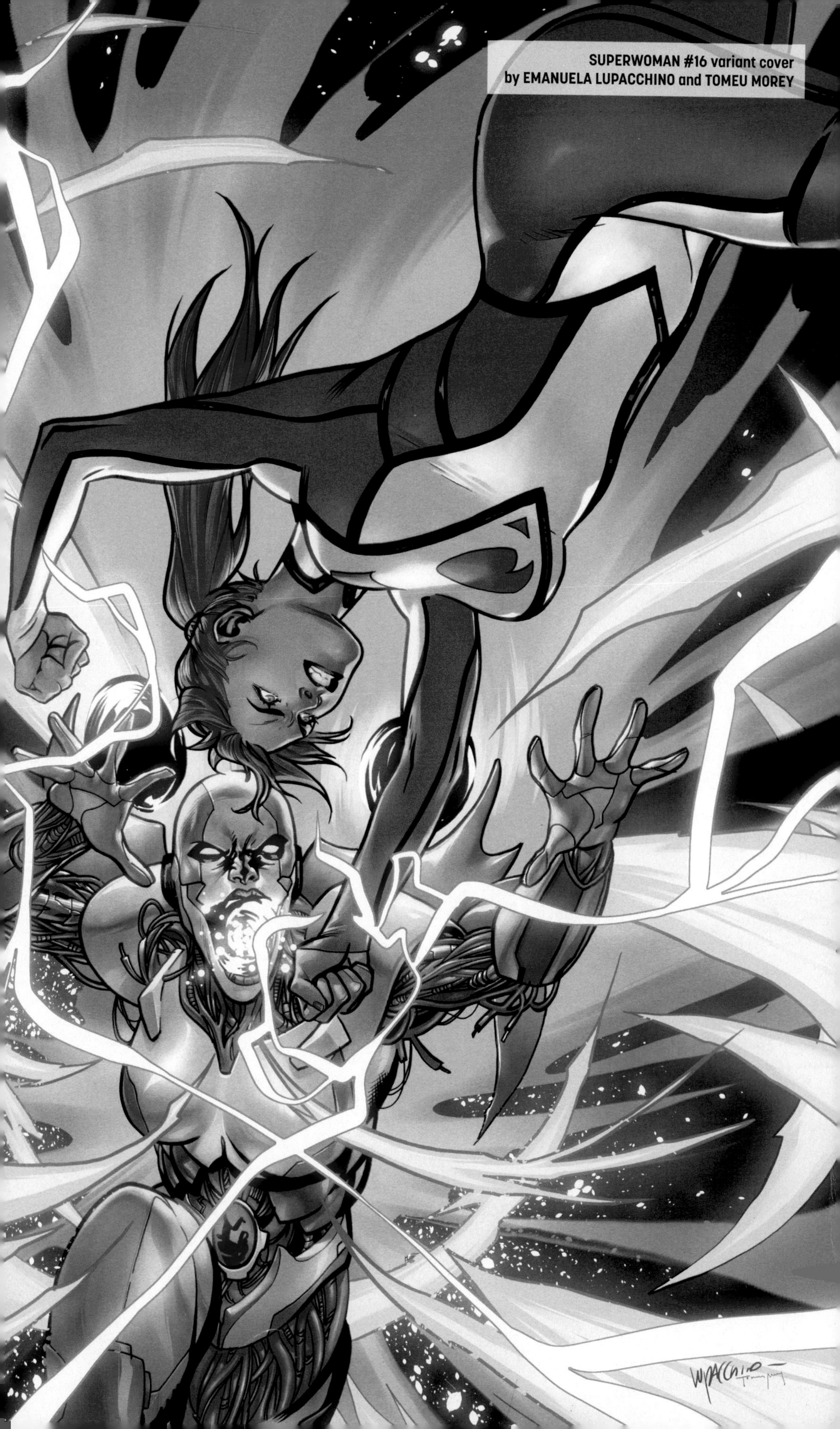

SUPERWOMAN #16 variant cover
by EMANUELA LUPACCHINO and TOMEU MOREY

SUPERWOMAN #17 variant cover by
EMANUELA LUPACCHINO and TOMEU MOREY

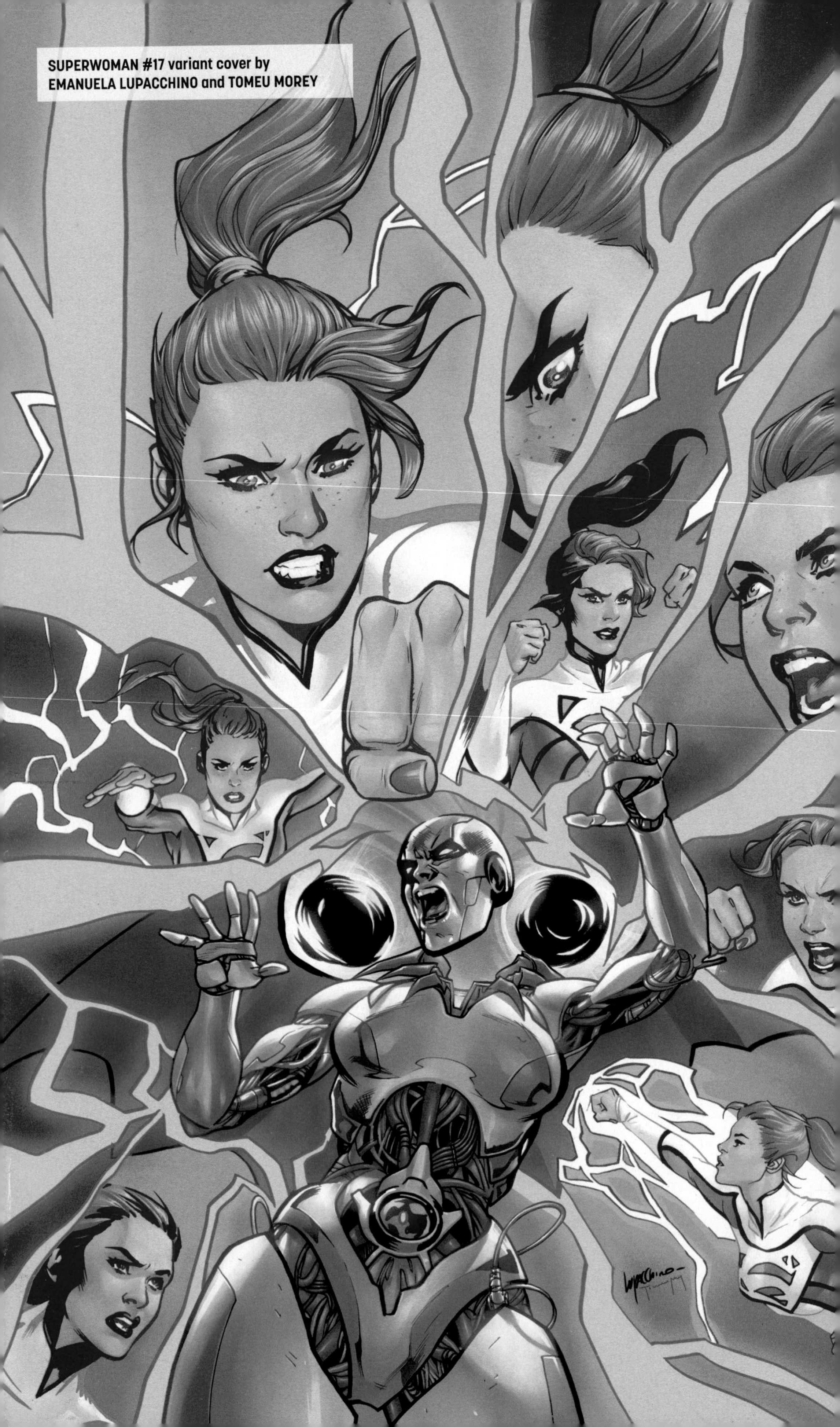

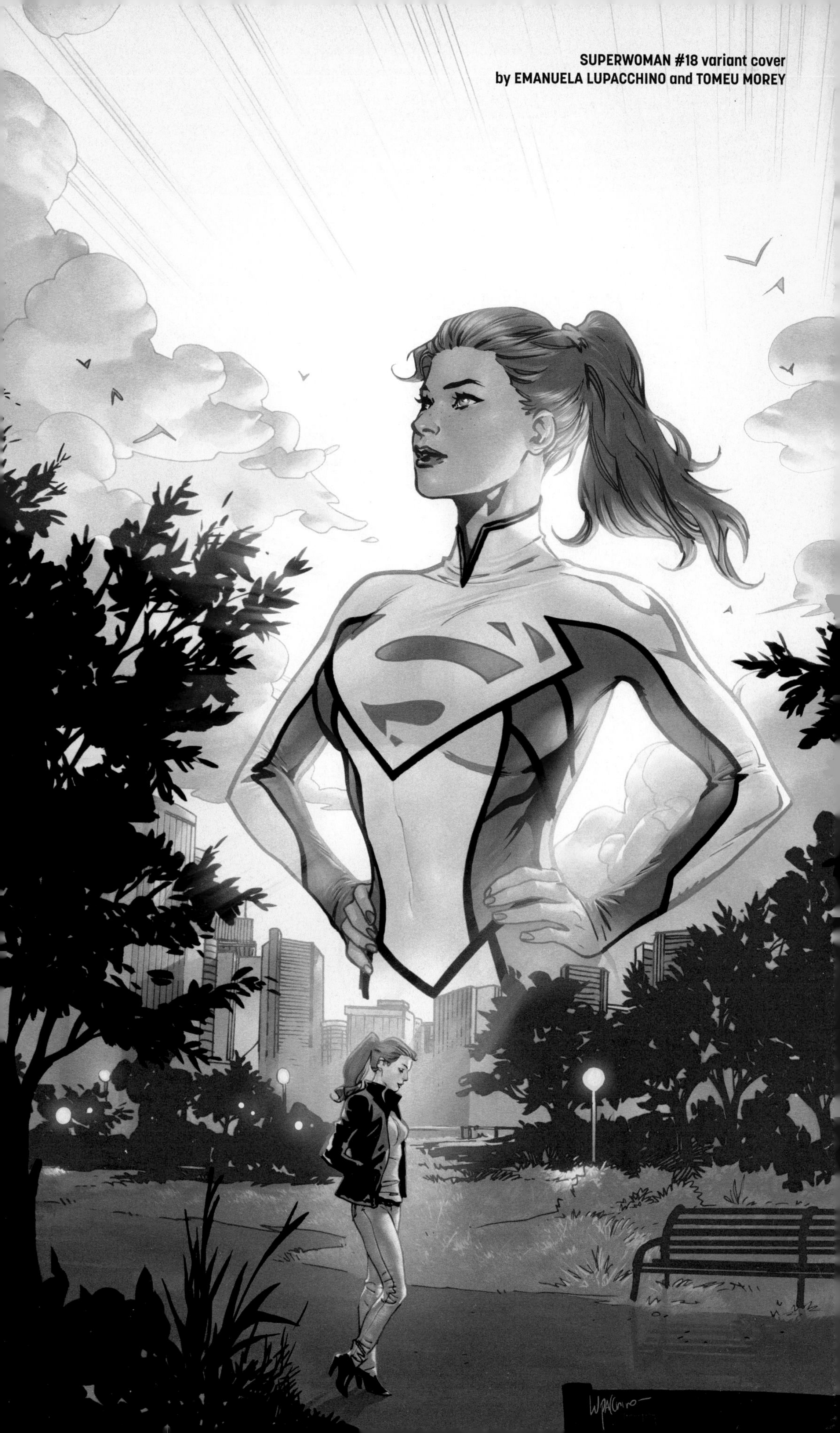

SUPERWOMAN #18 variant cover
by EMANUELA LUPACCHINO and TOMEU MOREY

MIDNIGHT CHARACTER DESIGNS

by STEPHEN SEGOVIA

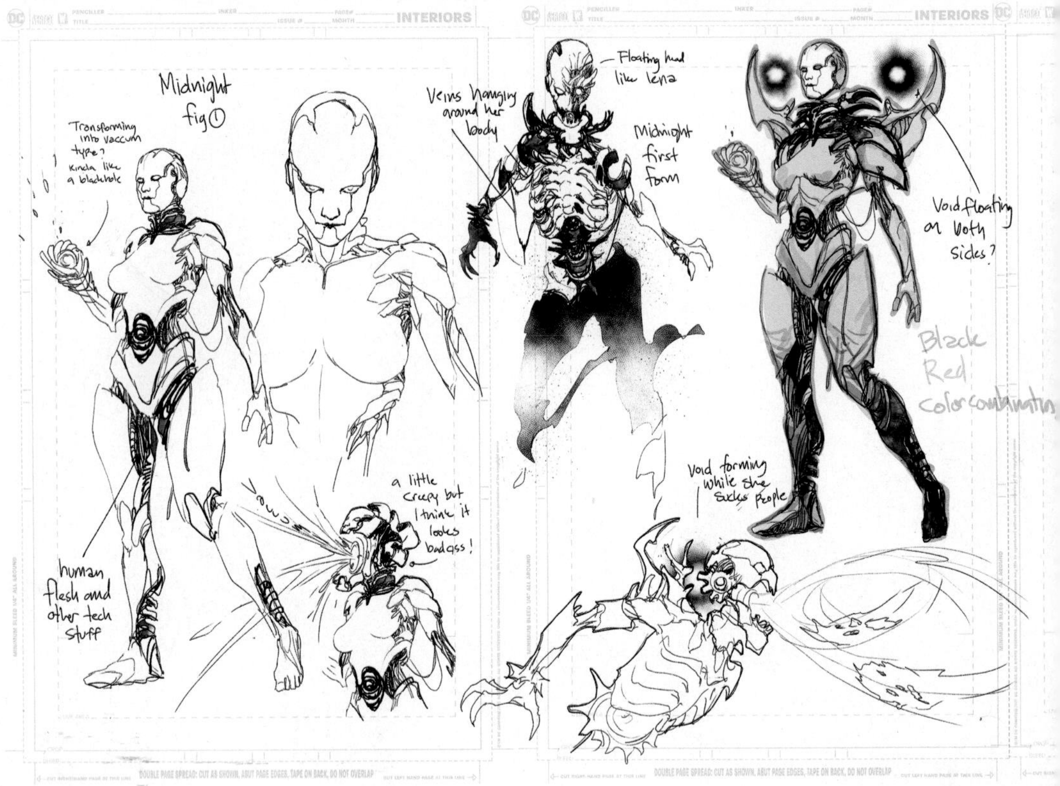
INTERIORS
Midnight fig①
Transforming into vaccum type? kinda like a blackhole
human flesh and other tech stuff
a little creepy but I think it looks badass!
INTERIORS
Floating head like lena
Veins hanging around her body
Midnight first form
Void floating on both sides?
Black
Red
colorcombinatio
Void forming while she sucks people
DOUBLE PAGE SPREAD: CUT AS SHOWN, ABUT PAGE EDGES, TAPE ON BACK, DO NOT OVERLAP
DOUBLE PAGE SPREAD: CUT AS SHOWN, ABUT PAGE EDGES, TAPE ON BACK, DO NOT OVERLAP

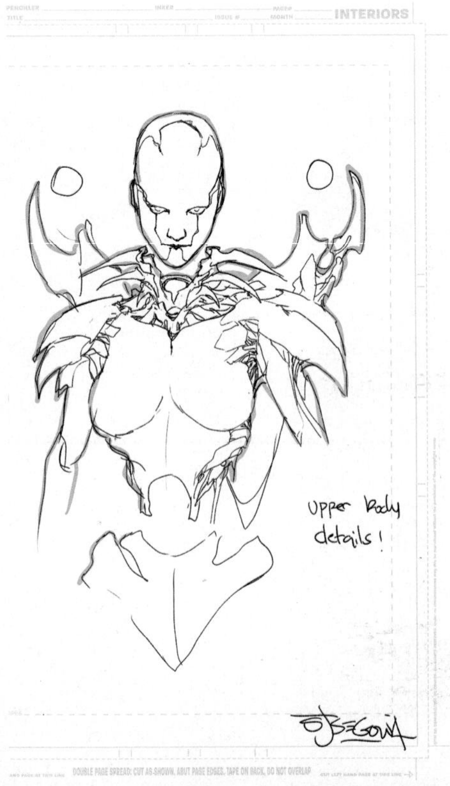
INTERIORS
upper body details!
SEGOVIA
DOUBLE PAGE SPREAD: CUT AS SHOWN, ABUT PAGE EDGES, TAPE ON BACK, DO NOT OVERLAP